The Political Economy of European Union Competition Policy

New Political Economy

RICHARD MCINTYRE, *General Editor*

The Political Economy of European Union Competition Policy

A Case Study of the Telecommunications Industry

Tuna Baskoy

Routledge
Taylor & Francis Group
New York London

HE
8085
.B39
2008

First published 2008
by Routledge
270 Madison Ave, New York, NY 10016

M

Simultaneously published in the UK
by Routledge
2 Park Square, Milton Park, Abingdon, Oxon OX14 4RN

Routledge is an imprint of the Taylor & Francis Group, an informa business

Typeset in Sabon by IBT Global.
Printed and bound in the United States of America on acid-free paper by IBT Global.

Library of Congress Cataloging in Publication Data
Baskoy, Tuna, 1972-
   The political economy of European Union competition policy : a case study of the telecommunications industry / Tuna Baskoy.
      p. cm.—(New political economy)
   Includes bibliographical references and index.
   ISBN 978-0-415-96525-5
1. Telecommunication policy—European Union countries.   2. Competition—European Union countries.   I. Title.
   HE8085.B39 2008
   384.094—dc22
   2008004914

ISBN10: 0-415-96525-X (hbk)
ISBN10: 0-203-89289-5 (ebk)

ISBN13: 978-0-415-96525-5 (hbk)
ISBN13: 978-0-203-89289-3 (ebk)

Contents

List of Figures

List of Graphs

List of Tables

Abbreviations

AT&T:	American Telephone and Telegraph
BT:	British Telecom
CAP:	Common Agricultural Policy
CBEMA:	Computer and Business Equipment Manufacturers Association
CEC:	Commission of the European Communities
CEN:	Comité Européen de Normalisation
CENELEC:	Comité Européen de Normalisation Electrotechnique
CEPT:	Conférence Européenne des Administrations des Postes et des Télécommunications
CFI:	Court of First Instance
CGE:	Compagnie Générale d'Electricité
CGCT:	Compagnie Générale Constructions Téléphoniques
C&W:	Cable & Wireless
DG:	Directorate-General
DGT:	Direction Generale des Telecommunications
DM:	Deutsche Mark
DMC:	Dynamic Market Competition
DT:	Deutsche Telekom
EC:	European Community
ECJ:	European Court of Justice
ECSC:	European Coal and Steel Community
ECU:	European Currency Unit

EDC:	European Defense Community
EEC:	European Economic Community
EITO:	European Information Technology Observatory
EMS:	European Monetary System
EP:	European Parliament
ERDF:	European Regional Development Fund
ESPRIT:	European Strategic Programme for Research and Development in Information Technology
ETSI:	European Telecommunications Standardization Institute
EU:	European Union
EUROATOM:	European Atomic Energy Community
EUROSTAT:	European Statistical Agency
EUTELSAT:	European Telecommunications Satellite Organization
FT:	France Telecom
GCE:	Generale Compagnie d'Electricité
GEC:	General Electric Company
GDP:	Gross Domestic Product
GSM:	Global System for Mobile Communications
GTS:	Global Telecommunications Services
HER:	Hermes Europe Railtel
IBC:	Integrated Broadband Communications networks
IBM:	International Business Machines
ICT:	Information Communication Technology
ISDN:	Integrated Services Digital Network
IT:	Information Technology
ITT:	International Telephone & Telegraph
ITU:	International Telecommunications Union
M&A:	Merger and Acquisition
MCR:	Merger Control Regulation
MCI:	Microwave Communications Inc.

NATO:	North Atlantic Treaty Organization
NRA:	National Regulatory Authority
OECD:	Organization for Economic Cooperation and Development
OEEC:	Organization for European Economic Cooperation
ONP:	Open Network Provision
QMV:	Quality Majority Voting
PSDS:	Packet-Switched Data Services
PCN:	Personal Communication Network
PTO:	Public Telecommunication Operator
PVN:	Private Virtual Networks
PTT:	Post, Telephone and Telegraph
RACE:	Research and Development in Advanced Communications-technologies for Europe
SEA:	Single European Act
SEL:	Standard Electric Lorenz
SES:	Société Européenne des Satellites
SIT:	Societá Italiana Telecommunicazione
SOGT:	Senior Officials Group on Telecommunication
SPAG:	Standards Promotion and Application Group
STAR:	Special Telecommunication Actions for the Regions
STC:	Standard Telephone and Cables
STET:	Societá Finanziaria Telefonica per Azioni
TA:	Telecommunication Administration
TEN:	Trans-European Networks
TEU:	Treaty on European Union
TO:	Telecommunication Organization
UK:	United Kingdom
UMTS:	Universal Mobile Telecommunications System
VANS:	Value-Added Networks
VAS:	Value-Added Services
WWII:	World War II

Preface

In the European Union (EU), competition policy occupies a central place amongst other EU public policies as the first truly supranational public policy regulating market competition. This book investigates the political economy of EU competition policy by taking the European telecommunications industry between 1980 and 2004 as a case study. It takes the often-ignored concept of 'workable' or 'effective' competition as a starting point. As one of the central supranational public policies, EU competition policy has several objectives including market integration; maintaining undistorted competition; ensuring the 'right amount of competition' in order for the EEC Treaty requirements to be met and its aims attained; the *diffusion of economic power*; and other broader public interest aims such as preserving the principle of fairness in the market.

There are three overarching arguments put forward in this study. The first is that there is a disjunction between the stated objective of EU competition policy (establishing and maintaining decentralized markets) and its actual practice (loosely oligopolistic markets). The second contention is that EU competition policy failed to establish and maintain even modest 'ideal' markets in the telecommunications equipment and services markets for two reasons. First, the theory of effective competition as the economic model for EU competition policy is primarily concerned with assuring the profitability of firms in order to prevent supply-side instabilities. Second, the theory of effective competition falls short of providing EU institutions with clearly defined conceptual and analytical tools to grasp the processes of competing and monopolizing and to create and maintain decentralized markets. These two factors suggest that EU competition law enforcers had problems understanding the dynamics of market competition. The third and final argument is that the objectives of corporate power for control of the market superseded such socially progressive objectives as decentralized markets, better and cheaper services, as well as employment in telecommunications.

Acknowledgments

This book is a revised version of my doctoral dissertation. As such, it is the product of a collaborative process, although as the author, I am ultimately responsible for the work in its entirety. In the first place, Greg Albo, my supervisor, deserves generous acknowledgment as he significantly contributed to the formation of my ideas and the completion of this work. I am grateful to Jonathan Nitzan, Kurt Huebner, and Edelgard Mahant, who were my dissertation committee members for guiding me through the labyrinths of political economy and European Union politics. I must thank Mike Burke and Vincent Mosco for their suggestions and recommendations during my defense. Additionally, I am grateful to Richard McIntyre, General Editor, for his constructive comments and suggestions. I would like to thank Benjamin Holtzman, Routledge Editor, for being patient with me during the review process. I am indebted to Carey Nershi, Page Composition Supervisor of IBT Global, for her swift and meticulous editing work.

I would like to thank Professor Carla Cassidy, Dean of the Faculty of Arts, at Ryerson University for her generous financial support to complete this work. I am also indebted to all of my colleagues in the Department of Politics and Public Administration at Ryerson University for their support. Gail McCabe deserves special thanks for spending countless hours to improve the language of this work. Nevertheless, the usual disclaimer applies here. My friends Serkan Gürses and Sirvan Karimi warrant special thanks for their friendship throughout the project. Finally, I would like to thank Stephanie Li for her generous support and understanding. This book is dedicated to my mother Fikriye and father Mustafa Necati, as well as my relatives Uğur Toçsoy, Gülsüm Türkmen, Bayram Şifael, Mete İplikçi, Hami and Ayşe (Neriman) Türkmen. I would not be where I am now without them.

Tuna Baskoy
June 2008
Toronto

1 Introduction

Electronic communications function like the *central nervous system* or the *arterial system* in a human body, and the information carried over the system is the *lifeblood* of contemporary societies. As an essential part of our daily lives, telecommunications is defined as "[t]he transmission and reception of information of any type, including data, television pictures, sound, and facsimiles, using electrical or optical signals sent over wires or fibers or through the air" (Microsoft Corporation, 2002, p. 513). Parallel to the increasing significance of electronic communications, the market value of telecommunications has also risen significantly over the past quarter century.

The European Commission estimated that the global market for telecommunications was ECU (European Currency Unit) 390 billion in 1986 and the European Union (EU), formerly European Community (EC), accounted for ECU 82 billion or 21 percent of the world market (CEC, 1988a, p. 5). The world-wide market value of telecommunications reached €1.137 billion in 2007 (191.54 percent growth), and the market value of the EU's telecommunications was €348 billion, an amount equal to 30.61 percent of the world market (European Information Technology Observatory (EITO), 2007, slides # 6 and 10). In addition to a 10 percent rise in the EU's share of the world telecommunications market between 1986 and 2007, the EU telecommunications market grew by 324.39 percent, almost doubling the growth of telecommunications world-wide, in part because of the geographical enlargement of the EU itself.

As part of neo-liberal economic policies and intensifying economic globalization in the 1980s and 1990s, the years 1980 to 2004 have seen an important domestic, as well as international, push towards marketization through deregulation and liberalization (Nitzan, 2001; Albo, 1997). These policies were carried out swiftly to open up formerly regulated industries to market competition in both advanced industrial and developing countries. The promotion of 'efficiency' through market competition has become the fundamental political aspiration around the world. Establishing and maintaining competitive markets in formerly monopolistic industries by replacing vertical or industry-specific regulation with horizontal or competition/antitrust law was the primary goal. Telecommunications was one of the many monopolistic industries that experienced this sort of radical transition along with transportation, water and electricity.

Like elsewhere around the world, telecommunications in the EU had been a tightly regulated monopoly before 1980. The industry had been perceived as a 'natural monopoly' and state- or privately-owned national monopolies controlled the industry for decades. With a dramatic shift in public policy in the 1980s, the industry underwent a drastic restructuring owing mainly to EU competition law. Eliassen, Mason, and Siovaag (1999, p. 23) noted that EU competition rules served as the principal public policy instrument to reorganize the telecommunications industry by subjecting state-owned monopolistic services firms to market competition, thereby facilitating the transition from monopolistic to competitive markets. Moreover, European Commission officials as well as member state regulators relied heavily on European competition law to regulate market competition in the industry in the post-liberalization period.

Former EU competition commissioner, Mario Monti (2004) stated that the goal of liberalization and deregulation of the industry was the establishment of market competition. As an important field, telecommunications policy has attracted the attention of scholars. However, there are discernible differences regarding their analysis. It is possible to group the scholars in three camps. Scholars in the first group, like Von Weizsiicker (1984, pp. 208–9), argue that market competition promotes innovation, reduces telecommunications costs, and spurs growth in the demand for network services. New technologies and new products are beneficial not only for firms, but also for the society. The rationale behind the positive attitude towards competition in the telecommunications industry is based on the logic that a competitive market with free entry promotes technological and product innovation, as competitive pressure motivates firms to be aggressive, entrepreneurial and risk-taking (Thimm, 1992). For them, deregulation and liberalization provide openings for reaping the benefits of competition.

The second group of scholars, a dominant group in European telecommunications studies, focuses on the impact of institutional structures and processes on policy making and outcomes. They emphasize the cultural and historical contexts of regulatory policies, thereby analyzing policy processes to identify central policy actors. There has been an intense debate among the students of EU telecommunications policy regarding the level of analysis and the significance of the actors in EU electronic communications policy. These debates coalesce within three main subgroups. The first subgroup treats national political institutions as an independent variable contending that they provide a framework within which public policies are developed (Thatcher, 1999, p.1; Dyson & Humphreys, 1990, p. ix). With the priority on the 'arts of statecraft', they analyze policy processes to understand whether states can preserve their autonomy and hence their capacity to act independently by re-establishing their competence to govern. For scholars like Dyson (1986), Humphreys (2004), and Humpreys and Simpson (2005), EU institutions as agents of the member states exerted power to the extent that the member states or the principals delegated them. The EU's role was secondary in that it was not a propelling force behind reform. Rather, its role can be summarized as 'a further reason for reforms' (Thatcher, 2004a, p. 285).

The second subgroup, consisting of researchers like Schneider and Werle (2007), concentrates on European levels of governance and singles out the European Commission, not the member states, as the leading actor of EU telecommunications policy. These scholars argue that the European Commission responded to counter the immediate American threat. Increasing competitive pressures led the European Commission to convince the member states to cooperate with each other to develop a common policy against the expansion of American Telephone and Telegraph (AT&T) and the diversification of International Business Machines (IBM) into telecommunications markets. Goodman (2006) extends this analysis to the other two important EU institutions, namely the European Court of Justice (ECJ) and the European Parliament (EP).

Within the second subgroup, there are scholars who concentrate on the supranational level with a focus on the implementation of competition rules in the telecommunications industry. Their analysis essentially tackles procedural questions such as how competition policy can be implemented, as telecommunications, mass media and information technology (IT) industries converge, new market structures replace the old ones, and firms re-position themselves in the telecommunications, broadcasting and IT industries (Larouche, 1998; Styliadou, 1997). Convergence among these three industries raises competition issues when a firm, which is dominant in one of the areas makes use of or extends its dominance into a related market, especially through a joint venture with another dominant firm from that market (Lang, 1997). The EU competition rules, which specifically focus on individual product and geographical markets in their analysis of market power, rarely capture the market power of conglomerates that actively operate in different industries, not only in national, but also in international markets (Just & Latzer, 2000; Lera, 2000; Latzer, 1998; Clements, 1998). Competition is taken for granted and the question of what kind of competition is not raised in this literature, either (Garzaniti, 2003).

The third subgroup considers the EU as a polycentric and multilayered political system in evolution. In contrast to the first two groups, which perceive power as concentrated either at the national or supranational level, scholars like Natalicchi (2001, pp. 211–3) conceptualize political power as dispersed across three types of actors: supranational institutions, national states and social forces. Moreover, subnational,

national, supranational actors at the European-wide and international levels should be considered simultaneously because political power is spread among different actors at different levels. EU telecommunications policy is explained within the logic of demand and supply for supranational regulation by integrating an analysis of the role of multiple actors at different levels.

Taken as a whole, scholars in the second group examine the processes of EU electronic communications policy-making and implementation informed by a detailed, historical approach, albeit with differences in their emphasis on actors and levels of analysis. The goal is to pinpoint the most important actor and the appropriate level of analysis to shed some light on the process of European integration. Schneider and Werle (2007, p. 280) observed that students of European telecommunications policy have yet to question the nature of competition to be established, policy outcomes, or winners and losers.[1]

Scholars in the third group are interested in the political economy of telecommunications policy. They take competition and profitability, not institutions, as independent variables and analyze their impact on telecommunications. For instance, Lüthje (1993) argued that the crisis of Fordist accumulation in telecommunications, as opposed to new technologies or international competition, triggered the problem of profitability that resulted in the redefinition of the roles of communications and computer companies. According to Locksley (1986), market competition and the profit imperative were the two significant factors for understanding the demand for and development of information and communication technologies. State-owned telecommunications service providers were privatized in order to generate private capital to exploit profit opportunities in the telecommunications industry. The end result of deregulation and privatization, which were deemed necessary for healthy capital accumulation, was the concentration and centralization of capital in information communication technologies (ICTs). Although scholars in the third group pinpoint policy outcomes and winners as well as losers, the problem with their analysis is that it is very broad and vague. Instead of providing a detailed industry level analysis, they provide sketchy empirical evidence. In addition, they are silent about EU telecommunications policy. Nor do they raise questions regarding the type of competition that policy makers and law enforcers targeted.

As this succinct review illustrates, the literature on telecommunications is rich and complex, but it is hard to find answers to the following vital questions: How was competition established? What kind of market was it aimed at: i.e. decentralized with many competitors or oligopolistic with few competitors? Who are the winners and losers? Given that EU competition law was the principal public policy instrument for deregulation and liberalization of the industry to establish competition, analysis of EU competition policy may provide some clues to answer these questions.

1.1. EU COMPETITION POLICY AND *WORKABLE* OR *EFFECTIVE* COMPETITION

Competition policy is often referred to as symmetric regulation that provides firms with a level playing field, as it regulates their behavior and conduct in the market.[2] According to Chang (1997): "Regulation is usually defined as the government (or the state) directly prescribing and proscribing what private sector agents can and cannot do, so that their actions do not contradict the 'public interest'" (p. 704). Regulating market competition is based on the idea that the market is imperfect and there are incidences of market failures. The state is therefore given the responsibility to correct these imperfections and failures to align the private interest with that of the public, at least in theory (Trebing: 1969, pp. 87–8).

Many countries around the world adopted competition law to stimulate and protect competition after the 1970s. Between 1945 and 1973, only 27 countries in the world had competition policy. This number suddenly jumped to 70 by the end of 1996 (Palim, 1998, pp. 105–45). Over 90 countries had competition law and policy by 2002 (Kolasky, 2002). In the process of spreading competition law and policy to other countries, the EU has played a major role, by obliging candidate countries to adopt its competition policy as part of *acquis communautaire* (the body of common rights and obligations which binds the member states together within the EU), as well as by promoting the idea of a multilateral agreement on competition within the World Trade Organization (WTO) (Holscher & Stephan, 2004; Monti, 2003a).

A free market economy was identified as the appropriate economic system for the European Economic Community (EEC) in the treaty establishing the EEC by the founding member states. For Sauter (1998): "The economic order protected by a liberal economic constitution is essentially that of a private law society (based on freedom of contract) supplemented by minimal public intervention. Within this framework, competition plays a central role" (p. 47). Nevertheless, the Commission of the European Communities (CEC) found that a *laissez-faire* model of a capitalist market was not a panacea for all problems due to its self-destructive nature (1958, p. 59).

For correcting market failures, the European Commission often perceives competition policy as the EU's central public policy. As such, it lies at the centre of the EU constitution. "Competition policy is therefore both a Commission policy in its own right and an integral part of a large number of European Union policies" (CEC, 1997, p. 17). Indeed, as a structural policy, it is the central public policy to which other EU policies have to adjust to ensure consistency (CEC, 1980, p. 11). In sum, EU competition policy is a public policy tool to realize the goals of the EU. It is the central public policy that determines the direction of all other policies as well. Wilks and McGowan (1996) characterized EU competition policy as "one element determining the evolution of European capitalism, an element with a potential to take pre-eminence over other areas of Community law" (p. 226). Thus, understanding EU capitalism entails comprehending its competition policy in the first place.

The history of EU competition policy starts with the history of European integration. The EU itself was founded by the six West European states of France, West Germany, Italy, Belgium, the Netherlands and Luxembourg as the European Economic Community (EEC) with the signing of the EEC Treaty in 1957. Competition policy was so important for the founding member states that they included competition rules (Articles 81 to 89 or ex-Articles 85 to 94) to regulate the markets in the EEC Treaty. EU competition policy is one of the earliest supranational policies in the EEC, along with the common agricultural and cohesion policies, according to Mahant (2004). The EU was created with the Treaty on European Union (TEU) signed on February 7, 1992, which came into effect in November 1993. The current membership of the EU is 27 after the accession of 12 new members, mainly from Central and Eastern Europe, in May 2004 and January 2007 respectively (Dinan, 2004).

The importance of EU competition policy has amplified with the twin processes of deepening market integration and geographical enlargement over the past quarter century. As one of the central supranational public policies, EU competition policy has several objectives including market integration; maintaining undistorted competition; ensuring the 'right amount of competition' in order for the EEC Treaty requirements to be met and its aims attained; *diffusion of economic power*; and other broader public interest aims such as preserving the principle of fairness in the market. Fairness is an issue in distributing state aids, subjecting all firms to the same laws, adapting competition rules to the needs of small- and medium-sized enterprises, and taking into account the interests of users, consumers and customers (Sauter, 1997, p. 117).

Preventing market concentration and the centralization of economic power is crucial for EU competition policy in order to protect economic and political freedom (Korah, 2004, pp. 13–4). According to the European Commission (1980):

> It is an established fact that competition carries within it the seeds of its own destruction. *An excessive concentration of economic, financial, and commercial power* can produce such far-reaching structural changes that free competition is no longer able to fulfill its role as an effective regulator of economic activity. (p. 10)

In checking the adverse effects of market concentration, EU competition policy regulates the market behavior and conduct of firms (Hildebrandt, 1998, p. 16; Frazer, 1988, pp. 3–4; Smith, 1982, pp. 169–70). As part of its objective of setting up competitive markets, EU competition policy has also been the key public policy tool used to deregulate and liberalize formerly regulated industries such as finance, transportation, electricity and telecommunications over the past quarter-century.

What does the 'right amount of competition' mean? What kind of competition does EU competition policy strive to develop in order to realize the goals stated in the EEC Treaty? Even though the treaty did not specify the type of competition, Hans von der Groeben, the first head of the EEC Commission's Directorate for Competition, maintained that EEC competition policy aimed at 'an effective and workable competitive system' as early as 1966 (CEC, 1966, p. 59). The European Court of Justice (ECJ) backed him in *Hoffman-La Roche & Co. AG v. Commission of the European Communities* (1979, p. 229) on the grounds that Article 3(f) of the EEC Treaty envisaged the establishment as well as the maintenance of a market structure suitable for workable or effective competition. The ECJ defined workable competition in *Metro-SB-Groß-Märkte GmbH & Co. KG v. EC Commission* (1978) as "the degree of competition necessary to ensure the observance of the basic requirements and the attainment of the objectives of the Treaty, in particular the creation of a single market achieving conditions similar to those of a domestic market" (p. 2). This definition is very vague and general. Naturally, Veljanovski (2004) concluded: "Yet it is rare to find in EC antitrust texts, or in statements by the Commission, a clear expression of the nature of effective competition" (p. 179). The term workable or effective competition remains a mystery in official documents.

The literature on EU competition law and policy is not very different from EU official documents. It is widely acknowledged amongst students of EU competition law and policy that effective or workable competition is the economic model behind EU competition policy (Kapteyn & Van Themaat, 1998, pp. 1–2; Raines, 1985, p. 137; Jacqueming & De Jong, 1977, p. 201; McLachlan & Swan, 1963, p. 56). Lindahl and Roermund (2000) stressed that "the core of EC law consists in arranging, adapting, applying, and enforcing the default setting of competition, and which the ECJ has elaborated by reference to what it terms 'workable competition'" (p. 15). Despite the importance of the concept for unravelling the political economy of EU competition law and its enforcement in new fields like telecommunications, even students of EU competition law and policy have paid scant attention to the concept.

It is possible to see three consistent patterns in regards to the treatment of effective or workable competition in the literature. The first pattern is that scholars like Swan (1983), Fishwick (1993), Kemp (1994), and Petrella (1998) do not mention the notion of workable or effective competition in their analysis at all. The second group, consisting of scholars like van Gerven (1974), Cini and McGowan (1998), and Korah (2000) insist that EU competition law promotes and maintains effective competition. Surprisingly, they do not provide a detailed analysis of effective competition.

Those who study EU competition policy in the third group attempt to define effective or workable competition, but they not quite successful. For instance, Carchedi (2001, p. 124) defined effective or workable competition as a model of competition that targets a market where an 'acceptable' degree of competition exists. Nevertheless, his definition was not very different from the way the ECJ defined it. Goyder (1998) drew attention to the difficulty of distinguishing workable competitive markets from oligopolistic markets without expounding in detail. For Goyder, workable competition means fewer firms in the market, which differs from oligopolistic competition in that it represents 'a sharper degree and different tempo of mutual reaction' between firms (p. 11). De Jong and Jacquemin (1977, p. 201) equated workable competition with market structures. In addition to the structural dimension, Lasok and Lasok (2001, p. 615) pointed out that effective competition refers to firm behaviour. In sum, there is no agreement among the students of EU competition law and policy regarding a definition of workable or effective competition.

Generally speaking, the literature on EU competition policy is vast, and written from economic, legal, political, public administration, as well as political economy perspectives. Economists usually analyze the formal neoclassical economic theories of market competition to explain the economic rationale behind individual competition law cases without providing a coherent analysis of effective competition in detail (Young & Metcalfe, 1997; Swann 1983). In a different way, lawyers often describe the competition rules as well as the procedures for implementing them from a legal perspective. They often compare a few cases with the objective of finding similarities and differences between them to explain the novelty in new cases (Albors-Llorens, 2002; Jacobs & Stewart-Clark, 1991).

Similarly, political scientists and those who study the public administration aspects of EU competition policy focus on political and administrative variables, rather than economic variables such as the type of competition (McGowan & Cini, 1999; Cini & McGowan, 1998; Wilks & McGowan, 1996; Brittan, 1991). Finally, the emerging political economy perspective investigates the economic, political and social motivations behind EU competition policy together with its distributional outcomes for different societal forces, but seldom provides any substantive analysis of effective competition, and its manifestation in the enforcement of EU competition rules in specific industries and sectors, from a historical perspective (Petralla, 1998, p. 292).

Except for a few critical scholars, the common flaw in the writings of students of EU telecommunications and competition policies is that they take for granted *competition* in general and *workable* or *effective competition* in particular. Naturally, they do not investigate the implications of effective competition for the political economy of EU competition law and policy, or the policy outcomes of enforcing competition law in the telecommunications industry. As a result, there is a serious gap in the literature. To address the gap, this study investigates the political economy of EU competition law with the help of the term workable or effective competition as an entry point by taking the telecommunications industry between 1980 and 2004 as a case study.

There are three overarching arguments put forward in this study. The first is that there is a disjunction between the stated objective of EU competition policy (establishing and maintaining decentralized markets) and its actual practice (loosely oligopolistic markets). The second contention is that EU competition policy failed to establish and maintain even this modest 'ideal' market form in the telecommunications equipment and services markets respectively for two reasons. First, the theory of effective competition as the economic model for EU competition policy is primarily concerned with assuring the profitability of firms in order to prevent supply-side instabilities. Second, the theory of effective competition falls short of providing EU institutions with clearly defined conceptual and analytical tools to grasp the processes of competing and monopolizing and to create and maintain decentralized markets. These two factors suggest that EU competition law had problems understanding the dynamics of market competition. The third and final argument is that corporate power expanded against other possible social objectives such as decentralized markets, better and cheaper services, as well as employment in the area of telecommunications. Thus the question turns to how market competition should be studied theoretically in order to evaluate EU competition law and policy successfully.

1.2. MARKET COMPETITION AND POWER

Referring to a particular type of relationship between economic agents in the market, free market competition is the cornerstone of capitalism (Tyson, 1997, p. xiii). It is the fundamental principle on which the capitalist market economic system is based. As stated by McNulty (1968), despite the centrality of the concept and phenomenon of market competition, there is no consensus on its definition or its outcomes among scholars. Neither is there a comprehensive debate about the implications of the diverse perspectives on competition policy in particular and state-market relations in general, as the existence of different approaches to market competition depicts the problem.

The notion of power is the entry point both for analyzing market competition and classifying the major approaches to it. Lukes (1974) defines power as A's ability to control or influence B's behavior through making decisions or not making decisions openly; through working behind the scenes to manipulate the agenda; or through persuading B to accept his/her agenda by shaping the perceptions and preferences of B of which B is not necessarily aware, even though they may be against or contrary to B's own best interest. Decision-making, agenda-setting and preference-shaping are the three main dimensions of power (Dyrberg, 1997). Hay (2002) elaborates this notion of power as follows:

> Power is then about context-shaping, about the capacity of actors to redefine the parameters of what is socially, politically and economically possible for others. The ability to influence directly the actions and/or choices of another individual or group is but one special case of this more general capacity. More formally then we can define power as the ability of actors (whether individual or collective) to 'have an effect' upon the context which defines the range of possibilities of others. (p. 185)

As this definition clarifies, both behavioral and structural or systemic aspects of power are equally significant in terms of its effects. The concept of power used here is broader than what mainstream economists mean by this word. The analytical distinction among *market, economic* and *political* power, as different forms of social power, is critical not only for studying how EU competition law was designed (political versus economic power), but also how it was historically implemented (political versus market power) in the telecommunications industry.

Market power, as stated by Montgomery (1985, p. 790), refers to the ability of an individual firm or group of firms to influence price, quality and the nature of a commodity in the marketplace or in the industry. Competition policy is mainly aimed at controlling and regulating this form of power. By contrast, *economic power* is "the degree to which individuals or individual units affect the decision-making process" (Klein, 1988, p. 394). What is meant by the decision-making process here is primarily political decision-making processes for deciding broader public policies. Economic power is broader in its scope and aims to influence public policies such as adopting competition law. Compared to market power, economic power is more general and comprehensive regarding its sphere of influence, as its scope is not solely restricted to the marketplace.[3]

Political power is organizational power designed to coordinate the actions of the people and to promote public interest. According to Neumann (1950), "Political power is a social power focused on the state" (p. 162). As such, it permeates all social activities in all spheres of life one way or another. In contrast to economic power that emanates from ownership, political power has its origins in people's consent. There is a reciprocal relationship between those who exert political power and those whose actions are coordinated. Political and economic power is interdependent as well as intertwined. For Neumann: "Economics is as much an instrument of politics as politics is a tool of economics" (pp. 172–3). Despite the ontological separation between them, the boundary is blurred in day-to-day interactions and the nature of power is so flexible that one form of power can be translated into another easily, especially economic power into political power.

Borrowing the classification by Carson, Thomas and Hecht (2002, ch. 2) of major approaches in social science literature, it is possible to distinguish three main groups of theories to study market competition with reference to power in its three forms. These are the *conservative* (advocated by those who defend *laissez-faire* capitalism), *liberal* (those who accept market failures and defend market interventions) and *radical* (critical of capitalism) paradigms of market competition. Power in three different forms—*market*, *economic* and *political* power—is the pivotal concept in that it reveals not only how different approaches theorize market competition and its consequences, but also in that it provides hints about the way these theories deal with the adverse effects of power, explicating the rationale behind competition policy and hence, state-society relations.

Conservative theories of competition consist of the classical theory of market competition advanced by Adam Smith and David Ricardo, the neoclassical theory of perfect competition, and the Austrian and Chicago theories of competition. They assert that market power exists in the short term, but it is temporary, as the invisible hand of the market, i.e. market competition, eradicates it in the long run. The conservative approach to market competition is against competition policy in general because of the belief that the market allocates resources more efficiently. As a result, they are not fond of competition policy as they advocate minimal state intervention. Conservatives perceive competition policy as 'populist' in its origin, protecting the interests of farmers, laborers and small-business owners who influence politicians by means of their votes (Torelli, 1955, p. 58–62). In other words, the state and its public policies are, in a sense, 'captured' by these segments of society and the market is consequently distorted in its normal operations. The problem with the conservative approach is that it represents market and economic power as a short-term problem.

The liberal approach to market competition, comprising the theories of imperfect, monopolistic and effective competition (which is the economic model for EU competition policy), acknowledges not only the existence of market and economic power in the long run, but also its resilient nature and wider adverse economic, political and social effects. The starting point in this view is that economies of scale and scope, a function of modern technology, require a few large firms for efficient production and distribution. Naturally, these firms have control over the markets in which they operate. Individually or collectively, they often use their market power to manage the flow of commodities, their quality and/or prices. Because of their strong position in their respective industries and sectors, they have significant economic power besides their market power. As a way of overcoming the trade-off between efficiency and negative effects of market and economic power, the liberal position asserts that political power can exert control over both market and economic power as long as it is not used arbitrarily. As a result, regulating market power through competition policy is seen as a remedy, assuming that the state can control market power and harness it for the public good. However, the liberal approach overlooks how economic power interacts with political power and affects the way individual public policies are designed in the first place.

The radical perspective of market competition that encompasses the theories advanced by Karl Marx, Rudolf Hilferding, Vladimir Il'ich Lenin, Thorstein Veblen and their followers pictures market and economic power as permanent and influential in the market as well as in policy-making and implementation. The nature of influence depends on the balance between social and economic forces. In contrast to their conservative and liberal counterparts, not only do the radicals explain the origins of market power by providing a wider framework for understanding the dynamics and working logic of market competition which is essential for comprehending market power and its effects, but they also offer a theoretical framework to study state-market relations that are necessary for investigating the interactions between economic and political power historically. There are, however, two major problems with the radical approach. First, it represents the state as a relatively weak institution and as such, capitalists or elite social forces can easily manipulate it. Second, the radicals do not discuss the implications of the radical theory of market competition for evaluating competition law and policy. To overcome these two shortcomings of the radical view, a new theoretical framework, referred to as *Dynamic Market Competition* (DMC), is suggested to evaluate the political economy of EU competition through the case study of the telecommunications industry.

1.3. A THEORY OF DYNAMIC MARKET COMPETITION (DMC)

In order to lay the groundwork for a brief explanation of DMC, it is useful to clarify the following frequently used concepts that are integral to theorizing DMC: competition, firm, industry, sector, monopoly, and monopolization. The central concept is that of *market competition*, a dynamic process "which both enforces and expresses the attempt of individual capitals to maximize their profits" (Eatwell, 1987, p. 539). There are two key aspects of this definition that correspond to different levels in the competitive process—expression and enforcement. On the one hand, *expression* refers to the individual firm level. Competition is a way through which firms express their strategies and behaviors to gain an edge in a market vis-à-vis their competitors in their attempt to make a profit. In the process, they also modify their organizational structures to adapt themselves to the changing market environment. On the other hand, *enforcement* insinuates that competition functions as a mechanism that forces firms in the relevant market or industry to follow a certain path. Perceiving competition as both expression and enforcement requires analysis of individual firms and industries simultaneously. It is essential to capturing the internal working dynamics of competition as well as its consequences, the core task in implementing competition law.

The principal actors in the process of competition are firms. A *firm* is a business unit formed to carry out some kind of economic activity (Hanson, 1977, p. 200). Its fundamental objective is to make a profit.[4] Firms usually offer more than one commodity (i.e. product or service), which may be similar or different, while representing various ownership structures and organizational forms, depending on the state of the market and the industry in which they conduct their regular business activities. Firms strive against each other to make a profit in a market, which can be defined as "a group of buyers and sellers exchanging goods that are highly substitutable for one another" (Shepherd, 1990, p. 54). The function of the market is to enable an exchange of commodities by bringing buyers and sellers into contact with one another. Markets are usually defined with reference to a particular product or service and a geographical location (i.e. local, regional, national, European, global), which is essential for understanding the business strategies of firms.

Individual product markets are usually part of a larger unit, called an industry, such as telecommunications. *Industry* basically refers to a group of firms that compete against one another on the basis of similar products (Sawyer, 1981, p. 31; Hanson, 1977, p. 262). An industry may consist of firms located in different geographical locations producing identical, similar or different commodities within a range. A *sector* means a division of a national economy and encompasses individual industries (Hanson, 1977, p. 410). A national economy is usually divided into two main public and private sectors, or into a number of smaller sectors such as agricultural, financial and industrial. The case in point in this study, telecommunications, falls into the industrial sector.[5]

In competing with each other, firms use their *market power* to gain an edge vis-à-vis their rivals to make a profit or to maintain the status quo in the market, if they are already profitable. One source of market power is a monopoly. All firms desire the elimination of competition in order to become a monopoly—a striking paradox of market competition. However, monopoly does not simply mean a market position, market structure or condition in which there is only one firm that controls the supply of a commodity for which there are no close substitutes, as scholars such as Black, (2002, p. 306), Shim and Siegel (1995, p. 236), and Knopf (1991, p. 210) define it. What is meant by *monopoly* in this study is borrowed from Gilpin (1977), i.e. a firm that "produces a sufficiently large proportion of the total output of a commodity to enable it to influence the price of the commodity by variations in output" (p. 150). In other words, there can be a monopoly even in markets where there is more than one competitor.

Competition is not absent in monopolistic situations. On the contrary, competition and monopoly are two sides of the same coin, as Marx (1963) observed a century ago (p. 152). *Market concentration* or *monopolization* illustrates the extent to which the production of a specific commodity is limited to a few large firms in a particular market (Ferguson & Ferguson, 1994, p. 39). What changes is the nature and form of market competition in monopolistic markets, compared to competitive markets. Being a monopoly is also a source of economic power, and monopolistic firms often use their power to influence decisions made by political actors. Whereas monopoly refers to a condition, monopolization insinuates a process. This study investigates 'the process of *competing* and *monopolizing*' in the first place, not 'the state of *competition* or *monopoly*' (Miller, 1955, p. 123). How then can one theorize the complex as well as dynamic processes of competing and monopolizing?

Within the radical paradigm, DMC is an attempt to theorize the dynamic and complex processes of *competing* and *monopolizing* in the market as well as state-market interactions by focusing on the notion of power in its three forms at three levels. At the first and general level, DMC investigates how economic and political power interacts with each other to shape discrete public policies such as competition policy. The subject matter of the second and intermediate level is to analyze the relations between market and political power at the industry level. At the third and micro level, DMC explains the complex and dynamic processes of competing and monopolizing between firms in the industry to provide some clues for the gap between the vision of competition in EU competition law and the actual processes of competition.

Borrowing the analytical distinction made by Hilferding (1981), DMC distinguishes three major markets: competitive, transitional, and oligopolistic markets. Whereas firms in competitive markets determine the price of their products independently, price leadership is the dominant practice in oligopolistic markets. In that sense, transitional markets are similar to competitive markets, albeit with one significant distinction: they are very unstable and prone to rapid consolidation. In their analysis of the evolution of competition, both Karl Marx and Thorstein Veblen, as Chapter 2 investigates in detail, identified four major stages or phases of market competition with reference to the profitability of firms within transitional markets—increasing (exaltation), intense (prosperity), destructive (crisis), and waning (depression)—during which fluctuations in profitability result in vacillation in the intensity of market competition.

Understanding the behavior of firms and the dynamics of competition in each phase is essential for the effective implementation of competition law in that they unravel business strategies, the conduct of firms in the market and the state's reaction to them in rapidly evolving markets such as telecommunications after deregulation and liberalization of the industry. The rationale for using this kind of framework in studying the political economy of EU competition policy is to evaluate policy outcomes in the telecommunications

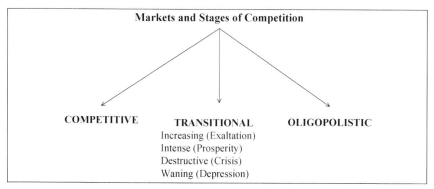

Figure 1.1 Dynamic market competition.

industry empirically to show the divergence between what Pal (2006, pp. 8–11) calls the 'policy goals' and 'real goals' of EU competition law.

1.4. METHODOLOGY AND RESEARCH DESIGN

The EU telecommunications industry is chosen as a case study for three major reasons. First, state-owned monopolies, known as Post, Telephone and Telegraph (PTTs), dominated the industry before the 1980s in Europe, and the member states had given them an exclusive right to offer telecommunications services in their respective countries. These monopolistic service providers had strong ties with monopolistic equipment producers in domestic markets, backed by the national states. Both service and equipment markets were concentrated at the national level. Thus, there was a chance for creating genuinely competitive markets. Second, the industry underwent a major 'boom and bust' cycle over the past fifteen years with significant long-term reverberations, which is essential for understanding the dynamics of the industry. Finally, EU competition policy was used as the principal public policy tool to deregulate and liberalize the industry with the aim of establishing effective competition and regulating market power by means of competition law rather than industry-specific regulation (Baimbridge, Harrop & Philippidis, 2004, p. 87). The structure of the industry in the post-liberalization period is a perfect witness to what EU institutions mean by effective competition. In other words, the policy outcome reflects the real policy goals as well as the limitations of EU competition policy.

   Profitability, essential for capital accumulation and a stable capitalist market economy from a supply-side point of view, played a significant role in EU competition policy decisions. There are two main research hypotheses to be tested in this study. First, whenever profitability declined, the EU institutions relaxed the implementation of Articles 81 and 87 (which deal with cartels and state aids respectively) and the merger control regulation (after 1990) the application of Article 82 (which prevents dominant firm(s) from abusing their power) to prevent powerful firms from squeezing out their smaller counterparts. In the case of serious drops in profitability as in the late 1970s, EU institutions deployed Article 86 (which aims to establish the supremacy of market competition by liberalizing formerly regulated industries) to open up new areas to boost the profitability of European firms. The second hypothesis is that there was a divergence between the dynamics of market competition and the way the European Commission perceived it. As a result, the European Commission, as the responsible EU institution for applying competition rules, often failed to grasp correctly the actual intention behind the particular market conduct of firms.

To provide evidence for these two hypotheses, a case study method was implemented because many features of social life and historical outcomes require complex, causal and combinatorial explanations that cannot be captured by statistical techniques alone (Ragin, 1987, pp. 13–32). In particular, a 'single case, embedded' design is used in this study. It allows for an in-depth analysis of a single case by concentrating on a number of different units of analysis (Gray, 2004, p. 132). The case study of the telecommunications industry is enhanced with a longitudinal approach to assess whether there was a genuine transition from monopolistic to competitive equipment and services markets in the post-liberalization period. The time frame of the study mainly covers the period between 1980 and 2004. The European Commission first applied competition law in the telecommunications industry in the early 1980s, and both the EU and its competition policy underwent a significant transformation in 2004, ushering in a new era, which goes beyond the scope of this study.

As for operationalization and measurement of the first hypothesis, the independent variable is profitability, which affects competition law decisions mainly made by the European Commission.[6] The dependent variable is the level of market concentration in the equipment and services markets respectively, which provides a measure of whether the EU established competition in these markets successfully. In analyzing the intensity of market competition, the rate of profit is taken as the benchmark rather than structural properties of the market such as the number of firms, since the former determines the latter and market competition is not simply a function of the number of firms (Marx, 1952, p. 41). Moreover, the present rate of profit and future profit expectations have a significant effect on the number of firms. As a result, available profit opportunities as well as the rate of profit are taken as explicating the variation in the behaviour of firms, their organizational structure, and intensity of market competition.

Two main profit indicators are used to study the relationship between market competition and the behaviour of firms in the market. The first, the net rate of return as a percentage of net total assets, is used to investigate the link between the rate of profit in the EU economy and the historical evolution of EU competition policy. The second profitability indicator, deployed in conducting telecommunications equipment and services market analysis, is based on the net rate of return as a percentage of the total assets of the largest four and three firms respectively. There are three factors in selecting the second index. First, it measures profitability as a percentage of assets, like the previous index, which assures consistency. Second, the largest firms usually play a significant role in shaping the intensity of market competition. Finally, the largest firms are usually taken as a benchmark by financial institutions to analyze market trends in lending money to firms. Overall, the two indices complement each other by revealing trends at the macroeconomic, industry, and firm levels, while making comparisons possible.

As for the second hypothesis, the explanation given by the European Commission, about particular firm conduct in its competition decisions is compared with what the business media reported about a particular case to see whether there is congruence between the two explanations. Finally, measuring the outcome of EU competition law is accomplished through analyzing the equipment and services markets in terms of number of firms and their market shares, price and quality of services, and employment over the past quarter-century.

The scope of this study is limited to market competition and its outcomes, as well as the activities of supranational institutions, especially those of the European Commission, with occasional comparisons with the position of the Court of First Instance (CFI), which was established in 1989, and the ECJ, unless otherwise specified, in the sphere of competition law and policy. This is due to the fact that the European Commission has been the main body to implement competition law. Competition policy at the national level is not discussed for four reasons. First, EU law has supremacy over national laws. Second, EU law has a direct effect in the member states, meaning that citizens anywhere in the EU can sue their own national governments in their own national courts for non-enforcement of the treaties. Third, EU law has pre-emptive powers vis-à-vis national laws. Finally, the ECJ and CFI have the right to review the constitutionality of legislative and executive acts of governments, subjecting them to EU law (Gillingham, 2003, p. 131).[7] Focusing on the activities of supranational institutions in the field of competition policy is therefore adequate for investigating the political economy of EU competition law and policy.

Primary as well as secondary sources are used in the phase of data collection. Major primary resources are official documents in various forms, including treaties between the member states to create the EEC, the EC and the EU; and documents prepared by the EU institutions such the European Council, the Council of Ministers, the European Commission, the ECJ and the CFI in the form of regulations, directives, decisions, recommendations and opinions. Statistical figures prepared by the European Statistical

Agency (Eurostat), telecommunications reports and statistics prepared by the Organization for Economic Cooperation and Development (OECD), and statistics from the International Telecommunications Union (ITU) are used to demonstrate whether EU competition policy has created genuinely competitive markets in the EU telecommunications industry and whether citizens have benefited from such policies. Moreover, company reports and major international business, economic and telecommunications news-papers and magazines, such as the *Financial Times, Wall Street Journal, The Economist, Business Week,* and *Telecommunications* are surveyed to explain the dynamic processes of competing and monopolizing over time. Secondary sources include the major journals and scholarly books about the EU.

1.5. CHAPTER OUTLINES

This study is based on three levels of analysis—the theoretical, European, and industry levels. The second chapter develops the first and more abstract aspect of these levels and critically maps out the existing economic theories of market competition and their implications for state-market relations by examining power in its three forms (i.e. market, economic and political). In the same chapter, DMC as an alternative theoretical framework explains how the three forms of power work in the politics of public policy-making.

Dealing with the second level of analysis, the third, fourth and fifth chapters analyze state-market relations, and by extension, the interactions between economic, market, and political power by focusing on EU competition and telecommunications policies. The third chapter initially summarizes the state of competition policy in the principal EU member countries before the Treaty of Rome, and describes individual EU competition rules to show how the contradictions of the theory of effective competition are manifested in the design of these rules. It also evaluates the historical evolution of EU competition policy.

The fourth chapter elucidates the political economy of EU telecommunications policy with a similar objective of identifying the norms, values, policy objectives and strategies of EU telecommunications policy. The fifth chapter deals with the competition law cases decided by the European Commission in the telecommunications industry over the past twenty-four years. The chapter has two objectives. First, it illustrates empirically the principal motivations of EU competition policy that are suggested by the theory of effective competition. Second, it demonstrates how EU institutions perceive market power, and thus, the weaknesses, contradictions, and ambiguities of EU competition policy that manifest themselves in the actual implementation process.

The sixth chapter tackles the industry level. It specifically focuses on the relations between firms by distinguishing between telecommunications equipment and services markets. The purpose is to explicate how market competition and power work in reality, and how that reality differs from the vision of market competition portrayed by the EU institutions in their decisions. The structure, dynamics and evolution of each industry component is evaluated. Key individual firms are selected from the respective individual markets and investigated to explain the processes of competition as well as its outcomes. Finally, the last chapter evaluates the findings regarding market competition, in general, and EU competition and telecommunications policies, in particular. A discussion of market trends in the industry together with their wider economic, political, social and democratic implications is undertaken to complete the study.

2 Theories of Market Competition
Towards a Theory of Dynamic Market Competition (DMC)

Market competition is a ubiquitous, yet controversial, concept in the literature. As Sawyer (1989) noted, diverse theoretical approaches to competition have a significant impact on the analysis of market dynamics and outcomes, hence, the desirability of capitalism as an economic system (p. 141). The literature is enriched by a range of market competition theories in economics. Recent theories rather examine the market environment shaped by ethical, social and governmental factors, or outcomes, as opposed to competition itself (Hunt, 2000; Foss, 2000). The focus of this chapter is on the major theories of market competition in the economics literature to understand the nature of the relationship between free market competition and monopolization.

Geisst (2000) stated that monopolization is "a natural consequence of free market capitalism" (p. 4). Profit is the link that connects competition to industrial concentration. It may appear paradoxical that competition destroys its own foundations, but Sawyer (1994) put it as follows:

> The battle over profits stimulates competition and rivalry, but the act of competition helps to destroy profits. If the search for profits is the prime force and competition the derived effect, then it would be expected that when competition and profits conflict, competition will be diminished. (p. 9)

Understanding the dynamics of competition and concentration with reference to profit is only possible through analysis of examining power relations in the market. With reference to the treatment of power in its three forms (*market*, *economic* and *political*), it is possible to classify the existing theories into three main groups: conservative, liberal and radical theories of market competition. Each group can be also divided into subgroups, as Figure 2.1 below indicates.

This chapter has three objectives to accomplish. The first is to make a detailed investigation of the model of *effective competition* proposed by the theory of effective competition and taken by EU competition policy as a guide to clarify its real purpose as well as identify its significant flaws. The second aim is to demonstrate that neither the *conservative* nor

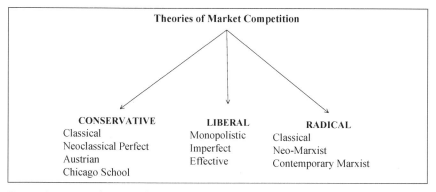

Figure 2.1 Main theories of market competition.

the *liberal* view offers an adequate framework to study the complex and dynamic processes of competing and monopolizing. The final objective is to demonstrate the strengths and weaknesses of the *radical* approach before proposing a new theoretical framework—a theory of dynamic market competition (DMC). DMC is derived mainly through a synthesis of Marx and Veblen's views on market competition applied to an analysis of the dynamic and complex processes of competing and monopolizing while still accounting for the nature and outcome of interactions between economic and political power over time in their historical context.

The first section of this chapter focuses particularly on the theory of workable or effective competition, despite its classification within liberal theories of market competition. The rationale for the separate treatment is to analyze effective competition in detail because as the model for EU competition law and policy, it deserves a closer look. The next two sections critically evaluate the conservative and liberal views respectively. The fourth section analyzes the radical perspective, before sketching a theory of DMC and suggesting how it can be applied to the study of the political economy of EU competition policy, which is taken up in the fifth and final section.

2.1. THE THEORY OF WORKABLE OR EFFECTIVE COMPETITION

Effective competition is a very controversial and ambiguous concept, which is defined in a number of ways in the literature. For instance, Shepherd (1990) defined it as striving between a 'sufficient' number of more or less equal rivals for market shares (p. 14). This definition implies three things. First, there are not many competitors. Second, competitors have more or less equal power and there is not much difference between them. Finally, competition as striving implies a gentle process. This definition points to a consolidated market where there are few competitors, more or less equal in power, competing with each other without serious harm. Contrary to Shepherd, Pearce (1986) equated effective competition with market structure. For him: "Workable or effective competition is a set of relevant criteria which purports to provide guidance on the competitive nature of markets, and can thereby instruct the formulation and execution of competition policy" (p. 458). The second definition indicates that effective competition deals with structural properties of the market, not with the process itself. Which definition is correct? Does effective competition refer to process or structure?

John Maurice Clark, one of the first American institutionalist economists, advanced the theory of effective competition under the name of 'workable' competition in 1940. He replaced the term 'workable' with 'effective' in 1961 due to the former's static implications (Clark, 1940 and 1961). He found supporters in continental Europe among German ordoliberals who played a critical role during the formative as well as initial years of European integration in the 1950s and 1960s.[1] In the specific historical setting in which economists and politicians alike saw large-scale enterprises as a solution to the economic crisis of the 1920s and the deep depression of the 1930s, the theory of effective competition was an attempt to answer the negative public policy implications of the theories of imperfect and monopolistic competition (Barry, 1989, pp. 109–10; Clark, 1969, p. 488; Clark, 1961, p. xi; Clark; 1960, p. 22; Clark, 1955, pp. 453–4). Clark and the ordoliberals opted for a middle way between a pure laissez-faire capitalism and communism within the neoclassical theoretical framework by developing the theory of effective competition (Oliver, Jr., 1989, p. 134; Clark, 1967, ch. vi; Clark, 1961, p. 39).

The theory of effective competition is concerned with "the conditions necessary for competition as a process to exist" in the first place (Ferguson & Ferguson, 1994, p. 29). In this sense, it is not very different from its brethren such as the theories of perfect, imperfect and monopolistic competition (as demonstrated below) in that they concentrate on the structural properties of the market. According to Ferguson and Ferguson (1994), Clark did not reject the static neoclassical theoretical framework entirely. On the contrary, "[he] attempted to work within the conventional analysis, with modifications to create a broader view of competition" (p. 29). Although the ordoliberals and Clark observed the monopoly-producing character of capitalism empirically and were concerned about its economic, social and political outcomes, their starting point was the economies of scale internal to the firm. They believed that there is a tendency to a market situation during which price is above marginal cost, and competition thus cannot eliminate some form of market power (Barry, 1989, p. 111). Efficiency versus justice was the principal dilemma they had to solve.

Despite the fact that the primary motivation in the theory of effective competition was a search for market conditions, Clark and the ordoliberals defined competition as a process, as part of their attempt to separate them-selves from the static neoclassical theory of perfect competition, as well as to inject dynamic elements into the static neoclassical framework without abandoning it.[2] They defined market competition as a price rivalry between business units and sellers with the motivation of seeking maximum net revenue under the circumstances of limited market power (Clark, 1943, pp. 283–300; Clark, 1940, p. 243).

Competition appears in aggressive and defensive forms, creating, reduc-ing, eliminating and recreating profits in different sectors of the economy (Clark, 1955, p. 454). Nonetheless, it is a kind of gentle 'neutralization process' in the last instance in that the responding firm eradicates the initial market power of the first mover, restoring the *status quo ante* in the market and maintaining an overall equilibrium position. What this picture suggests is that the theory of effective competition recognizes market power, but it implies a consolidated market in that firms have more or less equal market power, and power parity alludes to markets in equilibrium in general.

The theory of effective competition is concerned with market competi-tion and its implications for profitability at the industry level. The starting point is that industry does not operate at full capacity or at a point where marginal cost is equal to marginal revenue, as the theory of perfect compe-tition asserts. In actual competition, demand fluctuations cause industry to operate below full capacity in the short run. According to Clark (1940):

> A price which at all times covers only short-run marginal cost would lead to large operating deficits whenever demand is short of capacity, and would bankrupt most industries, no matter how shock-proof their capital structures. And since the horizontal individual demand curve of pure competition leads to a price that covers only marginal cost, it is not one of the conditions. *Instead, the requirement is an individual demand curve with sufficient slope to bring price, on the average, far enough above marginal cost so that average cost may be covered, over the run of good times and bad.* Along with this should go, presumably, enough price flexibility to afford a stimulus to demand in dull times, and the reverse in boom times. (p. 250, italics added)

Basically, the theory of effective competition is aimed at preventing supply-side market instability in the short term by ensuring the profitability of firms through toleration of mild market concentration, essential for market power to control prices. In the long term, potential competition and product sub-stitution are the factors that are thought to mitigate the problem of mar-ket instability, as the slope of the curves are flatter and hence, the effect of market power is less (Clark, 1940, p. 246). Moreover, cost and supply price curves of commodities are much flatter in the long run. In the case of the price curve, firms cut prices to boost sales volume, even at the expense of sacrificing their immediate profits. Concerning the cost curve, changes in plant capacity, not changes in output within the physical capacity of an existing plant, dominate the long-run cost curves of firms. Such costs do not vary significantly considering the average optimum size of the firm (Clark, 1940, pp. 248–9).

Profitability in the short term is the critical factor. That is the rationale for the theory of effective competition to focus on the structural properties of the market. Not every market is suitable for effective competition (Sosnick, 1958, p. 380). An 'adequate' number of producers, price-sensitive quality differentials, free entry to the market, free access to information, and some uncertainty about meeting price reductions are some of the preconditions for effective competition to exist. A transparent and stable market environment may cause open or tacit collusion between firms (Asch, 1970, pp. 120–1). The term 'adequate' is not clear, but it definitely suggests 'a few firms', not many. It also hints that concentration should not be excessive, which would facilitate tacit market collusion. In short, the theory of effective competition advocates loosely oligopolistic markets to assure profitability in the first place (Sosnick, 1958, p. 419).

Backing loosely oligopolistic markets, the theory of effective competition does not have any rule against concentrated economic and financial power as long as there is no significant change in the desired market structure (Sosnick, 1958, p. 419). It is clear that the ideal structure is one of loosely concentrated oligopolistic markets, and market concentration is not permissible after that threshold. Effective competition prohibits outright collusion, the shielding of inefficient rivals, and using tactics such as unfair, coercive, exclusionary, predatory and misleading sales promotion (Asch, 1970, pp. 120–1; Clark, 1955, p. 461). Cooperation and collaboration in every form such as interlocks, joint ventures and technological pools are acceptable, providing they do not harm competition or cause the concentration of economic power. Free market entry is thought to force firms to offer new and good-quality products to stay in business (Sosnick, 1958, p. 418). In this regard, the theory of effective competition is similar to the Austrian and Chicago theories of competition (as explained in detail below).

In the theory of effective competition, there is little trust in competition alone to allocate resources efficiently, even though it is perceived to be the main regulator in the market. Indeed, Clark (1961) did not perceive competition as a simple and self-acting regulator with the capacity to maintain itself without any outside intervention (p. 1). A system of effective competition entails 'a framework of institutions as well as essential rules' (Lenel, 1989, p. 29). A specific solution advocated by Franz Böhm, a prominent adherent of ordoliberalism, was the conception of an economic constitution (Moschel, 1989, p. 151). Walter Eucken, the founding father of ordoliberalism, defined the two underlying principles of the economic constitution, as constitutive and regulative. Institutional requirements necessary for the constitution to be effective are established through constitutive principles such as private property, a stable monetary system, freedom of contract, 'open' markets, and personal liability for actions. The regulative principles safeguard and maintain the system by preventing it from developing spontaneously in undesirable directions. In short, the state is responsible for preventing the market system from destroying itself by means of stabilization, anti-monopoly and social welfare policies.[3]

According to the ordoliberals as well as Clark, state intervention should take the form of a few well-defined stabilizing measures (Sally, 1996, p. 240). Since the economy consists of interrelated parts, frequent and arbitrary interventions in some spheres may have deleterious repercussions for other areas. This insight is essential for isolating economic logic from political pressures (Oliver Jr., 1960, pp. 125–6). The theory of effective competition entails a strong and isolated state. As Vanberg (1998) put it: "The formula of 'strong state' was meant by them as shorthand for a state that is constrained by a political constitution that prevents government from becoming the target of special interest rent-seeking" (p. 178). Taken as a whole, the state has *autonomy* in making laws as well as in daily administration (Streit, 1992, p. 639). A regulatory state, established on the basis of the rule of law and market competition to coordinate activities in the market, makes up the theoretical core of the theory of effective competition, and hence, of ordoliberalism (Bernholz, 1989, p. 190).

It is possible to discern a number of problems with the theory of effective competition. First, effective competition bears the fundamental contradiction of integrating dynamic elements into the static neoclassical framework, yet still pointing to market equilibrium in already consolidated markets.[4] Second, the theory of effective competition essentially deals with 'desired' market structure by targeting the profitability of firms and market equilibrium, rather than analyzing the processes of competition and market concentration itself, even though it defines competition as a process. Third, the theory of effective competition draws attention to the conception of time in market adjustment, but the concept has not been integrated sufficiently because the *conditions* of competition have been prioritized over the *processes* of competition. Fourth, the vision of the state, as an omnipotent and autonomous institution independent of economic and social forces in the theory of effective competition, does not take into account the complexity of state-society relations. While market power is recognized, there is a belief that political power can check the emergence of economic power by preventing excessive market concentration.

Finally, the implied model of the state, and hence, political power is excessively centralized and undemocratic. Clark and the ordoliberals accepted the negative potential of the strong state for democracy in return for gains in efficiency in the economic and political spheres. For instance, Clark (1969) insisted that:

> If the state is strengthened against such pressures, something of what we are accustomed to think of as democracy may be lost. Bureaucracies

and centralized executive power and responsibility grow. But there is no reason to think we must go all the way to dictatorship in order to make control reasonably effective; in fact, we may lose little that we now have of the substance of popular control over government and its activities. (p. 488)

The trade-off between economic efficiency and democracy is very clear in the theory of effective competition, and centralized political power is a conscious choice. What this trade-off indicates is that economic and political efficiency, rather than democratic participation, is the source of legitimacy for the polity in the theory of effective competition.

In sum, the theory of effective competition comes up short of offering an adequate framework equipped with the conceptual and analytical tools to comprehend the dynamic and complex processes of competing and monopolizing. It fails to provide a clear direction for understanding the divergent behavior of firms or to contextualize such activities over time in line with the evolution of the markets. The next three sections evaluate the contributions of *conservative, liberal* and *radical* theories of competition.

2.2. THE CONSERVATIVE APPROACH TO MARKET COMPETITION

The conservative tradition embraces theories such as the classical theory of competition put forward by Adam Smith and David Ricardo, the theory of perfect competition, and the theories of competition put forward by the Austrian and Chicago Schools. The conservative view perceives competition as a mechanism that allocates economic resources efficiently. Conservatives contend that market power is either non-existent or temporary because competition eradicates it in the long term. The prevailing idea amongst conservatives is that competition is always present and works as a mechanism putting pressure on firms to compete efficiently. Accordingly, competition eradicates market power, as efficient firms replace their inefficient competitors.

For instance, the classical theory of competition, as put forward by Smith and Ricardo, concedes that market power may exist in the short run, but not in the long run because competition eliminates it, unless the state intervenes by establishing entry barriers. Both Smith and Ricardo perceived market competition as a 'striving' or 'rivalry' among economic units, functioning as a general organizing principle in the market (Smith, 1994, p. 283; Ricardo, 1981, pp. 16, 62, 137, 263; Dennis, 1977, pp. 96–7). Competition is a force that tends to equate the market price of commodities to their cost price. The effective price mechanism ensures allocative efficiency in resource use (Ricardo, 1981, pp. 16–7; McNulty, 1967, pp. 396–9). As the 'invisible hand', competition plays a disciplinary role in the market, adjusting the price of wages, raw materials and manufactured commodities, and allocating capital geographically.[5] Briefly then, the classical theory of competition insists that free competition works efficiently as a *clearing mechanism*, or as an *invisible hand*, at the macro level, ensuring efficiency in the sectoral and geographical allocation of resources.

There are three substantial problems with this theory. First, it accepts the existence of market power in the short term, but claims that competition eradicates it in the long run. In this sense, market concentration, and hence, market power do not exist (Von Wieser, 1927, p. 154). Second, it concentrates on competition at the level of exchange, while overlooking the production level (McNulty, 1968, p. 654). Underestimating competition at the production level results in the exclusion of a critical aspect of market competition in that production and exchange are the fundamental features of generating and realizing profit from the perspective of firms. Third, the high level of abstraction employed in the theory "entirely glosses over questions of where these competitive forces operate, since the language omits reference to specific businesses or to particular markets" (Addleson, 1994, p. 99). Overall, the classical theory represents competition as a mechanism, while neglecting it as an expression of individual firm behavior. As long as markets are open to competition, there will be no market concentration and thus, there is no need for state intervention in whatever form. Economic power is also out of question.

Unlike the classical theory of competition, the modern theory of perfect competition is primarily interested in the necessary structural conditions for competition to exist, rather than explaining how competition actually works, as it assumes that competition works as a mechanism putting pressure on firms in the industry. There are five major conditions necessary for perfect competition to exist: identical products, perfect knowledge, many producers and buyers, and free entry and exit without any sunk costs (Lipsey, Ragan, & Couragant, 1997, p. 210). The theory of perfect competition is based on the idea of an equilibrium analysis in that demand and supply determine the price and quantity of products offered in the market (Nicholson, 1997, p. 250). It does not recognize market power, as it treats both capital and labor in the market as *passive* agents (Palley, 1996, p. 63). As well, it does not explain the process of competition because it is concerned with the conditions of competition, not the dynamic and complex processes of competition itself. In addition to overlooking non-price forms of competition, the descriptive and static framework of neo-classical competition suggests that competition policy is unnecessary.

In contrast to the theory of perfect competition, but similar to the classical theory, the Austrian and Chicago theories of competition define competition as a process. There is a major difference between the latter and the classical theory in that competition is depicted as a behavior, not as a mechanism, turning the classical theory upside down because of its focus on entrepreneurs or individual firms. In contrast to the passive image of the firm in the theory of perfect competition and its absence in the classical theory, the Austrian tradition focuses on the active role of the firm or entrepreneur in the process of competition (Young, 1992, pp. 204–7). The market process is itself dynamic, changing and imprecise, all of which makes static equilibrium impossible (Young, 1992, p. 212). The Austrians define market competition "as a dynamic and faltering human process of rivalry and bargaining" (Endres, 1997, p. 145). It is a dynamic process of discovery and conflict over price and non-price elements (Hayek, 1978, p. 179). Both producers and buyers learn the best available production techniques, products and prices, etc., through the process of competition (Hayek, 1948, pp. 95–6). In fact, competition creates a kind of impersonal compulsion driving entrepreneurs to try new possibilities.

In his explanation of the dynamics of market competition, Schumpeter (1950) introduced new variables such as new types of firm organization, new commodities, new production techniques and technologies, new sources of supply and the like, rather than taking price as the only variable. According to him, firms compete with one another, not for margins of profits, but to challenge the very foundations and lives of their competitors by introducing new commodities (p. 84). As a result, Schumpeter characterized the market as a "perennial gale of creative destruction" (Littlechild, 1978, p. 33). Discovering and implementing innovations requires substantial market power in the form of firm size and influence as tools for stabilizing otherwise turbulent and unstable markets. Large firm size induces firms to discover and exploit opportunities in reducing costs, and introducing new products to customers (Littlechild, 1978, p. 37). Instead of promoting cutthroat competition among many small firms, Schumpeter and the Austrian theorists supported oligopolies and cartels, as they perceived market power to be essential for creativity (Endres, 1997, p. 132).

For the Austrian School, market power is temporary and competition increases over time with the development of markets as well as demand. Prominent members of the school such as Carl Menger, Friedrich von Wieser, Joseph Schumpeter and Friedrich August von Hayek insisted on the temporal nature of market power. They maintained that a monopoly may exist at the beginning of the formation of a new market, but it disappears through time, as market competition intensifies (Young, 1992, pp. 207–17). For this reason, the Austrians believed that entrepreneurs have much more expertise in identifying inefficiencies than economists, judges or legislators, as long as there is free market entry (Littlechild, 1978, p. 34; Kirzner, 1985, p. 142). Entrepreneurs bear financial responsibility for their decisions, not regulators (High, 1984–5, p. 31). Instead of instituting government regulation, abolishing it is one of the best ways to increase competition because competition produces "a continuing process of rivalry and adjustment in an uncertain environment" (Littlechild, 1981, p. 361–2).

The Austrian theory introduced the criteria of competitiveness other than price. Despite these enhancements, the presumption that market competition always exists and puts pressure on firms to be innovative overlooks the fact that the intensity of market competition fluctuates. The Austrian School does not recognize the existence of economic power, and therefore, falls short of offering a convincing explanation as to why a few firms dominate specific industries for several decades. Finally, the Austrian School does not explicate the interactions between economic and political power, as the members believed that competition is enough to discipline market power and prevent the formation of economic power.

The Chicago School's theory of competition characterizes market power as transitory and ephemeral due to the firm belief in Say's law of the automaticity of the capitalist market. Markets have the following foundations. First, prices of all goods and services are independent of their qualities. Second, market-clearing prices are consistent with optimization decisions by all sellers and buyers. The quantity of commodities bought and sold equates their marginal costs with their prices. Finally, neither government actions nor monopolies influence relative prices in the long term (Hunt, 1979, p. 431).

Like the Austrians, members of the Chicago School concede the possibility of monopoly, but perceive it as transitory and temporary (Reder, 1982, p. 15). The main concern for the Chicago School is free market entry, echoing Adam Smith's opinion about monopolies created by states through granting special rights. Baumol (1987), one of the most influential members of the Chicago School, developed a theory of 'contestable markets' to show that market power is short-lived insofar as market entry is absolutely free and market exit is absolutely costless, regardless of the number of firms in the market (p. 3; Bork, 1967, p. 253). Shepherd (1984) criticized the contestable market model as follows: "Deliberate *brief entry* (hit-and-run entry) is also rare and unproven. Similarly, *free exit* (zero sunk cost) is also virtually unknown in significant markets with substantial market shares" (p. 580). Because of the perception that absence of entry barriers will be enough for competition to thrive, the Chicago School's theory of competition implies that there is not much need for a competition law.

As a whole, the conservative theories of competition perceive market power, and hence, market concentration, as temporary phenomena, while underestimating the implications of market concentration for the nature of interactions between economic and political power. They insist on the temporality of market power, and therefore, the redundancy of competition rules, especially rules dealing with market concentration. For the conservatives, market regulation in general is not an outcome of correcting market failures. In fact, 'a group of like-minded people' such as farmers and industrialists aligning along with other urban social forces capture regulatory agencies to further their interests (Stigler, 1988, p. 210). At the same time as they ignore economic power, the conservatives underestimate political power by representing the state as a dependent actor always yielding to the demands of organized groups. There is also a widely-held belief that firms are accountable to a market limiting their power because of competition (Peltzman, 1988, p. 236).

2.3. THE LIBERAL APPROACH TO MARKET COMPETITION

As an alternative to the conservative theories, the liberal approach to market competition comprises the theories of monopolistic and imperfect competition, in addition to the theory of effective competition, which is analyzed in detail above. The common feature of these theories is that they accept the permanent nature of market power, but they treat political power as omnipotent under all circumstances, since it has the capacity to regulate market power, and hence, to prevent the emergence of economic power.

The theory of monopolistic competition recognizes the market power of firms by shifting the emphasis from price competition to quality and product competition (Chamberlin, 1950 and 1961). Firms differentiate their products and become 'competing monopolists'. For Chamberlin (1950):

> Where there is any degree of differentiation whatever, each seller has an absolute monopoly of his own product, but is subject to the competition of more or less imperfect substitutes. Since each is a monopolist and yet has competitors, we may speak of them as 'competing monopolists', and, with peculiar appropriateness, of the forces at work as those of 'monopolistic competition'. (p. 9)

Functional similarity between products limits the market power of monopolies to the same degree that their products are substitutes and compete against each other (Chamberlin, 1937, p. 572). Prices overall are higher in monopolistic markets in comparison to prices under perfect competition. There is waste as the cost of producing, advertising, and selling these differentiated products is higher. These two adverse outcomes insinuate that the state has a role to play in dealing with them through appropriate public policies.

The theory of monopolistic competition has three major innovations with two shortcomings. First, the theory recognizes limited market power as a steadfast feature of capitalist markets. Second, it acknowledges both price and non-price forms of competition. Finally, the theory of monopolistic competition shifts attention from the industry to the firm in competition compared to the theory of perfect competition (White, Jr., 1936, p. 643). Like the Austrian tradition, the theory of monopolistic competition is firm-centric in its approach. But like other conservative theories, it assumes that competition always exists as a force and puts pressure on firms to differentiate their products. It does not explain when and under what conditions firms differentiate their products. Although market power is recognized, its effects are restricted to the market, thereby, leaving economic and political power untouched.

The theory of imperfect competition put forward by Joan Robinson also emerged in the early 1930s as a reaction to an increasing dissatisfaction with the Walrasian-Paretian theory of perfect competition (Knight, 1951, pp. 198–9; Sraffa, 1926). Robinson formulated the theory of imperfect competition along the lines of the particular equilibrium economics of Alfred Marshal and Arthur Cecil Pigou (Gram & Walsh, 1983, p. 548; Triffin, 1947, p. 3). Instead of challenging the equilibrium analysis of perfect competition, Robinson (1965) attempted to understand equilibrium positions by developing a new technique that would accommodate increasing returns to scale within an industry (p. 16).

Not unlike Chamberlin, Robinson (1932) focused her attention on the firm and took into account its cost and revenue functions together with the implications for market competition and market power. Her central proposition was that firms may be of less than optimum size in equilibrium under perfect competition because of increasing returns to those economies of large scale (p. 544). Besides defining a firm as a producer of one commodity and as controlled by a single independent interest, Robinson (1965) equated an industry with "any group of firms producing a single commodity" (p. 17). In general, Robinson (1965) challenged the assumption of the necessity of a large number of firms as a requirement for competition to exist in the equilibrium analysis of perfect competition by focusing on the slopes of the marginal cost curves of the firms (Loasby, 1971, p. 877).

According to Robinson (1934), the essential number of firms for perfect competition depends on the slopes of the marginal cost curves of each individual firm within an industry (p. 120). She implied that there is no need to have many firms in the market depending on the scale of the industry, as a few of them are able to supply the same amount of a commodity even at cheaper prices, as their costs decline with an increase in quantities produced (1965, p. 127). Although the average costs of firms fall rapidly because of those economies of large scale, the decline in the supply price is smaller due to market power (Robinson, 1932, p. 544; Kalecki, 1971; Steindl, 1947). Large firms benefit from economies of scale not only through lowering their costs by improving the organization of the industry, but also through raising the price of their products by restricting output (Robinson, 1965, p. 170). Efficient production and wider income inequalities are the two contradictory results of economies of scale. As maintained by Robinson (1965): "The problem of the world of monopolists thus resolves itself into the familiar dilemma between efficiency and justice" (p. 324). By posing the dilemma, Robinson suggested that market power is permanent and dealing with market power is a political issue.

Despite the path-breaking innovation of the theory of imperfect competition, it suffers from several theoretical flaws. First, the theory of imperfect competition overlooks the phenomenon of the "strategic interdependence of competitors, either through time or otherwise" even in the same industry

(Keppler, 1994, p. 109). Second, it assumes firms produce a single product (Weintraub, 1955, p. 478). Third, it overlooks inter-industry competition (Triffin, 1947, p. 19). Fourth, the theory of imperfect competition is criticized for not taking account of the influence of the credit system on the activities and production decisions of firms (Weintraub, 1955, p. 479). Fifth, the theory of imperfect competition focuses on market structure in the final analysis, not the dynamic processes of competing and monopolizing, explaining industrial concentration solely with technological advances. Finally, the theory hints at the role of economic power, but provides no further analysis of how to deal with it.

In the end, the liberal approach to market competition, in its monopolistic, imperfect, and especially effective competition versions, recognizes the permanent nature of market power and the link between market and economic power. Nevertheless, the characterization of political power as omnipotent in its control of economic power and ability to regulate market power is problematic. Moreover, the liberal perspective, similar to the conservative view, does not offer a framework for investigating the dynamics of competition and industrial consolidation. In that sense, the radical approach differs from them.

2.4. THE RADICAL APPROACH TO MARKET COMPETITION

Political economists like Karl Marx, Rudolf Hilferding, Vladimir Lenin, and Thorstein Veblen are the forefathers of the radical approach to market competition. Within the radical school, neo-Marxists scholars such as Michal Kalecki, Joseph Steindl, and Paul Baran and Paul Sweezy synthesized the ideas of Marx, Hilferding, Lenin, Veblen and Robinson. Contemporary Marxists have also made a recent attempt to revive and reinterpret Marx's theory of market competition within the context of the internationalization of capital and economic globalization.

The radical theories of competition advanced mainly by Marx and Veblen hinted at a dynamic theoretical framework that treats market and economic power as permanent features, at the same time as it theorizes the cyclical evolution of competition and its impact on market power and concentration. They defined competition as consisting of dynamic and complex processes. Competition functions as a vehicle for the expression of individual firm behavior in addition to working as a mechanism disciplining firms through the benchmark of profitability. Radicals also link the market to the state and analyzed state-market and state-society relations in detail.

Marx (1967) conceptualized competition within the context of value and prices of commodities (pp. 3–40). Defined as 'striving' between economic units, competition is a process through which the production, realization and distribution of surplus value is carried out. Competition is not peaceful but warlike—the action of capital upon capital (Marx, 1973, p. 751; Marx, 1968, p. 30). In such a warlike environment, there is no room for cartels. Moreover, competition on the basis of price, especially pricing-cutting is dominant, as opposed to competition on the basis of product differentiation. For Marx (1967), competition functions as a mechanism that has coercive power over every individual capitalist (p. 270). It coerces individual capitalists to follow similar patterns of market behavior (Marx, 1967, p. 316). In that sense, his view is not very different from that of Smith or Ricardo.

In examining market competition, Marx (1976) considered interactions not only between firms of different sizes, but also the relations between different sectors (finance, industry and agriculture) as well as the connections between firms and states, as he explained in the third volume of *Capital* (pp. 534–5). In Marx's understanding (1976), it is joint-stock companies that bridge the relationship between financial and industrial sectors. Observing their emergence, Marx drew three conclusions for his theory of competition. First, the joint-stock company, as a new form of organization for production, made it possible to produce commodities on a very large scale at less cost. Second, since joint-stock company shares are owned by many shareholders, their development resulted in the socialization of capital. Finally, that managers, not shareholders, run the day-to-day operations of the joint-stock company resulted in the separation of ownership from management (pp. 567–8 and p. 571). As Marx (1976) perceptively observed, the joint-stock company:

> produces a new financial aristocracy, a new kind of parasite in the guise of company promoters, speculators and merely nominal directors; an entire system of swindling and cheating with respect to the promotion of companies, issue of shares and share dealings. It is private production unchecked by private ownership. (p. 569)

The emergence of the joint-stock company changed the parameters of market competition, and the theory of market competition had to be recast. Nevertheless, Marx's theory of market competition was not fully evolved, although it is possible to find the basic elements scattered in his writings.

In addition to defining competition as a dynamic process, Marx explained not only the formation of economic power through the concentration and centralization of capital, but also how economic power influences public policies and, therefore, state-society relations. In *The Communist Manifesto* (1994), he revealed his vision of the modern state as follows: "The executive of the modern State is but a committee for managing the common affairs of the whole bourgeoisie" (p. 161). The bourgeoisie who own the means of production establishes itself in the modern representative state. As a result, public power is nothing but "merely the organized power of one class for oppressing another" (Marx,

1994, p. 176). In *The German Ideology* (1994), Marx contended that the state is principally an institutional form within which a double process of integration of the entire civil society and an assertion of the common interests of the individual capitalist takes place. Acting as an intermediary in the formation of all communal institutions, the state gives these institutions a political form, even though the state serves the purposes of the dominant class (p. 154). In explicating the existence of different forms of market regulation, Marx's followers, like Kolko (1965), asserted that state regulation promotes the interests of dominant classes because the state is capitalist (pp. 3–5 and p. 239).

There are several problems with Marx's theory of competition. The first is that he focused on market competition on the basis of price while overlooking non-price forms of competition. Second, for Marx, prices are perfectly flexible downwards, and this contradicts the realities of today, even though it might have been true in his lifetime because market concentration has increased over time. Finally, his vision of state-society relations is problematic in that he underestimated the impact of political power on economic power.

Rudolf Hilferding's theory of market competition provided a remedy to some of these problems. In observing firm behavior after the consolidation of the markets in heavy industries, Hilferding (1981) took Marx's theory of competition a step further by elaborating on the obstacles for the downward movement of prices. Based on additional historical evidence, Hilferding clearly identified two market types: markets with many competitors and markets with few large players or oligopolies after the destruction of small firms. Firms in competitive markets compete with one another on the basis of price. Competition still exists in the oligopolistic markets that have only a few large and powerful players with more or less equal economic resources and market power, but more often in these cases, competition remains indecisive in terms of market outcomes. Competitors with more or less equal power have a difficult time defeating each other. To prevent declining profits, firms rely on cartels, restrictive practices, combinations, fusions, amalgamations, advertising and other selling efforts as the principal market practices (p. 189).

Like Marx, Hilferding (1981) also discussed the importance of adjustment through time for understanding such practices. For instance, he contended that firms usually form cartels when their market is growing. In times of crisis, however, there is no chance for collaboration as they scramble to save whatever they can. Therefore, every firm acts without regard to others (pp. 192–3). Despite the innovation he brought to the radical theory of competition, Hilferding (1981) did not challenge Marx's view of the nature of the relationship between economic power and political power: "Economic power also means political power. Domination of the economy gives control of the instruments of state power. The greater the degree of concentration in the economic sphere, the more unbounded is the control of the state" (p. 370). Hilferding's perception of political power as passive vis-à-vis economic power seems problematic.

Following Marx and discussing the implications of his theory of market competition, Lenin (1963) maintained that market concentration does not mean the disappearance of competition. A mixture of free competition and monopoly would be the case (p. 40). Competition still exists in the markets even after concentration, but it changes its form. Restrictive practices and cartels become the main characteristics of new competition. Some of these practices include curtailing or restricting supplies of raw materials labor, cutting off deliveries, closing and trade outlets, cartel agreements, price cuts, stopping credits and boycott (Lenin, 1963, p. 26). Lenin specifically highlighted the international implications of market competition through imperialism, but did not challenge the vision of state-society relations that Marx had put forward.

Like many others, Veblen (1932) defined market competition as a dynamic process of rivalry and contention (p. 218). In contrast to Smith, Ricardo and Marx, but similar to the Austrians, Hilferding and Lenin, he considered price as well as non-price forms of competition with a particular focus on sales competition, advertising, and cartels. According to Veblen (1964a), competition is no longer product competition between the producer-sellers, but is in the form of salesmanship and sabotage: "Salesmanship in this connection means little else than prevarication, and sabotage means a businesslike curtailment of output" (p. 78). In restricting the production and distribution of commodities, competitors become collaborators in the form of syndicates, coalitions, and trusts. Even though there is an attempt to restrict market competition, there are deviations from time to time (Veblen, 1965, p. 38).

Reminiscent of Marx and Hilferding, Veblen made a distinction between shorter periods of relative stability and peace during which competition is not intense, and longer periods of destructive competition. Viewing competition as a dynamic process, Veblen, like Marx, put the modern corporation at the center of his analysis (1964a, pp. 90–93; 1965, p. 38). He had in his mind a national economy consisting of financial, industrial, and agricultural sectors. While the first sector consists of stock exchanges and banks, the second embraces many industries (Raines & Leathers, 1996, p. 145). Veblen's theoretical framework for understanding business competition is also broad enough to include the state (1932, p. 293). Compared to Marx, he was clear about the stages of competition and distinguished four main phases: exaltation, prosperity, crisis, and depression. He explained these stages in different parts of his writings, but like Marx, he did not advance a theory of competition alone.

With respect to the question of state-market relations as well as the interactions between economic power and political power, Veblen (1932) shared similar views with Marx and his followers in contending that the state favors capitalist interests: "Representative government means, chiefly, representation of business interests" (p. 286). Businessmen control the state through a 'tacit ring or syndicate' loosely organized within it in the form of political parties. Even though political parties have differences in the details of their programs, permanent parties in the legislature defend different lines of business policy (Veblen, 1932, p. 269). Politicians represent business interests as national interests to secure majority support. Business politics can be expressed at the state level in different forms. The extreme form is war and armaments (Veblen, 1932, pp. 293–5). On the whole, Veblen, along with Marx, Hilferding and Lenin, provided a broader framework for studying the dynamics of market competition and for considering price and non-price forms of competition (Arrow, 1975, p. 7; Walker, 1977, p. 228). Nevertheless, he exaggerated the significance of the financial sector over the industrial sector and underemphasized the growth of internal corporate financing (Riesman, 1953, pp. 162–5; Sowell, 1967, p. 88). Additionally, he undervalued political power, while exalting economic power.

The third group within the radical approach consists of the neo-Marxist scholars who aim to synthesize the ideas of Marx, Hilferding, Lenin, Veblen and Robinson. Michal Kalecki, Joseph Steindl, and Paul Baran and Paul Sweezy further analyzed the sources and implications of the economic power of large firms for the market and the public at large (Kalecki, 1971; Steindl, 1947; Baran & Sweezy, 1968; Sweezy, 1984). They relaxed the meaning of monopoly by maintaining that monopolistic domination does not require a market controlled by one firm. In oligopolistic markets with few firms controlling a substantial proportion of the outcome, dominant firms can also exert similar monopolistic influence because the cross-elasticities of demand are finite (Steindl, 1947, pp. 9–23). According to this view, economic power, once obtained, is self-perpetuating and augmenting despite the existence of competition rules. In fact, competition law is incapable of preventing price leadership and tacit collusions (Steindl, 1947, p. 65). Different from the classical radicals, the neo-Marxists did not explain how dominant groups acquire economic power or whether there is change in the composition of these dominant groups.

Finally, since the 1970s, contemporary Marxists have revived interest in Marx's theory of competition. These scholars were not interested in Marx's theory of market competition *per se*. They tried instead to reconcile the emergence of oligopolistic or monopolistic multinational corporations with Marx's theory of value (Kay, 1986; Bryan, 1985; Wheelock, 1983; Semmler, 1982). In the most recent debate on Marx's theory of competition, scholars have sought to relate Marx's theory of market competition to the decline in the rate of profit, and economic globalization (Foster, 2002; Clarke, 2001; Weeks, 2001). In sum, these two recent debates reflect the effort within neo-Marxist thinking to adapt the Marxist theory of competition to changing conditions.

The radical approach, in comparison to the theory of effective competition or the conservative and liberal traditions, provides a better explanation for the linkage between market power, market concentration, and economic power by putting forward a dynamic theoretical framework whereby current profit rates and future profit expectations are at the center of the analysis. It distinguishes three forms of markets: competitive, transitional, and oligopolistic, as well as explaining how market power manifests itself at the firm and industry levels in the complex processes of competition and concentration. Moreover, the radical approach takes the time factor into account to analyze the evolution of competition over time and in stages. It is a crucial element for understanding the actual intention behind firm-led strategies, organization and behavior that is missing from the conservative, liberal and effective competition theories. Furthermore, the radical perspective suggests the means by which economic power influences political decisions.

In sum, there are three points that remain underdeveloped in the radical framework. First, the nature of the relationship between political and economic power needs further elaboration to take into account political power in order to clarify the role of the state in policy making and implementation. Second, a dynamic theory of market competition has yet to be built on the basis of Marx's and Veblen's writings on competition to show how competitive markets turn into oligopolistic markets by explaining competition in transitional markets. Finally, the implications of this new theory of market competition for implementing competition policy have yet to be spelled out clearly.

2.5. A THEORY OF DYNAMIC MARKET COMPETITION (DMC)

DMC is a theoretical framework to study market competition as a process by focusing on interactions between market, economic and political power within the radical perspective. It analyzes not only the social, economic and political environment within which competition takes place, but also investigates market competition as a complex and dynamic process without overlooking its implications for the market as well as for wider society. The starting point is that economic dynamics are politically and socially constructed, as Offe (1971) and Block (1987) rightly pointed out.

The capitalist market economy does not exist in isolation from the wider society. Instead, it is deeply embedded in it (Gadrey, 2003, p. 62). Likewise, state and society are intertwined in such a way that the dividing line between them is not clear-cut, as maintained by Block (1987): "The point is that state and society are interdependent and interpenetrate in a multitude of different ways" (p. 21). However, they are ontologically two separate entities. Cooperation, conflict, and competition are the three predominant modes of interaction within and between markets and states, as in the case of any social reality (Szotampka, 1994, p. 53). Because of their internal dynamics as well as constant interactions between them, both the wider society and the state that operates within it are in the process of constant change (Hudson, 2004, p. 100).

The state has a crucial role to play in capitalist market economies. Offe (1975) convincingly argued: "The state is no capitalist itself, and accumulation takes place only in private accumulating units" (p. 126). As an ensemble of institutions with the responsibility for managing society's affairs, the state is an entity with its own life and interests that may coincide with the interests of some social forces or not, contingent on specific historical circumstances. Effective control over the state by any single social force is absent in capitalism (Mecksroth, 2000, pp. 74–83). However, the state has a structural obligation as well as legitimate authority to create and maintain conditions of accumulation in capitalist market economies (Offe, 1975, p. 126).

Even though the state in a capitalist society is independent of capital, it is dependent upon the presence and continuity of capital accumulation for its existence and survival (Panitch & Gindin, 2005, pp. 102–3). Revenues derived from the accumulation process are central to the exercise of political power by elected officials and senior bureaucrats (Offe & Ronge, 1975, pp. 137–47). According to Offe (1975), "Accumulation, in other words, acts as the most powerful constraint criterion, but not necessarily as the determinant of content, of the policy-making process" (p. 126). The state has an 'internalized' obligation to create conditions for uninterrupted and continuous capital accumulation.

Ironically, the very same social and economic mechanisms that the state institutionalizes and protects constrain the state's power (Offe, 1996, pp. 63–4). In this sense, capitalist firms have structural power that influences public policy making to their own advantage.[6] Influence does not mean determination, however. Block (1987) pointed out that: "Processes of interest aggregation, in short, do not produce *the* business position, but *a* business position that is the result of political debate and strategic calculations" (p. 11). Besides structural exigencies, capitalists as citizens can exert more influence on public policies than other social forces because they have more resources and better organizational abilities. Ultimately, the degree of influence depends on the institutional structure of the state and the type of political regime (Offe & Ronge, 1975, pp. 137-47).

Assuring profitability does not mean that every firm is necessarily profitable. Market competition determines profitable and unprofitable firms in the long term. After creating a level playing field, the state plays a regulatory role with occasional direct interventions only during emergencies. Current profit rate as well as future profit opportunities shape the business strategies and market behavior of firms, which, in turn, determine the intensity and forms of competition. It is possible to observe a systematic pattern in the business strategies, organization, behavior, and market conduct of firms depending on the factor of profitability in the markets they operate. As discussed above, Hilferding distinguished *competitive* and oligopolistic markets, but there is also an implication in his, Marx's and Veblen's writings that some competitive markets are transitional. On the basis of this observation, it is possible to add *transitional* markets as a third type between competitive and oligopolistic markets. The rest of this chapter briefly summarizes competition in these markets and discusses implications for enforcing competition law.

2.5.1. Competitive Markets

In competitive markets, there are many firms with varying sizes, but they are still owned individually. Capital required in competitive markets is relatively small and the rate of profit is lower than the overall average. Production is spread out among many firms. In addition to many players that eat up profit margins, large advertising campaigns and sales expenditures increase costs, thereby reducing profit margins. Free competition can be seen in the spheres of retail trade, and petty capitalist production. Competitive struggle on the basis of price is prevalent. Independent pricing is the rule in competitive markets. Thus, firms in crowded competitive markets are under the constant threat of bankruptcy. Some competitive markets are more prone to consolidation than others, especially in the industrial sector. A firm that enjoys technical and economic superiority dominates the market after a successful competitive struggle to eliminate its competitors (Hilferding, 1981, pp. 190–191).

With respect to competition law implementation, there is not much risk for competition in competitive markets. Nevertheless, competition law enforcers should be concerned about one practice that is the abusive conduct of a monopsonist or oligopolistic firms on the buyer's or supplier's side. Small firms in competitive markets often face a monopsonist or few buyers or suppliers with significant power. These powerful firms often abuse their market power to set lower market prices or discriminate against some firms at the expense of others. As a result, competition authorities should pay attention to both sides to ensure that large suppliers or buyers do not exploit small firms.

2.5.2. Competition in Transitional Markets

Some markets are not stable after all and may evolve into oligopoly. Transitional markets are located between competitive and oligopolistic markets in that they are still new, unstable and evolving. These are the markets where major product innovations appear. This may lead to the emergence of entirely new industries. Previously deregulated industries in the post-liberalization period such as telecommunications, air transportation, and utilities constitute a good example for transitional markets as well, but the direction of the change is from monopolistic to competitive markets.

The chief characteristics of transitional markets are numerous firms pursuing independent pricing policies, relative ease of entry and exit, and product homogeneity. There is a greater disparity in the size of competing firms in transitional markets. Large dominant, and medium-sized, as well as marginal firms exist side by side. On the basis of Marx, Hilferding, and Veblen's writings, it is possible to distinguish four major phases of competition in transitional markets with reference to intensity, dependence on the available sources of profit, as well as rate of profit.

Following Veblen's categorization, increasing (exaltation), intense (prosperity), destructive competition (crisis), and waning (depression) competition represent the four prime phases of business activity during which the intensity and form of competition varies (Veblen, 1932, p. 190). These stages provide a roadmap for comprehending the dynamics of market competition both as an expression of individual firm behavior and as a mechanism, as well as revealing the dynamics of state-market interactions. The next section examines these phases of competition more closely as well as their reverberations for implementing competition law.

2.5.2.1. Increasing Competition and Exaltation

In the phase of exaltation and increasing competition, prices of commodities increase in one industry or several lines of industries with growing demand. This, in turn, causes a sharp rise in requests for closely related commodities, opening up abundant new profit opportunities. Initially, firms use their stocks and idle capacity to meet rising demand, after which they increase their output capacity by building new plants (Veblen, 1932, pp. 194–7). When prospects of increasing profits, because of growing demand, appear on the horizon, shares of joint-stock companies valorize. Capitalization of industrial property makes it easy to access credit in large quantities, as the inflated property secures a greater amount of credit (Raines & Leathers, 1996, p. 145). Accordingly, the financial sector lends credit to firms in this specific industry. Firms use large amounts of cheap credit for building new factories, as well as buying undercapitalized firms (Bolbol & Lovewell, 2001, pp. 538–9).

In the meantime, commodity prices accelerate slowly in the absence of many competitors. Increasing profit margins, because of low input costs and higher output prices, attract new entrants. However, factors such as initial sunk costs and barriers to entry determine the overall number of new entrants. New firms, in turn, stimulate competition. Market leaders with sufficient financial resources speed up their research and development efforts to offer new commodities. New commodities are essential for creating new demand, as well as changing the structural parameters of competition. Additionally, cooperative agreements and joint ventures are widespread during this stage of competition as industry players move to restrict competition and defend their markets against new entrants. Taken as a whole, competition still remains weak because new entrants try to avoid the existing firms by entering into newly opened markets instead of competing head-to-head in older areas.

From a competition law perspective, market openness is the most important factor that functions as a check on price increases. Defensive competition is the usual practice at this stage of competition. As part of this strategy, dominant firms often form joint ventures with strategic cooperation and alliances acting as a deterrent to new entrants. Price increases and acquisitions are harmless because the market is growing and there are new players. State subsidies are less frequent. Overall, there is not much risk to competition other than collaboration agreements between dominant firms to protect their home markets.

2.5.2.2. Intense Competition and Prosperity

The difference between production costs and selling price is the main force behind the era of prosperity (Veblen, 1932, p. 198). High profit expectations and actual profit rates swell with the rising demand for new product or service offerings. New product market openings mean new geographic markets as well (Kaminsky & Reinhart, 2000, p. 146; Kojima, 2000, p. 376; Huber, 1998, p. 136; Stockman, 1998, p. 73; Hess & Shin, 1997, p. 93). Firms tend to expand geographically at this stage. As Marx (1952) noted: "The more powerful and costly means of production that he [individual capitalist] has called into life *enable* him, indeed, to sell his commodities more cheaply; they *compel* him, however, at the same time *to sell more commodities*, to conquer a much larger market for his commodities" (p. 39, italics original). This intensifies competition, within and between countries, as firms strive to cover their expenses and make profits (Marx, 1976, p. 1014).

The financial sector accelerates this process of competition by extending credit to money-hungry firms (Veblen 1964b, p. 130). Firms that foresee the future direction clearly take advantage of this opportunity by augmenting their capacity to expand geographically through internal expansion or by buying out other firms. High profit rates attract new entrants from other parts of the economy in the form of start-ups or extensions of business lines, depending on the existence of government regulation, history of the industry, entry, exit and sunk costs, research and development costs, and profit opportunities in other industries and sectors.

Competition fosters the introduction of new machinery in an attempt to reduce production costs. In the words of Marx (1973): "The anarchy of competition is one of the factors that causes the development of productivity in different branches of industry" (p. 369). Every new production technique makes commodities cheaper initially. Those capitalists who apply new techniques first earn more profit due to declining costs. Nevertheless, competition equalizes profit rates by universalizing new production techniques within the industry by accelerating the process of the diffusion of technology (Marx, 1973, p. 776)

With respect to the implications of competition for enforcing competition law, price cutting and mergers are two activities to be approached with caution, although they do not pose a direct or an immediate threat to competition at this stage. Facing decreasing prices, firms boost their profitability through larger market shares. The dominant practice is to sell large quantities at smaller profit margins. As a result, mergers and acquisitions gain momentum, as larger firms make use of abundant credit provided by the financial sector to buy other firms, and thereby, establish a critical mass in the market (Bolbol & Lovewell, 2001, pp. 538–9; Hilferding, 1981, pp. 193–95). Firms perceive market concentration as the main solution to the problem of thinning profit margins, but there is not much space for cartels, as firms look for individual solutions to the problem of profitability.

2.5.2.3. Destructive Competition and Crisis

Three major factors signal the beginning of the end of an era of prosperity. The first is escalating costs of capital, labor, and raw material, while the second is the sharp decline in final output prices because of market glut. Scarcity of offering new products is the final cause (Corbet & Vines, 1999, p. 163; Yoo & Moon, 1999, pp. 264–7; Muellerbauer, 1997, p. 1; Veblen, 1964b, p. 130 and 220). These three factors drive down profit margins rapidly. Nonetheless, reckless expansion in industrial investment and productive capacity, without higher returns, continues for some time due to speculation and 'dirty tricks', i.e. firms inflate their profits and hide their losses in order to attract more capital. The credit system serves as a basis for speculative activities in the market because it enables the acts of buying and selling to be spread out over time (Marx, 1976, p. 567; Veblen, 1964b, p. 130).

Eventually, after realizing that promised profits are not real or cannot be delivered, the financial sector stops lending to the industrial sector despite its urgent need. In this regard, Marx (1976) maintained that the financial sector plays a crucial role in accelerating, as well as decelerating, investment:

> The credit system hence accelerates the material development of the productive forces and the creation of the world market, which it is the historical task of the capitalist mode of production to bring to a certain level of development, as material foundations for the new form of production. At the same time, credit accelerates the violent outbreaks of this contradiction, crises, and with these the elements of dissolution of the old mode of production. (p. 572)

Market competition becomes destructive, at this point, as firms start underselling to survive the crisis.

In times of crisis, a capitalist who is controlling a large amount of capital can make more profit in absolute terms compared to their smaller counterparts, as the former deliberately reduces prices to drive out the latter from the market (Marx, 1976, pp. 331–2). The first consequence of destructive competition is the extinction of small firms and farmers who do not have enough capacity to produce on a greater scale (Marx, 1967, p. 705; Marx, 1952, p. 44). A few large firms that expanded recklessly during the stage of intense competition become bankrupt as well, since they cannot finance their debt any longer (Marx, 1976, p. 535). Thus, Veblen (1932) defined crisis as "a period of liquidation, concealment of credits, high discount rates, falling prices and 'forced sales', bankruptcy and shrinkage of values" (p. 191). It is also a period of extensive liquidation and redistribution of ownership of industrial equipment and property through forced sales and bankruptcy, paving the way for industrial concentration and consolidation (Marx, 1976, pp. 331–2; Veblen, 1932, pp. 202–3).[7]

Destructive competition has a number of implications for the enforcement of competition policy. First, price wars are the predominant strategy in this stage of competition. Underselling becomes a predominant firm behavior towards the end of destructive competition. Second, dominant firms abuse their position by using 'dirty tricks,' such as spreading false information about their competitors, withholding some key equipment or intermediate products from their competitors, not allowing competitors to share their facilities, lending competitors low-quality equipment or withholding technical information they are supposed to share under industry regulations. Third, both existing firms and new entrants make use of mergers and acquisitions with the two objectives of stabilizing their market environment by reducing the number of competitors, and entering into newly opened markets immediately, given that they do not have enough time to build new plants themselves. Finally, depending on the severity of the crisis and its social consequences, the state intervenes and bails out several bankrupt firms, especially the biggest ones, to reduce the so-called systemic risk and restore the conditions of accumulation (Gertler & Gilchrist, 1994, p. 309; Yoo & Moon, 1999, p. 272). State interventions may provide an unfair advantage to some firms at the expense of others. Therefore, competition authorities should be concerned about state aids.

2.5.2.4. *Waning Competition and Depression*

Depression or a period of underproduction because of low demand is the time during which plants run at half volume or not at all (Veblen, 1932, p. 216). The intensity of competition declines with the fall in the number of competitors as well as the demand. Market consolidation brings about a short period of truce and peace during which competition is not intense or destructive, restoring the rate of profit gradually. As the number of competitors decreases, the remaining firms restrict their mutual competition by cooperating with each other. With trusts and combinations, collective selling replaces competitive selling as business coalitions fix prices on the basis of 'what the traffic will bear'. Indeed, the scale of prices brings the largest aggregate net earnings to members of the coalition. In short, firms deploy three strategies to enhance profitability: limiting supply, obstructing traffic, and intensifying advertisement and sales efforts.[8]

Of these, trusts, cartels and coalitions are not everlasting, even if they work well in the short term to restore profitability. Cartels and trusts carry the seeds of destruction within themselves for two reasons. First, cartels do not include all firms in the industry. There are always small fringe firms outside the coalition that challenge and destabilize the cartel. Second, firms inside the cartel change their mind and think their interests are better served outside the cartel. They exit the alliance if, and only if, they see more profit opportunities outside the cartel (Veblen, 1932, p. 264). For these two reasons, cartels and trusts are unstable in the long term. Market competition erupts between cartel partners from time to time, resulting in massive price cuts and re-evaluation of the market values of corporations.

After a crisis, re-rating of the value of intangible and tangible items of wealth ensues (Veblen, 1932, p. 205). An increasing rate of unemployment signals the intensification of competition among the workers, thereby reducing the cost of labor (Marx, 1967, p. 549). Stagnation in production, and cheapening input and labor costs prepare the ground for industrial expansion in the next capitalist cycle because devaluation "clears the way for profit opportunities by existing capital on the basis of less competition, less pressure on wages, and lower production costs" Bolbol & Lovewell, 2001, p. 540). There is no end to the process of competition as long as there are at least two competitors (Marx, 1952, p. 41). Nonetheless, the nature of competition changes drastically in oligopolistic markets, if the market is already consolidated.

In terms of competition law, low profit rates ensuing from destructive competition result in bankruptcies, mergers and acquisitions, and voluntary industry exits, contingent on the present structure of the industry. Consolidation brings transparency, which makes it easier for firms to protect themselves by predicting their competitors' next move. A transparent environment is conducive to restoring the profit rate in the industry in three ways. First, firms differentiate their products or specialize in certain markets in the industry by knowing their competitors' areas of concentration. Second, they offer bundled products or services to create customer dependency. Finally, firms stop aggressive price-cutting, and begin to stabilize prices, if they do not immediately increase then. Mergers, acquisitions, tacit collusions, product bundling, and customer abuses are some of the principal activities that warrant special attention by competition authorities because they are signs that the market is becoming oligopolistic. Finally, state aids can be injected into the industry, if the industry does not recover naturally from a depression in a timely fashion.

2.5.3. Competition in Oligopolistic Markets

Transitional markets are not permanent. As Marx, Veblen, and Hilferding observed a long time ago, they eventually consolidate and become oligopolistic. In these cases, firms exhibit different market behavior and the nature of market competition changes dramatically compared to competition in the earlier markets. In oligopolistic markets, there are fewer firms, but their size is overwhelmingly larger. This does not mean that small or fringe firms totally disappear. In addition, firms in oligopolistic markets are no longer independent.

A major distinguishing characteristic of the firms in oligopolistic markets is that they have significant market power due to the concentration of much of the output in few hands (Steindl, 1947, p. 65). In the absence of significant cost differentials among firms, competitors can withstand price wars, which eventually hurt all players in the market without any clear winner or loser (Steindl, 1952, p. 53). As a result, large firms avoid destructive competition on the basis of price. In place of price competition, price leadership develops in such markets where dominant firms determine prices and others follow suit. Cartels are also widespread and engaged in price fixing and limiting production. The emphasis on competition in oligopolistic markets shifts from price to non-price elements, such as research and development, new products, new organization, and new production methods.

There are a number of market practices that may be of concern to competition law authorities. The first one is cartels which seek to curtail output by cutting deliveries, increasing prices, boycotting, and negotiating exclusive purchasing agreements. The second is the use of abusive practices by dominant firms and cartels, especially against smaller firms. Systematic price cutting and selling below cost to drive non-compliant firms out of the market are prevalent market practices (Lenin, 1963, p.26). Finally, price leadership, which is very difficult to identify, is another widespread practice. It is possible to gauge the market by observing trends in cost structures and the timing of price hikes in the industry. If there is a consistent pattern in price movements, it suggests that price leadership is working.

2.6. CONCLUSIONS AND IMPLICATIONS

This chapter has demonstrated that the theory of effective competition, the economic model for EU competition policy, lacks the necessary conceptual and analytical tools to explain the dynamics as well as the outcomes of market competition due to its contradictory foundations. In addition to its theoretical problems, the theory of effective competition promotes industrial concentration up to a certain point with the objective of assuring profitability above the normal rate of return (i.e. loosely oligopolistic markets). Moreover, market competition is equated with market structure, even though the theory was a product of an attempt to inject dynamic elements into the static foundations of the neoclassical theories of imperfect and monopolistic competition. Finally, the theory of effective competition's treatment of the state as a powerful and autonomous entity is problematic in that it does not take into account the impact of social forces, especially large firms, on politicians and bureaucrats.

Conservative and other liberal theories do not offer a viable alternative to the theory of effective competition for a number of reasons. The conservatives treat market competition as an efficient mechanism and market power as a temporary phenomenon, in that *laissez-faire* market competition has the power to eradicate it, so long as the state does not disrupt the 'natural' flow and dynamics of market competition. The conservatives offer little practical advice because of the way they define competition, and they have difficulties in explaining market concentration and market power, persistent features of contemporary capitalist markets.

In contrast to the conservatives, the liberals acknowledge market power and its persistence. Market failures are not uncommon in liberal theories. As a result, they target particular market structures and aim to correct market failures, whenever they exist. This explains why the liberals equate market competition with market structure and believe that the state, with its own institutional structure and resources, has the power to establish desired market structures and regulate market competition. Put differently, the liberal tradition represents the state as an autonomous entity above and beyond social forces. The liberal analysis of state-society relations in terms of privileging the state vis-à-vis the society is highly problematic.

Compared to the conservative and liberal perspectives, the radical approach offers useful conceptual tools to study market competition as a dynamic process over time, essential for competition as an expression of firm behavior as well as a regulative force over firms. The radical view makes it possible to study the evolution of markets over time as a whole, which is essential for grasping the rationale behind individual firm behavior and market action. Nevertheless, there are three flaws in the radical perspective. First, it underestimates political power. Second, it does not bring together all the pieces required to articulate a dynamic theory of market competition. Finally, the implications of this new theory of market competition for implementing competition policy are not spelled out clearly.

DMC overcomes these difficulties by suggesting three propositions. The first is that market competition and concentration or de-concentration should not be seen as a mere market phenomenon. Understanding them satisfactorily requires the study of the wider regulatory environment and relevant public policies, which are created through myriad forms of interactions between political and economic power. Individual public policies, which are, in fact, an outcome of bargaining and compromise between the state and social forces, have an impact on the dynamics of the market.

The second proposition is that there is always a possibility that public policies may fail because of policy mistakes, shortcomings, faults and weaknesses in their design and/or implementation, along with the manifestation of the concessions in concrete terms. The final proposition is that market competition and concentration is a dynamic, but not a unilinear process. Comprehending the logic behind competition, concentration, and de-concentration requires an in-depth historical study of the four phases of market competition to get a clear picture of the evolution of markets, individual firm actions, and the outcomes of market competition.

On the whole, this chapter has proposed that competition and concentration are not a mere market phenomenon. Studying them adequately necessitates an in-depth analysis of public policies and framework laws, such as competition law, which regulate competition and concentration in the market in the first place. Unraveling how market competition and concentration are perceived in public policies is critical to studying the political economy of EU competition policy, before analyzing its day-to-day implementation. Another significant finding is that the theory of effective competition engenders centralized, political decision-making in order to form and preserve loosely oligopolistic markets to assure the profitability essential for supply-side stability. Besides, it fails to make available to EU institutions the necessary conceptual tools to analyze the dynamic and complex processes of market competition, mainly because of its contradictory theoretical foundations. To provide empirical evidence for this observation, the next chapter evaluates the objectives, conceptual design, and historical evolution of EU competition policy.

3 Competition Law and Policy in the EU

This chapter examines three aspects of the formation and historical evolution of EU competition law and policy. First, it demonstrates that the EU has had a centralized decision-making structure in general affairs as well as in applying competition law. Second, it aims to show that the design of EU competition rules in the treaty establishing the European Economic Community (EEC) was intended to create and maintain loosely oligopolistic markets as an ideal market form. Finally, this chapter illustrates that EU competition policy had to give up even the modest 'ideal' of loosely oligopolistic markets and became reluctantly open to market concentration, as it sought to assure the profitability of firms in the 1980s.

The first section of the chapter provides a brief survey of the history of European integration and main EEC/EU institutions, followed by the history of competition policy in Europe before the creation of the EEC in the second section. The third section summarizes the competition rules stated in the EEC Treaty. The fourth section presents the historical evolution of European competition policy by focusing on the EU institutions' attitudes about profitability and market concentration. Taken together the four sections establish the basis for a broader understanding of EU competition policy.

3.1. HISTORY OF EUROPEAN INTEGRATION

The founding of the EEC as a supranational organization was preceded by the formation of a number of other supranational organizations between various European countries in the aftermath of World War II (WWII). There were two significant initial attempts in the economic field. The first supranational organization was the Benelux Economic Union that arose out of a customs agreement signed in 1944 by Belgium, the Netherlands and Luxembourg to promote free movement of workers, capital and commodities within the Benelux region. The second was the formation of the Organization for European Economic Cooperation (OEEC) in 1948. Established initially by the European states as an intergovernmental economic organization, it had the responsibility of allocating, administering and delivering

American aid under the Marshall Plan with the purpose of accomplishing the goals of the so-called Truman Doctrine to reconstruct Europe. The OEEC became the Organization for Economic Cooperation and Development in 1961 (OECD), opening its membership to non-European countries such as Australia, Japan, Canada and the US (Hahn, 1962).

In the political sphere, the European states formed the Council of Europe in 1949. The Council did not have any real executive powers, but played a symbolic role as a forum for discussion. Cooperation for defense purposes emerged when France, the UK and the Benelux countries signed the Treaty of Brussels in 1948, expanding the previous year's defense cooperation agreement (the Dunkirk Treaty) between France and the UK to defend member states against possible military aggression by Germany. However, the North Atlantic Treaty Organization (NATO) established in April 1949 linked North America with these five European states in the military field such that cooperation took a distinctly 'Atlanticist' turn. Other European countries joined NATO in subsequent years (Walton, 1953).

The formation of the European Coal and Steel Community (ECSC) in 1951 was a major turning point in the process of European integration. The ECSC was established with the signing of the Treaty of Paris by six West European states (Federal Republic of Germany, France, Italy, Belgium, the Netherlands and Luxembourg). Different from previous attempts, the Treaty of Paris resolved the age-old conflict between Germany and France by pooling national coal and steel production. Even though the ECSC emerged as a common market for iron, steel and coal through the removal of all customs duties, tariffs, quotas and other market restrictions among the six signatory states, it was more than a common market (Gebr, 1953).

The most innovative feature of the ECSC was the establishment of a High Authority. This genuine supranational institution, with powers to regulate the coal and steel industry, was a remarkable achievement of the ECSC. The Treaty of Paris, which expired on July 23, 2002, reflected a continuing desire for European integration as well. In this sense, the ECSC was the first step toward comprehensive integration at the continental level (Shaw, 2000, p. 44).

This achievement encouraged other initiatives such as the European Defense Community (EDC) and the European Political Community (EPC) in the first half of the 1950s, but neither was successful (Pinder, 2001, p. 11). The failure of these two initiatives showed that the European states were not yet ready to give up their sovereignty in such important areas as the military and politics. Nevertheless, they continued to pursue the idea of European integration in other areas. The foreign ministers of the ECSC member states came together in June 1955 in Messina, Italy to discuss the objective of broadening and deepening economic integration by creating a general common market based on free market competition, while taking specific measures in the field of nuclear energy. The meeting culminated in the formation of a committee, responsible for elaborating one or more treaties to enact these proposals. The Committee prepared the famous Spaak Report, named after its chairman, Paul-Henri Spaak, and submitted the document to the foreign ministers of the six countries, who approved it in May 1956 (Yalem, 1959).

The report called for the creation of a common market with indispensable political institutions. A notable characteristic of the report was that it included draft rules relating to competition policy to be included in the EEC Treaty. According to Goyder (1998), the detailed drafting of the competition rules caused a sharp argument and complex negotiations between the states, especially between the German and French delegations. Besides the ideological dimension to the dispute, the French delegation did not initially want to open up the French market to German capital with the help of competition rules that would reduce all restrictions on trade because French firms were too weak to compete successfully with their superior German counterparts. As a middle position, the French dropped their objections after the Germans had accepted the idea of excluding the agricultural sector from the competition rules and adopting a common agricultural policy (Wesseling, 2000, pp. 13–4).

The six countries signed the EEC Treaty along with a treaty establishing a European Atomic Energy Community (EURATOM) in Rome on March 25, 1957 (coming into force on January 1, 1958). Each of the three Communities founded in the 1950s (ECSC, EEC and EURATOM) had their own separate commission until 1967 and this arrangement was not efficient. The treaty establishing a single Council and a single Commission of the European Communities of 1965 came into effect in 1967 merged the High Authority and the two Commissions into one Commission of the European Communities (CEC), consolidating the executive arm of the EEC (Weil, 1967).

A debate between the member states and the supranational institutions about the locus of power flared up in the mid-1960s as the CEC claimed more power. For example, Walter Hallstein, the first president of the Commission and an ardent German ordoliberal, attempted to make the EEC financially self-sufficient, extend the budgetary powers of the Parliament, and revise the financing of the Common Agricultural Policy (CAP). However, the most contentious issue was that Qualified Majority Voting (QMV) would replace unanimous decision-making in a range of areas after the ending of a transition period (1958–70) in the Common Market. French President Charles de Gaulle perceived the voting arrangements in the EEC Treaty as an assault on sovereignty.

Known as 'empty chair policy', Charles de Gaulle ordered his ministers not to attend meetings of the Council of Ministers, withdrew France's permanent representative to the EEC, and told Gaullist members of the European Parliament to be absent from Parliament in July 1965. France was fiercely resisting Hallstein's idea of the EEC as "a federation in the making" (Hallstein, 1963, p. 162). As Nugent stated (2001), the result was the so-called 'Luxembourg compromise', according to which the unanimity rule was to be maintained, whenever 'vital national interests' were at stake. This incident reinforced the power of member states in the evolution of European integration at the expense of paralyzing all decision-making in the EEC over the next fifteen years.

After the resolution of the empty-chair crisis led by France in the mid-1960s, the EEC expanded both horizontally and vertically. In the first place, the member states successfully accomplished the complete removal of customs duties in July 1968, ahead of schedule. Second, the EEC completed its first expansion in 1973, when Denmark, Ireland and the UK became members. Before that, however, General de Gaulle had rejected the UK's application twice in 1963 and 1967, respectively. In other words, the EEC continued horizontal expansion, even if the progress was slow. In terms of vertical integration, political leaders decided to deepen European integration at The Hague Summit in December 1969. Consequently, political leaders of the nine member states decided to form the European Council at the Paris Summit in December 1974 as well. The informal body would meet three times a year to deal with problems, which the Council of Ministers were unable to solve (Wallace & Edwards, 1976). In other words, the member states would steer the direction of the EEC informally, regaining their control at the supranational level, by establishing their dominance over the process of European integration.

The rosy economic atmosphere of the 1960s gave way to pessimism in the 1970s, with the economic slowdown in Europe, and the US decision in August 1971 to suspend the dollar's convertibility into gold. In addition, the oil crises of 1973 and 1979 aggravated the situation. As part of a broader plan for dealing with the economic slowdown, the EEC member states decided to pursue greater monetary integration by 1980, and agreed not to fluctuate exchange rates between their currencies by more than 2.25 percent (known as the 'snake'). These initiatives were part of the first stage of the monetary unification plan (Dinan, 2004). The EEC also introduced the European Monetary System (EMS) in 1979 (Eichengreen, 1993). Besides launching new social, regional and environmental policies, the EEC set up the European Regional Development Fund (ERDF) in 1975 to assist less developed regions. Despite such collaborative efforts to deepen vertical integration, the member states largely preferred to deal with their problems individually throughout the 1970s, almost halting the progress of European integration.

As stated by Albo and Zuege (1999), the world economic recession of the early 1980s caused a wave of 'euro-pessimism'. In order to overcome this negative outlook and rekindle the project of European integration, the member states signed the Single European Act (SEA) in February 1986, which came into force in July 1987. The SEA identified some three hundred necessary actions that would remove trade barriers between the member states and allow for the creation of the common market. Most of these actions had been blocked by the requirement for unanimous agreement in the Council of Ministers. With qualified majority voting, the Council of Ministers could speed up decision-making and turn the single European or common market into a reality by the end of 1992 (Grin, 2003). Having eliminated the need to gain consent for lawmaking from each member state, the SEA was also able to initiate market deregulation and liberalization policies to create more opportunities for European firms in areas such as transportation, utilities and telecommunications.

In addition to qualified majority voting, the SEA instigated a number of institutional innovations as well. First, it established European Council meetings as an official aspect of institutional practice, ensuring that the heads of governments and states would meet regularly to decide the future direction of the EEC. Second, it introduced the 'cooperation' and 'assent' procedures for Parliament to share legislative power with the Council.[1] Finally, the SEA created the Court of First Instance (CFI), which became functional in 1989, to deal with certain kinds of cases, especially actions brought by firms or private individuals against EU institutions, competition cases, and disputes between the institutions and their employees with the purpose of easing the burden on the European Court of Justice (ECJ) (Steiner & Woods, 2001). In the meantime, the EEC continued its expansion program in the 1980s by accepting Greece in 1981, and Spain and Portugal in 1986, as member states. With the SEA, it seemed that the member states surrendered some of their individual powers to make daily decisions with qualified majority voting as well as sharing some power with the European Parliament. Nonetheless, the members became officially in charge of shaping the future direction of the EEC through the European Council.

The fall of the Berlin Wall in 1989, the reunification of Germany in October 1990, and the collapse of the Soviet Union in 1991 signaled the end of the Cold War, dramatically changing the political landscape of Europe overnight. With the momentum gained in the second half of the 1980s, the EEC continued its rapid metamorphosis through the 1990s, despite the severe economic recession of 1992. The European Council decided to set up an inter-governmental conference in Strasbourg in December 1989 in order to complete economic and monetary as well as political union. As a major turning point in the history of European integration, the member states signed the Treaty on European Union (TEU) in Maastricht on December 9–10, 1991, which came into force on November 1, 1993 (El-Agraa, 2004).

The TEU, widely known as the Maastricht Treaty, laid the basis for common foreign and security policy, closer cooperation in justice and home affairs, and economic and monetary union by 1999, including a single currency (Nugent, 2001; Huebner, [n.d]). It also renamed the EEC, adopting the title of European Community (EC), while establishing the

European Union (EU) by adding the above-mentioned areas of intergovernmental cooperation to the existing Community system. Finally, the TEU also introduced a new 'co-decision procedure' with respect to legislative power, whereby the Parliament obtained equal power with the Council when legislating a number of significant issues, such as the free movement of workers, internal markets, education, research, environment, Trans-European Networks (TEN), health, culture and consumer protection (Hartley, 1993).

The Amsterdam European Council agreed on the Treaty of Amsterdam at a meeting on June 16–17, 1997. Signed in October 1997 and enforced on May 1, 1999, the new treaty brought innovations in the spheres of freedom, security and justice, the EU and the citizen, common foreign and security policy, and the EU's institutions in general. It added 23 new fields for the co-decision procedure, while creating a new post, High Representative for the Common Foreign and Security Policy. In other words, the treaty conferred on the EU new powers and responsibilities, but not yet a legal personality in world politics (Chryssouchoou, Tsinisizelis, Stavridis, & Ifantis, 1999). For the most part, the Treaty of Amsterdam achieved nothing more than fine-tuning of the TEU.

The EU carried on its expansion with Austria, Finland and Sweden joining on January 1, 1995. After completing the single market and monetary policy, and with new members, the EU decided to undergo a major institutional reform in the late 1990s, in response to criticisms directed against it as well as to prepare for even further expansion to the east by 2004. Accordingly, the Intergovernmental Conference on institutional reform opened in Brussels in February 2000 and ended with a political agreement, the Treaty of Nice, in France in December 2000.

The new treaty amended the TEU and the treaties establishing the European Communities with the objective of dealing with issues of qualified-majority voting and the co-decision procedure, the weighting of votes in the Council, the composition of the Commission and of the European Parliament, and closer cooperation in the areas of defense, human rights and justice. The new treaty added seven new fields in which the co-decision procedure applies (Yataganas, 2001). Nevertheless, EU competition policy was exempted from the co-decision procedure. In a historic expansion on May 1, 2004, Cyprus, the Czech Republic, Estonia, Hungary, Latvia, Lithuania, Malta, Poland, the Slovak Republic, and Slovenia joined the EU, increasing its membership to 25. With the accession of Bulgaria and Romania on January 1, 2007, the EU had 27 members.

As this brief history of European integration depicts, the EU constitutes a new polity formed through negotiations between the member states. As Hooghe (1999) aptly puts it, the EU is a polity in the making. The ECJ clarified the EEC's position in the *Flaminio Costa v E.N.E.L.* case in 1964 by drawing attention to the creation of a new sovereign federation-like entity through the EEC Treaty:

By contrast with ordinary international treaties, the EEC Treaty has created its own legal system which, on the entry into force of the Treaty, became an integral part of the legal systems of the member states and which their courts are bound to apply. By creating a Community of unlimited duration, having its own institutions, its own personality, its own legal capacity and capacity of representation on the international plane and, more particularly, real powers stemming from a limitation of sovereignty or a transfer of powers from the states to the community, the member states have limited their sovereign rights and have thus created a body of law which binds both their nation and themselves. (para. 3)

Instead of focusing on the supranational level and privileging the supranational institutions at the expense of the national level and the member states or vice-versa, this study takes the EU as a single entity.

In principle, European integration is an elitist project and an outcome of perceived interests of the member states as maintained by Chryssochoou (2001). This does not mean that economic factors did not play any significant role. As Willis (1978) stated: "At all stages of the process of integration, the political and economic facets have been closely interrelated" (p. 1). Nonetheless, as the structural-functionalists and Marxists claim, 'economic spillover' or 'internationalization of capital' does not alone explain European integration (Corbey, 1995). Haack (1983) pointed out three major factors behind European integration: internal (creating profitable regional blocks and preventing political conflict between France and Germany); external (increasing the competitiveness of European firms mainly against their American counterparts); and East-West conflict (capitalism versus socialism).

As Milward (1992) suggested and the brief history of European integration has demonstrated, the formation of the EU is a manifestation of the reassertion of the European nation-states themselves, at the European level. The EU has been a vehicle for the member states to extend their functions and ambitions as part of their ultimate strategy of regaining the loyalty of their citizens, and is essential for their legitimacy by improving their social and economic conditions. Of course, the member states could not impose their projects onto social forces unilaterally. They made promises and concessions to European economic and social forces to gain their support for the project of European integration in return for reestablishing their control and authority at the European level via the EU. Therefore, EU governance represents how the member states ensured their power collectively by acting through EU institutions at the supranational level.

3.2. EC/EU GOVERNANCE

Despite the geographical expansion over time, the institutional structure that was set up by the EEC Treaty has remained intact, albeit with minor modifications. The EEC Treaty designated supranational institutions responsible for making and implementing decisions. Article 7 (ex-Article 4) designates the Assembly or the European Parliament, the Council of Ministers, the Commission, the Court of Justice and national courts as the principal bodies that are responsible for carrying out the tasks entrusted to the EEC. Under the EEC Treaty, the European Parliament did not have any specific legislative powers, in contrast to national parliaments. Its powers were mainly limited to supervision and advising. The Parliament could ask oral and written questions of the Commission and Council, and vote the Commission out of office during the formative years. Nevertheless, it gained the right to co-decide with the Council in the making of laws in a number of policy areas in 1992 and the policy area coverage of its co-decision power has expanded ever since (Scully, 2003).

The Council of Ministers, which consists of one representative from each member state in specific policy sectors, has been the main legislative body (Peterson & Bomberg, 1999). Political leadership of the Council falls to the rotating Council Presidency. Since the unification of the three separate Commissions in 1965, the member states have rotated the presidency every six months. The Council makes a decision through qualified majority voting, simple majority voting or unanimous voting depending on the area in which it legislates. It enacts laws in the form of regulations, directives and decisions as well as ensuring coordination of the general economic policies of the member states.[2]

In contrast to the legislative function of the Council, the European Commission, as the executive branch, acts autonomously without instruction from any member state to defend the interests of the EU as a whole. In general, the Commission ensures the implementation of the regulations and directives adopted by the Council and the Parliament. In particular, the Commission is responsible for ensuring proper functioning and development of the Common Market. It has limited legislative power conferred on it by the EEC Treaty itself, as well as by delegation from the Council. In addition to being the only institution with the right to propose new legislation, the European Commission is responsible for managing the Community's common policies such as competition, research, development aid and regional policy, as well as managing the budget for common policies (Egeberg, 2003). While the member states nominate commissioners, the European Parliament confirms them. A civil service made up of 36 'Directorates-General' (DGs) and services located mainly in Brussels and Luxembourg assist the Commission. The Commission's financial resources enable it to act quite independently of the member states, but it is accountable to the European Parliament (Tomkins, 1999).

The ECJ is the institution that ensures the observation of law in the interpretation and application of the EEC Treaty. It has the power of judicial review over all Council and Commission acts other than recommendations and opinions. Besides the cases brought by natural and legal persons, the member states, the Council of Ministers, or the European Commission, may each institute proceedings against the other for lack of competence, or infringement of an essential procedural requirement, treaty or any rule of law affecting the misuse of powers. This also applies to competition policy. The CFI has been assisting the ECJ since its establishment in 1989 (De Búrca & Weiler, 2001).

The European Council with its summit meetings of heads of state and governments became an informal institution in and of itself at the Paris summit of December 1974. The main function of the European Council was to move the business of government forward when the Council of Ministers was deadlocked. It became a formal Community institution with the SEA in 1987 and the TEU assigned it a 'system-steering' role in 1992 (Bulmer, 1996). The European Council issues general policy guidelines, settles difficult issues on which ministers (meeting in the Council of the EU) fail to agree during their four meetings each year, and sets out new agendas for the development of the EU (Peterson & Bomberg, 1999). There are also other European auxiliary bodies such as the Court of Auditors, the European Economic and Social Committee, the Committee of Regions, the European Investment Bank and the European Central Bank. These institutions make a significant contribution to EU governance in their respective areas of responsibility.

The institutional structure of the EEC/EU clearly reflects the centralization of political power in the hands of the European Council, the Council of Ministers and the European Commission. While the member states control the first two supranational institutions directly, their control over the last one is indirect, through the appointment of commissioners. Besides their steering capacity via the European Council, the states are the dominant players in lawmaking through the Council of Ministers, despite the increasing powers of the European Parliament. The member states accepted the Reform Treaty, a scaled back version of the European Constitution rejected by Dutch and French voters in 2005, in June 2007. The treaty defines the EU as a single legal personality, sets up a permanent EU presidency to plan summits, and establishes a new foreign policy chief position. Additionally, it extends the scope of qualified majority voting in the Council of Ministers, while giving the European Parliament the right to elect the President of the European Commission, and extending its legislative and budgetary powers.

Overall, the new Reform Treaty does not significantly alter the basic institutional structure set up in the EEC Treaty of 1957, a centralized decision-making structure dominated by the member states, which embodies the institutional requirements of the model of effective competition. Nevertheless, the Reform Treaty is a decisive moment for EU competition policy in that the member states agreed to drop the phrase 'free and undistorted competition' from the list of EU objectives listed therein at the insistence of French president Nicolas Sarkozy, a departure from the EEC Treaty and the TEU (Buck, Blitz, & Bickerton, 2007).

3.3. COMPETITION POLICY IN EUROPE BEFORE THE EEC

Historically speaking, competition policy has always been on the public agenda in Europe. It is possible to identify three dominant practices in the member states before the formation of the EEC. The first was the absence of a stand-alone competition policy. This was the case with Italy, where there was no separate national competition policy until the early 1990s.[3] The second approach attempted to regulate cartels and trusts with the objective of maintaining competitive markets in countries such as France, Denmark, the UK, and Ireland. The third practice, prevalent in countries such as Germany and the Netherlands until the end of WWII, encouraged the formation of cartels in order to prevent the deleterious consequences of market competition. With this pattern, however, the two countries made a major u-turn in policy in the post-WWII period by declaring cartels illegal. In other words, there was a policy convergence, to some degree, just before the EEC Treaty, suggesting that EU competition policy did not emerge in a vacuum.

In the history of Europe, restrictive practices and cartels were widespread and seen as an enemy of the public. The first competition-related legislation introduced in France in 1791 assured freedom of trade and industry. The Le Chapelier Law passed in the same year made business coalitions an offense. Enacted in 1810, Article 419 of the French penal code condemned all business coalitions for price-fixing, without distinction. Elimination of business coalitions as an offense in 1864 opened the way for the establishment of professional organizations, unions and cartels. Although there were few policy measures to prevent excessive prices or concerted speculation to avert shortages until 1945, competition policy was not a priority in France. A price control ordinance adopted in 1945 empowered the state to freeze wages and all prices, while making illegal all concerted practices, conventions, expressed or tacit agreements or coalitions, regardless of their form or cause, if they impaired the exercise of competition. Complementing this ordinance, a new French competition law passed in 1953 annulled agreements to increase prices under the rule of reason principle. The new legislation required investigation of the rationale behind such actions before courts could declare them unlawful (Sounam, 1998).

The Danish case was similar to that of the French in that the aim was to control cartels and prices. Denmark passed its first piece of antitrust legislation in 1929 to prohibit agreements that limited the free entry of individuals to trades or jobs in an inappropriate manner. The purpose of enacting the Act on Price Agreements in 1931 was to investigate price agreements in trusts, cartels and other combines having a monopolistic character, if these agreements led, or could lead to excessive prices on commodities that were part of general consumption. It also stipulated the establishment of a three-member Price Agreement Committee. In the case of unreasonable prices, the High Court could annul the agreement and fine the participants to the agreement (Albeek, et al., 1998).

A new Act on Price Agreements (1937), annulling accords that caused excessive prices or restraints of trade, replaced these two pieces of legislation. The Price Act took the place of the Act on Price Agreements during WWII, empowering the Price Control Council to regulate prices directly. A new Price Agreements Act, introduced in 1952, conferred extra powers on the Price Control Council. The Monopolies and Restrictive Practices Act replaced it in 1955 to prevent unreasonable prices and business conditions, besides ensuring the best possible conditions for the freedom of trade through public supervision of monopolies and of restraints of trade (Albeek, et al., 1998).

British and Irish competition policies also have a long history. Common-law competition doctrines have their origins in the Magna Carta (1215) (Wilks, 1996; Merkin & Williams, 1984). Yet, there was no written competition legislation until the 1948 Monopolies Act. The principal objective of the new Act was to enable the state to investigate cartels and monopoly abuses, although the latter were of less significance. The Restrictive Trade Practices Act of 1956 followed, requiring the registration of most types of restrictive agreements, especially horizontal agreements between firms (Symeonidis, 1998). Subsequent amendment and extension in light of practice enhanced the capacity of the law. In the case of Ireland, the Restrictive Trade Practices Act passed in 1953 was the first competition law forbidding restrictive business practices, while laying down the establishment of the Fair Trade Commission (Barry & O'Toole, 1998).

The German and Dutch cases were quite different from the previous experiences. Instead of making cartels illegal, the first German and Dutch initiatives declared them legal. In 1897, the German Imperial Court of Law held cartels to be lawful devices to organize industry. A law against the abusive conduct of cartels was enacted in 1923 to curtail hyperinflation. It had two objectives of controlling unreasonable pricing and inhibiting undue restrictions on the freedom of cartel members such as threats against defecting members. The Nazi regime declared membership in a cartel as mandatory in 1933, and cartels became quasi-government agencies of the centrally planned war economy. The Allied Military Government applied American antitrust law in West Germany after WWII, declaring cartels illegal. The Act against Restraints of Competition replaced the US antitrust regulation in 1957 (Neumann, 1998).

Competition policy in the Netherlands followed a similar course as that of Germany, albeit with a shorter history. The Business Agreements Act of 1935, which was the first Dutch national legislation in the area, had the purpose of curtailing the deleterious effects of excessive domestic competition on prices and employment by endorsing restrictive producer agreements. It gave the government powers to force cartel membership upon dissenting firms, if necessary. After the Nazi government had occupied the Netherlands, it imposed the Cartel Decree in 1941. The new law established a compulsory confidential cartel register without any sanctions for non-compliance and established an independent commission as an advisory body. The law remained intact until the parliament passed a new legislation, the Suspension of Business Regulation Act in 1951, to use against cartels that harmed the public interest. Passed in 1956 and operative in 1958, the Economic Competition Law kept the cartel register intact and included industries such as banking, insurance and transport, while broadening the definition of cartel to cover all competition agreements (Brusse & Griffiths, 1998).

These individual country experiences point to three major patterns in competition policy in Europe. First, European states had competition policy in one form or another, indicating that EU competition policy was not formed in a vacuum. Second, the intensity and effects of market competition determined the initial individual country experiences. That is, competition law supported cartels to restrict competition in countries where competition was intense and had deleterious effects, whereas it targeted cartels to promote competition in countries with less competitive activity and strong cartel experiences. Finally, market concentration was not a policy concern in any European country. According to Dixon (1958), the prevailing doctrine in Western Europe before WWII was based on the 'abusive principle', that is, there was no outright condemnation of monopolies, only the prevention of their abusive practices.

The Treaty of Paris was an exception in that it included two novel clauses about market concentration and state aids.[4] As indicated in Article 4, the Treaty of Paris prohibited measures that restricted trade between the member states in coal and steel, discriminatory practices, unfair state subsidies, and restrictive practices. In line with Article 4, Articles 65, 66 and 67 of the Treaty aimed to protect market competition. While Article 65 dealt with cartels and cartel-like agreements that restricted competition, Article 66 focused on the problem of abuse of market power and future mergers and acquisitions in the coal and steel industries. Finally, Article 67 aimed to control state aids to the coal and steel industry. In conclusion, the Treaty of Paris included two innovative clauses dealing with *concentrations* and *state aids*. As the following section indicates, the EEC Treaty did not have any rules for regulating market concentration through mergers and acquisitions, largely due to its focus on facilitating market integration, increasing the competitiveness of European firms, and ensuring profitability.

3.4. COMPETITION RULES IN THE EEC TREATY

Compared to the ECSC and EURATOM, which were specialist communities, the EEC Treqty provided a broader mandate for the economic as well as political unification of Europe. The fundamental aspiration of the Treaty was "to lay the foundations of an ever-closer union among the peoples of Europe," as stated in the Preamble.[5] While Article 1 established the EEC, Article 2 specified the fundamental objectives of the EEC as follows:

> The Community shall have as its task, by establishing a common market and progressively approximating the economic policies of Member States, to promote throughout the Community a harmonious development of economic activities, a continuous and balanced expansion, and an increase in stability, an accelerated rising of the standard of living and closer relations between the States belonging to it.

Article 3 spelled out the means, one of which was "the institution of a system ensuring that competition in the common market is not distorted" (Article 3(g) (ex-Article 3(f)), to achieve the objectives stated in Article 2. The interdependence of the different parts of the Treaty meant that competition policy would influence most aspects of the common market (Van Themaat, 1963, p. 20). *In Istituto Chemioterapico Italiano SpA and Commercial Solvents Corporation v. EC Commission*, the ECJ ruled in 1974 that:

> The prohibitions of Articles 85 and 86 must in fact be interpreted and applied in the light of Article 3(f) of the Treaty, which provides that the activities of the Community shall include the institution of a system ensuring that competition in the Common Market is not distorted, and Article 2 of the Treaty, which gives the Community the task of promoting 'throughout the Community harmonious development of economic activities'. By prohibiting the abuse of a dominant position within the market in so far as it may affect trade between member-States, Article 86 therefore covers abuse which may directly prejudice consumers as well as abuse which indirectly prejudices them by impairing *the effective competitive structure* as envisaged by Article 3(f) of the Treaty. (p. 342)

The competition rules had a direct link to the objectives of the EEC, and Article 3(g) (or ex-Article 3(f)) envisioned an effectively competitive market environment to realize them.

Classifying the competition rules as 'regulative' and 'administrative' with reference to their functions facilitates greater understanding of EEC/EU competition law. On the one hand, Articles 81, 82, 86 and 87 of the EEC Treaty are the principal competition rules to achieve the objective set out in Article 3(g), i.e. establishing and maintaining market competition in the EU. On the other hand, Articles 83, 84, 85, 88, and 89, in the main, are the rules that designate the institutions as well as their responsibilities in implementing the articles in the first group, as Table 3.1 below indicates.

Article 81 (ex-Article 85) proscribes "all agreements between undertakings, decisions by associations of undertakings and concerted practices which may affect trade between Member States and which have as their object or effect the prevention, restriction or distortion of competition within the common market." It contains a number of examples of agreements such as: direct or indirect fixing of purchasing or selling

Table 3.1 EEC/EU Competition Rules

Regulative	
Article 81 (Ex-Article 85)	Regulates restrictive practices between firms
Article 82 (Ex-Article 86)	Bans abusive behavior of dominant firm(s)
Article 86 (Ex-Article 90)	Subjects firms with special rights to market competition
Article 87 (Ex-Article 92)	Regulates aids to firms by member stats
Administrative	
Article 83 (Ex-Article 87)	Grants the Council of Ministers the right to lay down guidelines for implementing Articles 81 and 82
Article 84 (Ex-Article 88)	Designates member states to apply Articles 81 and 82 until the Council of Ministers adopts the guidelines mentioned in Article 83
Article 85 (Ex-Article 89)	Authorizes the European Commission to apply Articles 81 and 82
Article 86(3) (Ex-Article 90)	Entitles the European Commission to implement Article 86
Article 88 (Ex-Article 93)	Authorizes the European Commission to apply Article 87
Article 89 (Ex-Article 94)	Bestows on the Council of Ministers the right to adopt guidelines for the application of Articles 87 and 88

prices or any other conditions; limiting or controlling production, markets, technical development or investment; sharing markets or sources of supply; and applying dissimilar conditions to equivalent transactions with other trading parties.

As stated in the second paragraph of Article 81, any agreements, concerted practices or decisions prohibited by Article 81 automatically become void. Yet, Article 81(3) declares inapplicable the provisions of the first paragraph, if any agreement, decision or concerted practice:

> . . . contributes to improving the production or distribution of goods or to promoting technical or economic progress, while allowing consumers a fair share of the resulting benefit, and which does not:
> (a) impose on the undertakings concerned restrictions which are not indispensable to the attainment of these objectives;
> (b) afford such undertakings the possibility of eliminating competition in respect of a substantial part of the products in question.

The third paragraph suggests that the negotiators of the EEC Treaty compromised with both firms and European consumers to gain their support, which was essential for the legitimacy of the EU. In cases of cost-benefit analysis, if the latter is larger than the former, Article 81 can permit restrictions or cartels that do not eliminate competition in a substantial part of the market. Nevertheless, the compromise brought with it the problem of ambiguity, according to Bellamy and Child (1987). Overall, Article 81 supports one of the premises of the theory of effective competition in that there are no rules to ban restrictive agreements between firms per se. The principle of the rule of reason applies to Article 81.

According to Article 82, "any abuse by one or more undertakings of a dominant position within the common market or in a substantial part of it shall be prohibited as incompatible with the common market in so far as it may affect trade between Member States". Article 82 also gives some examples of abuses such as imposing direct or indirect of unfair purchasing or selling prices, limiting production, markets or technical development that reduce consumer welfare, and applying dissimilar conditions to equivalent transactions.

Article 82 has three striking features. First, it does not target the firms with a dominant position directly, but only those that exploit their dominance individually or collectively. Article 82 does not punish a firm that holds a dominant position on the market, if that position results from its own competitive strength and effectiveness. Nevertheless, acquiring a dominant position by buying out competitors is unlawful under Article 82. In other words, Article 82 does not deal with the internal structure of dominant firms, but with their behavior on the market individually or collectively. Dominance is not limited to individual firms. Confirmed by the European Commission and the CFI in their *Italian Flat Glass* decisions of 1990 and 1992 respectively, Article 82 recognizes 'collective dominance' and abuse 'by one or more undertakings' (Korah, 2004, pp. 111–4). Such language insinuates that Article 82 anticipated market concentration long before the merger regulation.

Second, Article 82 does not have any power to require a firm with a dominant position to divest itself of some of its holdings (as is the case of American antitrust law). In *Europemballage Corporation and Continental Can Company Inc. v. EC Commission* (1973), the ECJ concluded " . . . the [EEC] Treaty tolerates even the absence of *all* competition, i.e., a complete monopoly" (p. 208). Levying a fine is the only option. Finally, as it is clear from the language of Article 82, the acts cited are not prohibited, if non-dominant firms conduct them. As stated by Friend and Ridyard (1991):

> Dominant undertakings are subject to a stricter regulatory regime under the EC competition rules than their smaller competitors. Forms of commercial behavior which may be acceptable when practiced by a non-dominant company will be regarded as an abuse under Article 86 when engaged in by a dominant firm. (p. 13)

To put all these in perspective, the actual intention behind Article 82 is not to protect competition per se, but to shield small competitors from the abusive behaviors of their bigger counterparts, especially in times of economic slowdown, while Article 81 allows small competitors to form cartels. There are also elements of compromise in the language of Article 81 and 82, as Del Marmol (1963) noticed:

> Articles 85 [81] and 86 [82] reflect the perplexity of the negotiators. The texts are the result of a compromise between the backers of a prohibition of restrictive practices per se and the advocates of the repression of abuses. Each delegation has received partial satisfaction, and the result is an indigestible legal cocktail which makes lawyers happy and businessmen unhappy. (p. 116)

Overall, the EEC Treaty, in contrast to the Paris Treaty establishing the ECSC and its Article 66 dealing with concentrations, was permissive of industrial concentration by contenting itself only with a prohibition of the abuse of market power, instead of preventing the formation of it (Spaak and Jaeger, 1961). McLachlan and Swan (1967) explained this major policy shift between 1951 and 1957 as follows:

> . . . [B]y the time the Rome Treaty was signed the opposite fear was beginning to be felt: that the scale of European business was too small to take full advantage of the large market being created. The path to *concentration* was therefore left almost entirely clear. An additional reason might also have been that by the time that the Rome Treaty was negotiated, the opinions of German industry could no longer be ignored. (p. 196, italics added)

The exclusion of a competition rule preventing market concentration in the EEC Treaty provides further evidence for the strategic calculation of encouraging the formation of loosely oligopolistic markets on the part of European elites, in addition to the structural power of German capital.

Article 86 (ex-Article 90) subjects both public and private undertakings, to which the member states granted special or exclusive rights, to Articles 81 and 82.[6] Article 86(1) states that:

> In the case of public undertakings and undertakings to which Member States grant special or exclusive rights, Member States shall neither enact nor maintain in force any measure contrary to the rules contained in this Treaty, in particular to those rules provided for in Article 12 and Articles 81 to 89.

Article 86 subjects a revenue-producing monopoly to the rules contained in the EEC Treaty, especially to the rules of competition, as long as such rules do not prevent the performance of the particular tasks assigned to public undertakings and private firms to which the member states grant special or exclusive rights. Article 86 asserts the prevalence of market competition over other concerns. It is indeed a tool for extending the rules of the market economy to state-owned economic enterprises or to private firms with special rights to operate services of a general economic interest. Article 86, along with Article 87, disciplines the state by controlling its activities in the market (CEC, 1973, p. 112).

Article 87 (ex-Article 92) invalidates any aid granted by a member state or through state resources in any form that distorts or threatens competition by favoring certain undertakings or the production of certain goods, if it influences trade between the member states negatively:

> Save as otherwise provided in this Treaty, any aid granted by a Member State or through State resources in any form whatsoever which distorts or threatens to distort competition by favoring certain undertakings or the production of certain goods shall, in so far as it affects trade between Member States, be incompatible with the common market.

Instruments of state aid are grants, tax exemptions, soft loans, equity participation, and loan guarantees. Not unlike Article 81, Article 87 also has exemptions such as aid having a social character, aid for the damage caused by natural disasters or exceptional occurrences, and aid to promote economic development in poorer regions.

The European Commission allows for state aids in three circumstances. The first is when market forces obstruct progress towards the Treaty's objectives: "Distortions of competition can still be caused through State aids, but these aids may also help to improve the balance of the economy, either between regions or over a period of time" (CEC, 1965, p. 60). The second is when market forces prolong the period of attaining the objective of delivering cheaper, good-quality goods and services, or of delivering them at unacceptable social costs. Finally, market forces that intensify competition to such an extent that competition can destroy itself justifies state aid. What these three conditions indicate is that both less and destructive competition are harmful. In evaluating individual state aid cases, one of the criteria for granting aid is to restore long-term viability of the industry or the sector by facilitating less painful restructuring (CEC, 1979a, pp. 124–5). As a result, Article 87 has been much more politicized than any other article, as we shall see below. Similar to Articles 81 and 82, Article 87 is consistent with the theory of effective competition as there is no rule *per se* against market concentration, cartels or state aids (Cocks, 1980, p. 13).

The EEC Treaty also broadly spelled out the institutional division of labor regarding the implementation of the regulative rules. As in the case of the overall decision-making structure of the EEC/EU, the European Parliament has the least say in regulating market competition. It has the right to require the European Commission to make general or specific policy statements, while reporting on the progress of investigations. It can also suggest new investigations to the European Commission. In its advisory capacity, other EU institutions are to consult the European Parliament prior to the adoption of any regulations or directives giving effect to Articles 81 (ex-Article 85) and 82 (ex-Article 86). The European Parliament still does not have co-decision making power in the field of EU competition policy.

In this field, the Council of Ministers is the main legislative body. The first paragraph of Article 83 indicates that the Council is the political body responsible for laying down the appropriate regulations and directives for implementing Articles 81 and 82, after consulting the Parliament on a proposal from the Commission. According to Article 87(e) (ex-Article 92), the Council may also decide whether an aid granted or intended to be granted by a member state is compatible with the common market. Article 89 (ex-Article 94) grants the Council the right to adopt appropriate regulations for the application of Articles 87 and 88 by a qualified majority voting on a proposal from the Commission and after consulting the Parliament (Merkin & Williams, 1984, p. 32). By following the same procedure, the Council also has responsibility for determining the conditions for the application of Article 88(3), and the categories for exempting aid from this procedure. All these show that the Council has power to design a framework for the allocation of state aids.

The European Commission functions as legislator, executive and judge in the process of enforcing EU competition law, given that it has the right to formulate and apply competition law according to Articles 85 (ex-Article 89), 86(3) (ex-Article 90) and 88 (ex-Article 93) of the EEC Treaty. Article 85 authorizes the Commission to apply the principles laid down in Articles 81 and 82. It can initiate applications or cooperate with the competent authorities in the member states in implementing such principles. If the Commission finds out that there has been an infringement, it has the right to propose appropriate measures to stop the breach by making decisions, publishing them, and authorizing the member states to take the necessary measures.

Article 86(3) also bestows on the Commission the right to address appropriate directives or decisions to the member states in ensuring the application of the provisions of Article 86. Furthermore, Article 88 deals with procedures for the application of the principles laid down in Article 87. As the first paragraph of Article 87 illustrates, it is the responsibility of the Commission to check and review all systems of aid existing in the member states in cooperation with their governments, besides proposing to the concerned member state appropriate measures. Paragraph 2 of Article 88 stipulates that the Commission may ask a member state to abolish or alter an aid granted by the latter, if the aid is incompatible with Article 87.[7]

Adopted in 1962, Council Regulation 17/62 for the implementation of the principles contained in Articles 81 and 82, as required in Article 83, conferred on the Commission an exclusive right to declare Article 81(1) inapplicable pursuant to Article 81(3), but its decisions would be subject to review by the ECJ. The second paragraph of Article 9 also bestowed power on the Commission to apply Article 82, but it was not the sole power as in the case of Article 81. Under Article 9(3) of the Regulation, the member states could implement Article 81(1) and Article 82 in agreement with Article 84, so long as the European Commission did not initiate any procedure (Council Regulation 17/62, 1962).

Additionally, Regulation 17/62 granted the Commission extensive investigatory and enforcement powers. Finally, in 1965, the Council adopted a regulation that conferred on the Commission the right to exempt certain specified groups of agreements from the application of Article 81, reinforcing exclusive Commission powers in the area of competition (Council Regulation 19/65, 1965). For Wesseling (2000), Regulations 17/62 and 19/65 led to the concentration of enforcement powers in the hands of the European Commission at the expense of national competition authorities and the member states until their replacement by a new legislation in 2003.

In implementing the competition rules, the European Commission acts as a collegiate body and each Commissioner has responsibility for one or more departments or Directorates-General (DGs) whose total number has changed over time. The DG IV, the directorate for competition, is the division responsible for implementing competition articles. DG IV was among the first established DGs in 1957. France wanted the member states to have a veto over the decisions of the DG IV originally through the establishment of an Advisory Committee, before they were sent up for approval by the Commission during the negotiations of Regulation 17/62. The Commission officials as well as the German delegates resisted because competition policy was at the heart of the project of European integration. Finally, the Advisory Committee, consisting of representatives of the member states, was established, but its power was limited to advising without the right to pronounce any formal veto powers (Goyder, 1998, p. 45; Gerber, 1998, pp. 350–1).

DG IV was very small and powerless in the beginning, with only about twenty officials in 1960, and barely growing to twenty-eight by 1964 (Goyder, 1998, p. 35). As the process of European integration accelerated in subsequent years, the size of the Commission and the DG IV grew. After the interim presidency of Manual Marin (July 1999—September 1999), who replaced the Jacques Santer College of Commissioners (1995–1999), Romano Prodi became president of the European Commission in September 1999 and decided to remove the numerals with the purpose of making the Commission and the EU more transparent and understandable. In consequence, DG IV is now referred to as the DG for Competition.[8]

The ECJ and the CFI (after 1990 to lessen the burden of the ECJ) are the two supranational courts making final decisions in competition law cases. Parties to whom the Commission addresses its decisions under Article 81 and 82, and other interested parties can initiate an appeal to the CFI within two months of the communication of a Commission decision. The CFI has the power to declare that a decision of the Commission is void, in addition to reviewing any penalty or fine imposed by the Commission. Parties can also appeal CFI decisions on points of law before the ECJ which may over-rule CFI decisions or refer the cases back to the CFI.

As for the member states, Article 84 (ex-Article 88) stipulated the application of Articles 81 and 82 by the authorities in the member states to the law of their country until the entry into force of the provisions adopted in pursuance of Article 83 during the period of transition (until 1962). Because, until recently, the European Commission had the exclusive right to implement Article 81(3), national courts could not implement the third paragraph of Article 81, granting exemptions to agreements between firms. National courts and competition authorities can apply Articles 81 and 82 fully now only by following the line of reasoning set in similar European Commission, CFI, and ECJ decisions. This indicates the centralization of decision-making power in applying the competition rules.

In summary, the design of the competition rules in the EEC Treaty reflects the blueprint of the theory of effective competition discussed in Chapter 2 in a number of ways. First, Article 86 declares the primacy of market competition over everything else. Second, the absence of a rule dealing with mergers and acquisitions in the EEC Treaty and the restriction of the scope of Article 82 to penalize only abusive practices by dominant firms demonstrates that EU competition policy was lenient to market concentration initially. Third, cartels, especially those formed by small firms, were also legal. Fourth, Article 87 demonstrates that the vision of market competition is imperfect and the state has the responsibility to correct it. Fifth, the EEC Treaty granted almost all rights to the Council of Ministers and the Commission to implement the competition rules exclusively vis-à-vis the Parliament and the member states (McGowan, 2000, p. 148). Finally, the role of the ECJ, and later the CFI, as the final arbiter indicates the significance of law in regulating market competition. The next section investigates the relationship between profitability and market concentration in the historical evolution of EU competition policy to provide support for the theory of effective competition.

3.5. HISTORICAL EVOLUTION OF
EU COMPETITION POLICY[9]

Historically speaking, profitability has played a significant, if not a determining role in the historical evolution of EU competition policy with the aim of ensuring supply-side stability (CEC, 1993, p. 13). The weight of each policy objective (market integration, consumer welfare, or profitability) has been complex in EU competition policy, but there seems to have

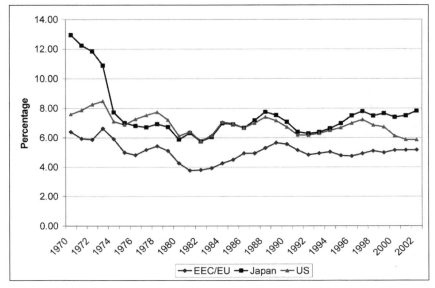

Graph 3.1 Net rate of return on net total assets, EEC/EU: 1970–2002.[10]

been a rough pattern in actual implementation historically. Whenever the rate of profit was high, EU institutions could pursue other goals such as market integration, consumer welfare, decentralized markets and international competitiveness, etc. In times of declining profitability, EU competition policy authorities relaxed the implementation of Article 81 and Article 87 to allow firms to collaborate with each other and receive aid from their governments, while strengthening the application of Articles 82 and 86 with the purpose of protecting smaller firms and creating new profit opportunities by opening new markets. Contrary to the stated goals of EU competition policy, preventing market concentration did not play a significant role in its development.

With reference to the rate of profitability as a key target for the EU regulatory mandate, this study divides the history of EU competition policy into three main periods.[11] As Graph 3.1 illustrates, while the first period covering the years between 1970 and 1979 was a time of declining profitability, the second between 1980 and 1992 was a period of restoring profitability. Finally, the period after 1993 has been and continues to be an era of maintaining high profitability.

3.4.1 The Period of Declining Profit Rate: 1970–1979

After the stability of the 1960s, the rate of return started to decline at the beginning of the 1970s. As Graph 3.1 illustrates, the rate of return on total assets went down from around 6.39 percent in 1970 to 3.77 percent by

1981. In the aftermath of decreasing to 4.81 percent in 1976, there was a small recovery in the rate of profit, peaking at 5.43 percent in 1978. This temporary recovery gave way to another period of declining returns at the beginning of the 1980s. This secular trend of decline in the 1970s sent EU competition officials a clear signal that the problem was not temporary, but permanent, and therefore indicating that structural changes to the operation of the economy were required to restore profitability.

Understanding the 1970s requires assessing what happened in the 1960s briefly. It is appropriate to characterize the 1960s as a period of institutionalization before serious enforcement. The Council of Ministers passed Regulation No. 17 to specify the rules for applying Articles 81 and 82 in 1962, four years after the EEC Treaty into force. Due to the lack of resources and past experience, the European Commission was very cautious in implementing the individual competition articles in order to avoid irritating the 'sovereignty-conscious' member states, especially France in the 1960s. Given that there were no problems regarding profitability in the 1960s, the primary policy objective was to integrate formerly isolated national markets.

A three-pronged strategy in implementing competition policy was put in place. First, assisted by the supportive decisions of the ECJ, the European Commission firmly applied Article 81 to open up formerly isolated national markets for competition and to facilitate trade between member countries. Second, there was no activity regarding Article 82 because the objective was to create a truly European economy through cross-border mergers and acquisitions. Third, the Commission was flexible in implementing Article 87 to foster economic development as part of its strategy of closing the gap between the regions, while being careful not to intrude into the policy realms of the member states through the deployment of Article 86 in the early stages of European integration.

During the initial years, Article 81 served as the tool for removing private obstacles to interstate trade within the EEC. Vertical restraints or restrictive practices, including collective mutually exclusive arrangements such as re-selling and re-importing which disturbed the development of the common market, received special attention from the Commission (CEC, 1964, pp. 69-70; CEC, 1963, p. 63). Concerted practices and agreements to raise prices and restrict production were the primary targets, as the cases of *Grunding* (1964), *Aniline Dyes* (1969) and *Quinin* (1969) demonstrated (CEC, 1966, pp. 66–76; CEC, 1965, p. 74). The European Commission was also against market-sharing agreements that did not provide any benefits to consumers. Nonetheless, cooperation agreements between producers for efficiency gains and technological improvement were permissible because consumers would eventually benefit from such decisions in the form of new products, better services, and lower prices, as cases such as *Van Katwijk's Industrieen N.V* (1970), and *Omega Watches* (1970) illustrated. Agreements between small- and medium-sized firms under Article

81, as in the case of *Transocean Marine Paint*, under the third paragraph of Article 81, were legal as well (Wesseling, 2000, p. 24).

Rapidly deteriorating economic conditions in general and profitability in particular in the 1970s led to a reversal in the application of the competition rules. In response to the general economic downturn in the 1970s, the first change was the lenient application of Article 81 with the purpose of allowing firms, especially small firms, to cope with economic recession (CEC, 1978a, p. 28; CEC, 1978b, p. 104; CEC, 1973, pp. 18–9; CEC, 1962, p. 18). In the 1970s, cartels or horizontal agreements between large firms, and abusive practices of dominant firms were the main targets. The latter created an opportunity for the application of Article 82 for the first time. Until the early 1970s, the European Commission did not deploy Article 82, in order to encourage firms to facilitate market integration as well as to reach economies of scale through mergers, acquisitions and the establishment of joint subsidiaries (CEC, 1966, p. 79).

Concurrent with the changing economic circumstances, the European Commission raised its concerns about economic concentration through mergers and acquisitions as a precautionary measure to prevent rising inflation as early as 1969. The upshot was to apply Article 82 to limit rising inflation by controlling the abusive behavior of dominant firms as well as by preventing market concentration (CEC, 1972, p. 97). In 1971, the Commission applied Article 82 in *Gesellschaft fur Musikalische Auffuhrungs-und Mechanische Vervielfaltigunsrechte (GEMA)* for the first time in history. GEMA was a German performing rights or authors' rights society. According to the Commission, GEMA abused its dominant position mainly by discriminating against nationals of other member states. Article 82 cases also included vertical relationships not covered by Article 81 (Gerber, 1998, p. 122).

Moreover, there was a clear trend of market concentration between 1971 and the early 1980s, as the largest firms increased their market share dramatically at the expense of smaller companies (CEC, 1984, p. 197; CEC, 1981a, p. 164). In response, the Commission took an innovative approach by applying Article 82 to mergers and acquisitions for the first time in *Continental Can* in 1972. Continental Can Company Inc. of New York (USA) and its subsidiary Eurobemballage Corporation of Wilmington, Delaware (USA) and Brussels (Belgium) acquired the majority of the shares in Thomassen & Drijver-Verblifa NV of Deventer (Holland) in 1970, after a series of acquisitions in Europe in the late 1960s, including one in Germany (Schmalbach-Lubeca-Werke). The rationale behind the decision was that Continental Can abused its dominant position by buying out its small competitor through its European subsidiary. The EU Commission's (1972) reasoning was that: "The purchase of a majority shareholding in a competing undertaking by an undertaking or group which has a dominant position may, in certain circumstances, constitute an abuse of that dominant position" (p. D11). Even though the ECJ upheld the Commission's ruling of to disallow the acquisition by relating the implementation of Article 82 to Articles 2 and 3(f) of the EEC Treaty in *Europemballage Corporation and Continental Can Company Inc. v. EC Commission* (1973), it found the Commission's analysis problematic, as the following excerpt indicates:

> Since, moreover, the Commission has obviously not undertaken a study of the market over a fairly long period, which seems to be essential for the purposes of Article 86, and in particular has not attempted to ascertain trends of development in an apparently rapidly changing market (including new accessions to that market), it must in fact be held, after all these considerations, that it is extremely doubtful whether the Commission has succeeded in proving that Schmalbach has a dominant position. (p. 214)

The *Continental Can* case illustrated that both the Commission and the ECJ were eager to maintain loosely oligopolistic markets and prevent excessive market concentration. It is important to note that Continental Can was an American, not a European company. This case was also interesting because the ECJ observed a serious flaw in the Commission's market analysis for the first time. It pointed out that the Commission did not take into account the time factor, illuminating the problems with the theory of effective competition.

Because of the limited juridical powers of Article 82 to deal with mergers and acquisitions, the Commission submitted a proposal to the Council in 1973 to regulate mergers and acquisitions with a Community dimension. However, since the member states did not want to give up their control over mergers and acquisitions, the Council was unable to codify the proposal in law until 1989, a full 16 years after its submission (CEC, 1974, p. 31). In short, the application of Article 82 in the 1970s targeted several objectives. These included preventing market concentration through mergers and acquisitions, especially American multinationals in Europe; protecting smaller firms from the abusive practices of larger firms; and controlling inflation. In this sense, the enforcement of Article 82 was a major turning point in the evolution of EU competition policy in the early 1970s.

During the 1960s and 1970s, the principal criterion with respect to the application of Article 87 was profitability under the name of 'promoting economic development' (CEC, 1966, p. 83). As Graph 3.2 below clearly demonstrates, overall state aid cases increased dramatically during the 1970s, as profitability declined.[12] Both the Commission and the Council supported state aids to the shipbuilding and textile industries throughout the 1970s with the purpose of restructuring them to decrease excess capacity and to restore profitability, essential for international competitiveness (CEC, 1976, p. 78; CEC, 1966, p. 88; CEC, 1960, p. 71; CEC, 1959, pp. 56–7).

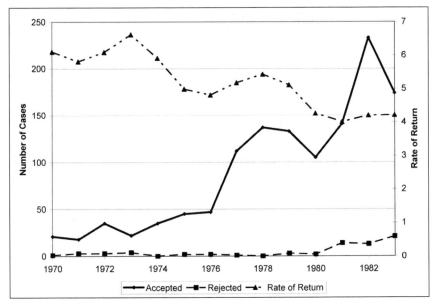

Graph 3.2 Number of accepted and rejected state aid cases, and rate of return: 1970–1983.[13]

For instance, the Commission, in *Ford Tractor (Belgium) Limited* (1964), asked the Belgian government to discontinue state aid to Ford Tractor (Belgium) Ltd. of Antwerp granted under the Law of 17 July 1959, even though the goal of the aid was to facilitate economic expansion and to create new industries. The rationale behind the Commission's ruling was the following: "On the Common Market in agricultural tractors, the production capacity is not smaller than the demand . . . The aid can only contribute to aggravating the already difficult situation in the Community production of tractors" (p. 35). Restoring profitability was prioritized in this decision.

In another case, the Belgian government's decision to grant state aids in the form of interest subsidies and tax exemptions for two oil company groupings was not acceptable to the Commission. The reason given was that the oil companies planned to extend and set up a new oil refinery in Antwerp in 1973:

> [S]econdly, given the situation of the industry, this aid seemed liable to distort trading conditions in the Community to an extent contrary to the common interest: surpluses, however small, on the petroleum products market, *depress prices and are therefore likely to upset the financial equilibrium* of the refining industry of the Community. (CEC, 1964, p. 160, italics added)

Similarly, the Commission had to approve the Italian government's aid to small firms during the early 1970s (CEC, 1975, p. 92; CEC, 1973, p. 107).

In the second half of that decade, when the economic situation worsened, the Commission had to approve more state aids to halt the economic decline in industrial activity and employment with the purpose of encouraging an economic upturn and enabling European manufacturers to manage through the crisis. The Council, at its meeting in Copenhagen in April 1978, underlined the need to restore the competitiveness of the industries in distress with the help of state aid (CEC, 1980b, p. 100; CEC, 1979a, p. 123; CEC, 1977, p. 133; CEC, 1966, p. 84). By and large, Article 87 was applied with the objective of establishing profitable market conditions for the existing firms at the expense of consumers as well as maintaining the 'equilibrium' in the market.

Article 86 was the only competition article that did not play any role at all during the first period. Nevertheless, the Commission raised the question of the direct applicability of Article 86(2) by the ECJ, for the first time, in 1971 (CEC, 1972, p. 146). The ECJ backed its 1971 stance and the Commission's initiative, through its decision in 1974 on the direct applicability of Article 82 to the market conduct of public undertakings and undertakings with exclusive or special rights according to Article 86 (CEC, 1965, p. 81). This decision would have a great impact on the telecommunications industry in the second period, as the next section will show. Both the Commission and the Council intensified their efforts to prepare the grounds for implementing Article 86 in conjunction with Article 82 during the first period in individual sectors and industries, including banking, insurance, and public utilities, transport and agriculture. Moreover, they aimed to use Article 86 to make the financial relationships between the member states and state-owned enterprises transparent, a prelude to the eventual control of state aid (CEC, 1973, pp. 58–72; CEC, 1966, pp. 80–88; CEC, 1979b, pp. 108–13).

What the first period indicates is that macroeconomic conditions and declining profitability significantly influenced the application of individual competition rules in the 1970s. Compared to the 1960s, the application of Article 81 was relaxed to permit the formation of cartels especially by smaller firms. Likewise, Article 87 was eased so that the member states could provide financial aid to firms experiencing financial difficulty in order to prevent massive bankruptcies and save jobs. As part of the attempt to protect smaller firms from the abusive practices of dominant ones, the Commission enforced Article 82 in 1971 for the first time, as well as extending its interpretation to preclude excessive market concentration. However, Article 82 provided limited juridical powers, as its main function is to control the abusive market conduct of the dominant firms against their smaller counterparts. Surprisingly, Article 86 was not popular during this period, but the steep decline in profitability in the mid-1970s pushed the member states to prepare the juridical ground for its application in order to open up new areas of profit for European firms under the pretext of strengthening the international competitiveness of the European industry in the second period.

3.4.2. The Period of Restoring Profitability: 1980–1992

After a sharp decline in the mid-1970s, profitability made a gradual recovery in the 1980s, as Graph 3.1 (above) depicts. The rate of return at 3.77 percent in 1981 began to rise thereafter, reaching the peak of 5.65 percent in 1989. Profitability declined to 4.83 percent by 1992 with deteriorating macroeconomic conditions. The decline was temporary and the trend quickly reversed, with the rate of return reaching 5.02 percent in 1994. Jumping from 3.77 percent in 1981 to 5.65 percent by 1990 was a remarkable achievement, as it represents an increase in the rate of return of approximately 50 percent over the nine-year period. Despite the deceleration of the rate of return to 5.15 and 4.83 percent levels in 1991 and 1992 respectively, it never fell to the level of the early 1980s.

In addition to temporary factors such as the oil shocks, the sharp decline in profitability in the 1970s, as the Commission correctly diagnosed, was the result of a new international division of labor in the world economy with the rise of the East Asian economies as world players (CEC, 1981a, p. 9; CEC, 1979a, pp. 9–10). The EEC institutions established new measures in the name of enhancing the 'international competitiveness' of the European industry, in contrast to the 'temporary' solutions of the 1970s (CEC, 1982b, p. 7; CEC, 1980a, p. 11). The Single European Act (SEA) of 1986 was a determined response. In particular, Article 130(g) of the SEA gave the EEC responsibility to implement common research and technological development policy to increase the international competitiveness of European companies (CEC, 1987a, p. 23).

In addition, the Commission changed its attitude towards market concentration in contrast to the rhetoric it had used to promote decentralized markets in the 1970s, as it started to characterize bigger firms as significant contributors to international competitiveness of the European industry (CEC, 1990a, p. 226; CEC, 1981a, p. 197). The Commission justified its tolerant attitude toward market concentration in the following words: "Keener competition within the Community is not in itself incompatible with a high degree of concentration and a strong trend towards oligopoly in a number of industries" (CEC, 1981a, p. 179). Encouraging market concentration publicly was a significant policy reversal in the historical evolution of EU competition policy.

Nevertheless, the Commission was not very clear about its course of action. It tried to establish a balance between competitiveness and competition: "The basic approach has been to seek the best possible balance between on the one hand a reinforcement of the competitivity of

European industry and on the other hand the maintenance of *workable competition*" (CEC, 1984, p. 44, italics added). One thing that remained clear to the Commission was the absence of a causal relationship between market structure and the intensity of market competition. There was an obvious shift in the Commission's goals towards maintaining the stimulus of competition, promoting structural adjustment and increasing competitiveness (CEC, 1985, p. 15). As a result, there was no single merger or acquisition case to which Article 82 was applied during this period. The implementation of Article 82 in conjunction with Article 86 in the telecommunications industry for the first time in history, was a landmark decision (as examined in the fifth chapter in detail).

In contrast to the Commission's lenient attitude towards mergers and acquisitions in the 1980s, the Council eventually adopted a new regulation for monitoring and prohibiting concentrations that create or strengthen a dominant position through mergers, acquisitions, and merger-like joint ventures in 1989. The scope of the regulation was limited to mergers, acquisitions and merger-like joint ventures having a Community dimension and impeding effective competition significantly. The Merger Control Regulation (MCR), which came into force in September 1990, was only concerned with mergers, acquisitions, and merger-like joint ventures with a Community dimension:

> For the purpose of this regulation, a concentration has a Community dimension where:
> (a) the combined aggregate worldwide turnover of all the undertakings concerned is more than 5000 million ECUs, and
> (b) the aggregate Community-wide turnover of each of at least two of the undertakings concerned is more than 250 million ECUs, unless each of the undertakings concerned achieves more than two-thirds of its aggregate Community-wide turnover within one and the same Member State (Council Regulation, 1989, p. 1).

The criteria for determining the Community dimension have remained a controversial topic between the member states and the Commission, as they have been revised periodically in the third period to bring more cases under the jurisdiction of the Commission.

The MCR aimed to prevent market concentration through mergers, acquisitions and merger-like joint ventures. Effective inhibition of market concentration required a clear definition of the concept in the first place. The concept of 'market dominance' was the key for applying the MCR, but this definition was problematic in itself, since it did not recognize the condition of interdependency between firms in the market (Kolasky, 2001, p. 10). It mainly focused on market shares and hence, market structure, at the expense of the dynamics of competition in the industry concerned ("Trustbusting: Will Economics Bless this Union,"

1997, p. 61). Nor did it provide any clear framework against which officials and companies alike could test mergers. This suggested opaque-
ness in the accessibility of the Commission's merger procedures ("Listen,
Mario," 2002). Moreover, the regulation uses a short time frame to evaluate the effects of mergers and acquisitions (Korah, 2000, p. 313). As a
result, it misses long-term implications of mergers and acquisitions for
relevant markets and industries.

The application of Article 81 was relaxed during the second period by
means of several regulations to exempt specialization, research and development, patent licensing, distribution and servicing agreements (CEC,
1989, pp. 45–8; CEC, 1987a, p. 43; CEC, 1983a). The purpose was to
facilitate the transfer of new technology as well as reinforce the 'competitiveness' of European industry. In the case of Article 87, the Commission
directed state aids to assist industries with some degree of viability at
the beginning of the 1980s (CEC, 1981a, p. 113). The Commission also
channeled state aid to promote research and development, education and
training, development of small firms, as well as to less-favored regions in
an effort to stimulate economic development and enhance international
competitiveness (CEC, 1992, p. 124; CEC, 1983b, p. 104). Sectoral aids
continued, but it became difficult for the member states to get approval
from the Commission (CEC, 1985, pp. 144–5). In emergency cases, the
Commission was flexible enough to extend the framework on state aid.
A case in point was the granting of permission to accept state aids to the
European vehicle and airline industries in the early 1990s (CEC, 1992, p.
37; CEC, 1991a, p. 159).

A major turning point in the historical evolution of EU competition
policy came with the application of Article 86 in the early 1980s. After
preparing the legal infrastructure in the first period, the Commission
finally implemented Article 86 by adopting a new directive on the transparency of financial relations between member states and their public
undertakings in June 1980 (coming into force in January 1982). The
new directive obliged the member states to supply the Commission with
information on transfers of public funds to their public undertakings at
the latter's request. France, Italy and the UK applied to the ECJ for the
annulment of the directive under Article 230 (ex-Article 173), but were
opposed by Germany and the Netherlands (CEC, 1981b, p. 117; CEC,
1982a, p. 155).

The countries in the first group contended that the Commission usurped
their legislative powers in the sphere of state aids by adopting such a directive
under Article 86(3). The Council, they argued, had the right to exercise such
powers under Article 87 (ex-Article 94). Furthermore, both France and Italy
disputed the need for greater transparency in the public sector, whereas
the UK sided with the Commission. Eventually, the ECJ (1982) dismissed
the request in *France, Italy and the United Kingdom (France Intervening)
v. EC Commission (Netherlands and Germany Intervening)*. The ECJ's

decision encouraged the Commission to extend antitrust enforcement into the following sectors: banking, insurance, transport, energy, postal services and telecommunications, public credit institutions, public water authorities, the building industry and the organization of sports events (CEC, 1993a, p. 19; CEC, 1991a, pp. 58–9; CEC, 1985, p. 13). Opening the previously exempted industries to competition or market liberalization through Article 86 created new profit opportunities, thereby helping to restore profitability in the second period.

In sum, the second period was an era during which profitability was restored with the slogan of increasing international competitiveness. In addition to allowing industrial concentration, the Commission was lenient towards restrictive practices in the form of cooperative agreements for research and technological development. Furthermore, state aids were directed to the finance, research and development activities of firms, while the liberalization of new industries such as transportation, electricity and telecommunications with the help of Article 86 created new profit opportunities. Finally, the Council of Ministers agreed to pass the MCR to prevent 'excessive' market concentration, with the real intention of freeing European multinationals from the control of the individual member states and facilitating market integration by means of mergers and acquisitions.

3.4.3. The Period of Maintaining Profitability: 1993–2004

The completion of the internal market by January 1993 and the signing of the TEU were major achievements for the EU, but the economic downturn of 1992 and 1993, and the lack of support for the TEU in several member states, created widespread pessimism. Economic recovery after 1994 and geographical expansion, however, soon provided new enthusiasm for the EU.[14] In terms of profitability, the turbulence of the late 1970s and early 1980s had been resolved. Graph 3.1 (above) illustrates the restoration of profitability, as the rate of return reached the 5 percent level in 1988 for the first time in nine years. A decline to 4.83 percent in 1992 was temporary, as the rate of return jumped to 5.02 percent in 1994, before reaching 5.15 percent in 2000 and 5.16 percent in 2002 respectively. In other words, the level of profitability in the third period became comparable to the level achieved in the 1970s as it hovered around 5 percent during both periods compared to 4 percent in the second period. What this suggests is the stabilization of profitability in the third period.

Restoration of profitability to former levels allowed room for the EU institutions to follow other policy objectives such as enhancing consumer welfare and stimulating the international competitiveness of the European industry. The member states inserted a new title, "Title XIII, Industry" into the Treaty on European Union (TEU), signed in 1992, with the aim of strengthening the goals of the SEA and deepening market integration. Article 130 of the TEU under this title urged the Commission as well as the member states to put in place all necessary policies and measures to improve the competitiveness of the European industry.

Accordingly, the Commission shifted its emphasis from competition within the EU to the international competitiveness of the European economy and began to treat EU competition policy as a tool for industrial policy (CEC, 1996a, p. 15). The Commission noted: "On the contrary, because of the emphasis placed on the responsibilities of industry, *competition policy is an essential instrument of industrial policy*" (CEC, 1994a, p. 23, italics added). This change would have a serious impact on the implementation of the individual competition rules. In the first place, it meant a further relaxation of the implementation of Article 81, especially in the case of vertical agreements (CEC, 1999a, pp. 21–2; CEC, 1998a, p. 25; CEC, 1997a, pp. 22–6; CEC, 1994a, pp. 20–31).

As economic globalization and the pace of technological progress intensified, the need for more dynamic markets and internationally competitive European firms increased in the 1990s. Thus, the Commission adopted a lenient attitude towards horizontal agreements because they perceived cooperation between firms as an essential means of sharing 'risk', saving costs, pooling expertise, and launching new products faster. This is clear from the following statement of the Commission (CEC, 2001a):

> The new rules embody a shift from the formalistic regulatory approach underlying the current legislation towards a more economic approach in the assessment of horizontal cooperation agreements. The basic aim of this new approach is to allow collaboration between competitors where it contributes to economic welfare without creating a risk for competition. (p. 16)

Putting this macro policy shift in action, the Commission and the Council of Ministers, in addition to new guidelines for horizontal agreements, adopted several new regulations dealing with specialization agreements, and research and development under Article 81 (CEC, 2001a, p. 18). New rules increased the thresholds of market share to exclude more firms from the coverage of supporting cooperative agreements under Article 81 (CEC, 1994a, pp. 23–4). Graph 3.3 above shows that the implementation of Article 81 was less stringent between 1993 and 2002, at a time when especially dominant public telecommunications operators collaborated with each other and formed joint ventures to defend their domestic markets (as investigated in Chapter 6).

Even though there was a sharp rise in the number of cases banned under Article 81 between 1999 and 2001, the abrupt economic slowdown in this period forced the Commission to relax its attitude towards cartel-like cooperative agreements and joint ventures, as is clear from Graph

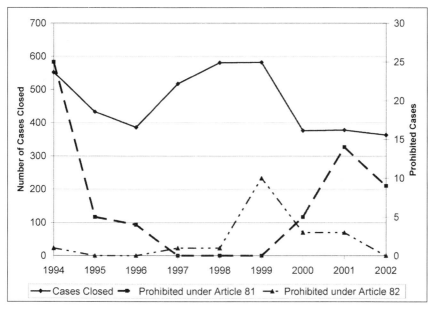

Graph 3.3 Implementation of Article 81 and 82: 1994–2002.[15]

3.3. Similarly, the implementation of Article 82 was relaxed throughout the 1990s as well, even though there was a sudden rise in the number of prohibited cases under Article 82 between 1998 and 2000. After this short period, it was possible to see the same lenient attitude, not unlike the implementation of Article 81, to deal with the prolonged economic recession.

The regime governing the implementation of Article 81 underwent a major change in 2003. Council Regulation No. 1 of 2003, which replaced Council Regulation No. 17, brought about a number of changes to the implementation of Article 81. First, the new regulation eliminated the system that required prior notification of agreements between firms as a precondition for individual exemption. Second, it expanded the Commission's evidence-gathering and investigation powers. Finally, it ended the Commission's monopoly over the granting of exceptions under Article 81(3), decentralizing the implementation of Article 81 (Venit, 2003). The new regulation stipulates that the competition authorities and courts of the member states can also apply Article 81(3), besides Article 81(1) and Article 82. However, this does not mean the devolution of real administrative power for implementing competition policy to the national authorities. The regulation makes that clear:

> The principles laid down in Article 81 and 82 of the Treaty, as they have been applied by Regulation No. 17, have given a central role to the Community bodies. This central role should be retained, whilst

associating the Member States more closely with the application of the Community competition rules. (Council Regulation No 1/2003, 2002, p. 6)

By and large, the Commission still maintains its extensive powers and plays a supervisory role in the process of the implementation of Articles 81 and 82 by the member states. Whenever deemed appropriate, the Commission has the right to make a final decision. In such circumstances, member states will automatically be relieved of their competence or authority in the area.

Moreover, member states do not have the right to interpret the laws in their own way. Rather, they are obliged to implement them in light of Commission, CFI, and ECJ decisions. Moschel (2000) expressed his opinion about the implications of the new regulation in the following words: "Ultimately, the organs of the Member States mutate into auxiliaries of the Commission" (p. 497). Briefly, whereas Council Regulation No. 1 of 2003 lessens the substantive role of national competition laws and institutions in interpreting EU competition law, it bolsters the controlling powers of the Commission over national institutions.

As for the MCR, in the first place, the Council adopted a regulation in June 1997, amending Regulation No 4064/89 on the control of concentrations between undertakings. The revised regulation included a new category of merger cases and full-function joint ventures, although the Council did not accept the Commission's proposal to lower the old turnover thresholds. For a new category of merger cases to be under the surveillance of the Commission, four conditions had to be satisfied. The first two were turnover thresholds (the combined worldwide thresholds of the merging firms had to be more than ECU 2.5 billion, while their combined turnover had to be more than ECU 100 million in each of at least three member states). Furthermore, each of at least two of the merging firms had a turnover of more than ECU 25 million in each of those same three member states. Finally, each of at least two of the merging companies had a Community-wide turnover rate of more than ECU 100 million. A second innovation brought about by the amended regulation was the inclusion of all full-function joint ventures under the new merger regulation (CEC, 1998a, pp. 60–1).[16]

A second revision of the MCR was adopted in 2004 as part of a package of comprehensive reforms introduced in December 2001. The package included guidelines on the assessment of horizontal mergers or mergers between competitors; a set of best practices on the conduct of merger investigations in order to ensure transparency; and finally, the appointment of a Chief Competition Economist and the formation of a panel to inspect the investigating group's conclusions. In the first place, the new regulation reworded the substantive test for the assessment of mergers, shifting the emphasis from "concentrations which may significantly impede effective competition in the common part or in a substantial part of it" to protect effective competition directly. In other words, creation or strengthening of a dominant position does not necessarily mean the significant impediment of effective competition in the new law anymore (Schmidt, 2004). Put simply, the rewording provides further justification for concentration.

The revised regulation also clarifies that the Commission has the power to investigate all types of mergers, ranging from dominance by a single firm to the effects of oligopoly on the market. Finally, the new regulation revamped the mechanism for reallocating cases from the Commission to the member states and vice versa (Council Regulation No 139/2004, 2004). In sum, what the revised regulation implies is that the Commission will not automatically prohibit a concentration that creates or strengthens a dominant position, if it does not significantly impede effective competition.

Implementation of the MCR after its passage was not strict. As Graph 3.4 shows, the number of prohibited cases dropped sharply with the prolonged economic slowdown in 2002 and 2003. Despite the existence of the MCR, the Commission prohibited very few mergers, showing that the problem was not the absence of the regulation itself, but the attitudes of the supranational institutions toward market concentration.

In the field of Article 86, the third period witnessed the liberalization of the internal market in electricity as of February 19, 1999, by allowing 25 percent of consumers in 15 member states to opt for suppliers of their choice (CEC, 1999a, p. 53). In the area of state aids, the Commission

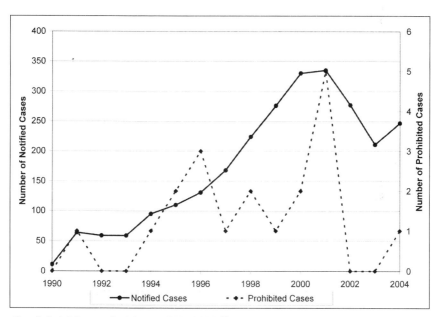

Graph 3.4 Merger decisions: 1990–2004.[17]

implemented its policy of reducing the amount of aid as proposed in 1993, as well as reducing the budget deficits of the member states (CEC, 1995, p. 163). As Graph 3.5 demonstrates, there was a significant drop in the total amount of state aid from around 1.2 percent of GDP to 0.5 percent between 1992 and 2005. It is also apparent that the Commission was sensitive to the fluctuations in the European economy in that the total amount of state aids increased in 1992 and 1993, while the decline was not as much in 2002 and 2005 as in 1998 and 1999.

To summarize, the third period was a period of maintaining profitability around the 5 percent level. Despite the slight fluctuation in 1997 and 2001, the rate of return was healthy. The higher rate influenced the application of individual articles. In contrast to the relaxed enforcement of Article 81 until 2001, the Commission put more emphasis on the application of Article 82 to prevent the abusive practices of dominant firms. The revised merger regulation followed a similar pattern in that the number of prohibited decisions peaked in 2001 before starting to decline back to the 1990s level. State aid declined significantly after 1992, but was sensitive to fluctuations in profitability in 1997 and 2001, indicating that the fundamental rationale behind permitting state aids did not change very much. Finally, the Commission enforced Article 86 to deepen market integration in the areas of electricity and postal services. With the maintenance of stability in profitability, EU competition policy entered into a new period with reforms

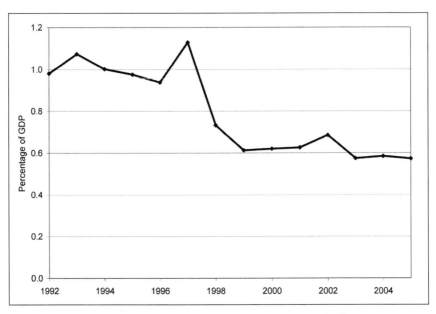

Graph 3.5 Amount of state aid as % of GDP, EU15: 1992–2005.[18]

that became effective in 2004. The impact of the new regulations on EU competition has yet to be seen.

3.5. CONCLUSIONS

This chapter has illustrated that socio-economic conditions, along with political and social forces, exerted a significant role in shaping EU competition policy. Occurring in specific socio-economic conditions, the policy was an outcome of intense bargaining and compromise between political actors and diverse social forces, each of which had its own power. Therefore, it is not surprising to observe that EU competition policy was born at the end of intense negotiations among the six member states as well as between the member states and domestic social forces, especially capitalist firms. The design of the individual competition articles in the EEC Treaty indicates that there was not a significant rupture with the competition policy experiences of individual member states before the EEC.

This chapter has three significant findings. First, the EEC had a centralized decision-making body, and the Council of Ministers and the Commission were the key legislative organs, despite the existence of the Parliament as an elected assembly. The EEC/EU was reformed a number of times over the past forty-five years, and this centralized structure remained intact, even though the Parliament has gained significant legislative powers, especially over the past fifteen years. Despite these reforms, the Parliament still does not have any legislative power in the field of competition policy. EU competition policy is, therefore, still sheltered from direct democratic control.

Second, the design of the competition rules in the EEC Treaty supported the claim made in the second chapter that EU competition policy favored loosely oligopolistic markets during the first twenty years of its existence. The absence of a rule regulating mergers and acquisitions in the EEC Treaty supports this contention. Finally, as the key official documents indicated, the EU institutions became tolerant to highly concentrated markets under the name of international competitiveness after the 1970s, in part, to restore the profitability of the European firms. As a result, the implementation of Article 81 was more flexible to allow firms to restrict competition. In a similar way, Article 87 was another tool to keep firms solvent in the short term by allowing the member states to aid the firms financially during an economic crisis. State aid was also provided for ailing industries to restructure themselves and restore profitability in the long term.

Under conditions of healthy profit margins, it was possible to observe the rigorous implementation of Article 81 and 87 in contrast to the less stringent application of Article 82 and the MCR. Article 82 was a tool to protect small firms against the abusive behavior of larger firms during the economic slowdowns of 1992–93 as well as in 2001–2. Finally, Article 86 served as the principal public policy instrument throughout the 1980s and 1990s to open up new profitable areas, thereby helping to restore profitability. For this reason, the next chapter analyzes the implementation of EU competition policy in the telecommunications industry, primarily, through Article 86. As the next chapter illustrates, Article 86 was the public policy tool around which the EU institutions developed a common strategy of controlled liberalization to protect former monopolies, while ensuring new revenue sources for newcomers in industries such as telecommunications.

4 EU Telecommunications Policy

The previous chapter has shown that Article 86 (ex-Article 90) of EU competition law was the key public policy tool to open up new industries such as airlines, electricity and telecommunications, among others, for market competition and subject them to Articles 81 and 82 after the economic slowdown in the 1970s. This chapter investigates how EU competition law shaped EU telecommunications policy and, therefore, the European telecommunications industry between 1980 and 2004, in broader terms. The underlying argument is that EU telecommunications policy was aimed at creating new oligopolistic equipment and services markets in the telecommunications industry, as part of the overall goal of restoring profitability through establishing 'effective competition'. The EU authorities assumed the policy would eventually be beneficial to European consumers as well.

There were three components to EU telecommunications policy to establish effective competition: adopting common technical standards at the EU level; progressive liberalization and deregulation of the equipment and services market; and finally, gradual privatization of former state-owned telecommunications services monopolies without breaking them up into a series of competitive firms (as AT&T had been broken up). Whereas EU institutions carried out the first two components of EU telecommunications policy at the supranational level, member states implemented the third part at the national level at varying speeds.

The first part of the chapter explains how EU institutions perceived the market in the eighties and early nineties; the second section focuses on the rationale for adopting common technical standards in the telecommunications industry. The historical evolution of EU telecommunications in the third part explains the convergence of the interests of the EU authorities, member states, major telecommunications firms, and heavy corporate users in the 1980s and 1990s. The fourth section examines the motivations behind the privatization of state-owned national telecommunications operators (TOs) by the member states.

4.1. EUROPEAN INTEGRATION AND
EU TELECOMMUNICATIONS POLICY

The prevailing thesis in the existing literature about EU telecommunications policy is that its aim was to improve the competitiveness of the European telecommunications industry, especially that of manufacturers at the global level.[1] Lalor (1987) observed that:

> Altogether, the EC standardization, deregulation, and tariff harmonization policy should, if not by 1992 then by 1995, give Europe the integrated telephone market that would give its leading telecommunication companies, Alcatel, Ericsson, Philips and Siemens an improved basis for international competition. It is this aspect of integration that European planners value most. (p. 115)

The argument that EU telecommunications policy aimed to improve the international competitiveness of the European telecommunications industry does not seem convincing insofar as the industry was already competitive in the 1970s and early 1980s, even before liberalization and deregulation efforts (Thimm, 1989, p. 90). Indeed, in terms of sales figures in 1980–1981, eight telecommunications equipment makers out of the top 13 firms in the world were European.[2] In addition, the literature falls short of offering any convincing explanation for its often-stated assumption of "the irreconcilable conflict between the aim to deregulate and liberalize telecommunication markets and the aim to build up a strong European telecommunication sector" (Fuchs, 1992, p. 644). These issues, as well as why EU authorities selected the telecommunications industry to focus their energies, instead of tackling many others such as computers that needed help, are critical to examining the EU telecommunications industry since 1980 (Zysman and Borus, 1994).

To explicate the fundamentals of EU telecommunications policy, one should move beyond a constricted focus and overly general conclusions, and turn to the grand project of European integration in which EU competition policy has played a crucial role, as a broader frame of policy reference. The policy objective that would elucidate the anatomy of EU telecommunications policy, as part of competition policy itself, is profitability. The European Commission stated the primary rationale for implementing EU competition law in the telecommunications industry in the following way: "Pursuing *effective competition* in telecoms is not a matter of political choice. The choice of a free market and a competition-oriented economy was already envisaged in the EEC Treaty, and the competition rules of the Treaty are directly applicable within the Community" (CEC, 1991b, p. 4). Applying competition rules to the telecommunications industry was part of putting the liberal EEC Treaty into practice to establish a competitive capitalist market in accordance with the principles of ordoliberalism.

In addition to the implementation of the EEC Treaty, EU telecommunications policy was part of a series of measures to revive the stalled European economy in the 1980s. The Commission predicted the telecommunications industry alone could generate up to 6 percent of regional GDP by the end of the 1990s (CEC, 1993b, p. 94).

The situation was not as optimistic as the European Commission forecast in the 1980s, but the industry was growing fast enough, as Graph 4.1 demonstrates. The Commission followed three apparent goals in its telecommunications policy: the promotion of an advanced European telecommunications infrastructure; the stimulation of a homogeneous region-wide market for services and equipment (i.e. accelerating the process of European integration); and finally, the encouragement of international competitiveness of the telecommunications industry (Williamson, 1991a, p. 6). In other words, EU telecommunications policy reflects the objectives of both competition and industrial policies.

As the previous chapter clarifies, EU competition and industrial policies were no longer in conflict with one another by the 1980s, in contrast to common perceptions of the 1970s. Indeed, competition policy became a means for realizing industrial policy in the 1980s. EU industrial policy in this period had three key targets. The first was to establish stable and long-term conditions for an efficiently functioning market economy, i.e. forming and maintaining market conditions suitable for effective competition (read profitable markets). The second was providing the main catalysts for

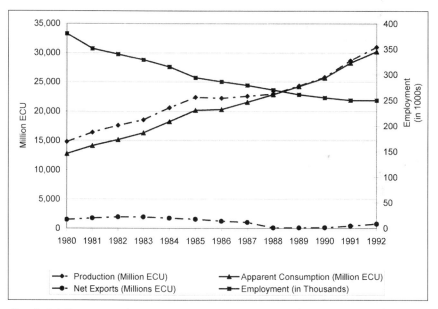

Graph 4.1 European telecommunications equipment market: 1980–1992.[3]

structural adjustment of the whole economy. Finally, developing policy instruments that would accelerate structural adjustment and enhance the so-called competitiveness of the European industry was the third objective (CEC, 1990b, p. 5). EU industrial policy singled out EU-wide technical standards as a key solution for industrial restructuring, creating a single market in telecommunications and improving the international competitiveness of the European telecommunications industry, as part of a general strategy of restoring profitability.

4.2. COMMON TECHNICAL STANDARDS IN TELECOMMUNICATIONS

The EU telecommunications policy objective of common technical standards raises several questions. Why were common technical standards so important? Who benefited from them? How did they influence market structures? What was the connection between common technical standards and effective competition?

Common technical standards at the European level were crucial for a number of reasons. First, they created larger markets for companies, as Breton (1987) observed that: "An increasingly important role of standardization is the reduction of costs by the creation of a larger market" (p. 166). Second, common technical standards reflected the priorities and interests of those who created them. In other words, they produced 'firewalls' to protect the interests of a small group vis-à-vis those who did not take part in their creation. According to the OECD (1991):

> The strategic implications of IT [information technology] standardization are now broadly recognized to be enormous because they will determine the future of individual firms, affect competitive advantages of countries, and even influence the development of whole technologies and their diffusion. (p. 9)

In essence, common technical standards would be the source of power for a company, an industry, a country or a trading block, as they helped to determine the industry's potential scale of operations (Drake, 1994, p. 71).

How could common technical standards determine the scale of operations, and hence the market power essential for international competitiveness? The key concept to comprehend in this is 'systems competition'. For Bohlin and Granstrand (1991):

> By systems competition we mean a set of technologically different and at most weakly compatible systems competing on the telecommunication services markets, with cooperating groups or families of firms (equipment manufacturers, TAs [telecommunication administrations],

etc.) supplying each system in competition with other such families or groups of firms. (p.475)

All players within a system strive as a block to replace the technological system of their competitors with the purpose of increasing their respective market shares. Since there are only a few systems, the nature of competition is oligopolistic. Unless companies agree to cooperate, competition between oligopolistic systems is usually fierce, inducing investments in first-mover advantages until one of them establishes its dominance. Leading firms protect their respective markets, but usually endeavor to raise their market share by increasingly deploying strategic behavior regarding switching costs and common technical standards (Dalum et al., 2000, p. 123). The state takes an active role in this competition between different systems by promoting one system of standards against another explicitly or implicitly.

EU institutions often financed projects for the creation of European technical standards, especially in telecommunications, from the 1980s on. In Europe, development costs of new products in the telecommunications industry increased sharply in the 1970s with the growing complexity of telecommunications equipment, especially central public switching equipment. The national telecommunications administrations and/or public network operators were less willing to completely reimburse the basic development costs incurred by their preferred suppliers. As Schnoring (1994) emphasized, national telecommunications equipment manufacturers felt increasing pressure to gain access to other markets in order to recover sunk costs.

Common technical standards were a double-edged sword: on the one hand, they would help firms gain instant market shares; on the other hand, they would cause firms to lose their market share, if they could not play a role in creating the standards or commercializing technology rapidly. In other words, standardization was a very risky business and many European firms hesitated to undertake this on their own. As a result, EU institutions financed research and development projects to facilitate the creation of new pan-European technical standards, as shown below.

Common technical standards played a crucial role in European industrial policy for three reasons. First, they would remove the technical barriers to trade between the member countries that were essential for European integration, while creating new ones at the European level to protect the European firms against their non-European counterparts, a new form of non-tariff protectionism. Second, common technical standards became new public policy instruments for promoting industrial competitiveness. Common standards promoted competitiveness by lowering costs for producers, shaping customer preferences for products through their familiarity, while enabling the emergence of new markets, new products and new services (CEC, 1990b, pp. 12–3). Third, common standards aided market restructuring by driving out 'unnecessary' competitors and leaving larger and financially sound firms in the market, contributing their competitiveness at the global level.

The European Telecommunication Standards Institute (ETSI) was established in 1988 to act as the arbiter of standardization for the EU. Gagliardi (1989), the ETSI's first director, perceived common technical standards as a tool for the European telecommunications industry to extend its market outside the national boundaries, essential for supporting high research and development expenses. Adoption of common technical standards in Europe was the foundation of EU telecommunications policy. By establishing these standards, the EU had the opportunity to combine its interests in computing and telecommunications, while establishing a European information communications technology (ICT) industry and telecommunications infrastructure (Shearman, 1986, p. 152). By establishing new technical standards, the EU institutions planned to boost the profitability of the EU telecommunications equipment manufacturers by indirectly facilitating the industry's restructuring through mergers and acquisitions. At the same time, common technical standards facilitated the potential for cooperation and competition. Nevertheless, this was not an easy to task to accomplish before the 1980s, given the absence of urgent pressure, as the historical evolution of EU telecommunications policy illustrates in the next two sections.

4.3. THE HISTORICAL EVOLUTION OF EU TELECOMMUNICATIONS POLICY

Schneider (2001) captured the essence of EU telecommunications policy over the last thirty years in the following words: "Essentially, the European Commission promoted institutional adaptation through a strategy combining elements of neoliberalism with neomercantilism, i.e., state-led adaptation of industrial sectors through the introduction of competition" (p. 76). This section demonstrates how this double-tracked policy was first implemented by focusing on the adoption of common technical standards, progressive liberalization, and privatization in the telecommunications industry.

It is possible to distinguish three major periods in the historical evolution of EU telecommunications policy. The first phase spanned from 1957 to 1979 during which the ideas for a common market that would favor the European manufacturers emerged, but there was no concrete action. In the face of a number of pressures, EU institutions as well as member states adopted the goal of creating common technical standards and a new EU-wide regulatory framework in the second period (1980 to 1992). In the third period, 1993–2004, liberalization of the telecommunications services market was phased in along with the consolidation of the new regulatory framework.

4.3.1. Towards a Common Telecommunications Market: 1957–1979

Until the mid-1970s, there were few direct policy initiatives in the telecommunications industry by EC institutions. However, three major institutions were established at the European level to coordinate the telecommunications activities of European states and their membership extended beyond EC member states. The first two institutions responsible for the standardization of European telecommunications and computer technology—Comité Européen de Normalisation Electrotechnique (CENELEC) and Comité Européen de Normalisation (CEN)—were established in 1958 and 1961 respectively. The third was the Conférence Européenne des Administrations des Postes et des Télécommunications (CEPT), or the European Conference of Postal and Telecommunication Administrations, founded by 19 countries across Europe in 1959 (Natallichi, 2001, p. 31).

Created as an independent forum, the CEPT was primarily responsible for achieving a broad measure of regional comparability for tariffs and operating procedures through consensual decisions and voluntary recommendations, while leaving each Postal, Telephone and Telegraph (PTT) authority in the control of national markets (Schneider and Werle, 1986, pp. 86–7). Its activities also included cooperation on commercial, operational, regulatory and technical standardization issues between the PTTs. The CEPT did not have any interest in the sphere of standardization at the European level, for individual PTTs did not want to lose their control at the national level.

As part of an attempt to establish a customs union, the European Commission put forward an initial proposal in 1966 to set rules for domestic and international tariffs for basic postal services. However, the Council of Ministers could not reach a decision on the subject at that time. Similarly, the Commission advanced another proposal in 1968 to create a Postal and Telecoms Committee for the harmonization of postal and telecommunications tariffs. After five years of discussion in the Council of Ministers without any concrete results, the Commission eventually withdrew the proposal in 1973 (Natallichi, 2001, p. 32).

The situation started to change in the mid-1970s. The Council of Ministers adopted a resolution in 1974 based on a Commission proposal, recommending the establishment of a common market for the whole ICT industry where effective competition would prevail. In one of its resolutions, the Council of Ministers (1974) noted: "Aware that *effective competition is desirable* and that the present situation makes appropriate measures necessary to encourage European-based companies to become more competitive . . ." (p. 1, italics added). The goal was to establish effective competition in ICTs and make European companies more competitive internationally. Establishing market conditions suitable for effective competition by adopting common standards and applications, and collaborating on public procurement policies, would be the focal areas for joint action.

A year later, the European Commission called on the CEPT to pursue rigorous regional standardization policies as part of an attempt to achieve greater technical harmonization in accordance with the EEC Treaty. This call did not yet include a comprehensive liberalization policy, but the CEPT established a committee for that purpose in 1975 (Drake, 1994, p. 85). The Committee did not achieve its standardization goal for two reasons. First, harmonization attempts often came into conflict with entrenched national sovereignty concerns. Second, the CEPT did not have the power to enforce national compliance with harmonized standards (Hawkins, 1992, p. 344).

Another initiative in the ICT industry came at the EC Dublin Summit in 1979. In the face of a rapidly worsening economic situation, the Commission responded with a communication that drew attention to the significance of ICTs for the European industry and society. The European Council invited the Council of Ministers to investigate a common strategy for the development of ICTs in Europe (Solomon, 1984, p. 220). At the same time, the Council of Ministers invited the Commission to examine methods and possibilities for coordinating projects at the national level in the microelectronic sector and to submit specific proposals for joint European projects to the Council before March 11, 1980 (Council of Ministers, 1979, pp. 1–2). Furthermore, Etienne Davignon, Industry Commissioner from 1977 to 1985, arranged a meeting with the chief executive officers of the twelve largest ICT firms and asked them to develop a program for cooperation in new information and communication technologies in 1979 (Natallichi, 2001, p. 34). However, his effort did not produce substantial immediate results.

In summary, the direction of future policy took its basic shape in the first period of EU telecommunications policy-making. Common technical standards and common procurement policies were identified as areas where common action could be taken to create a single European equipment market, while preventing non-European firms from conquering the newly opened markets. That is why, initially, the policy did not imply liberalization of the telecommunications services markets. Deregulation would be the next step to follow after adopting common European technical standards.

4.3.2. Adopting Common Technical Standards: 1980–1992

The second period was a turning point in EC telecommunications policy during which the supranational institutions adopted, as well as implemented, concrete policy measures at the European level, especially in the realm of common technical standards and common procurement policies. External and internal developments in telecommunications pressured actors at different levels to develop a common position. In other words, factors such as external pressures, especially from the US, failure of national efforts, technological convergence, the Commission's enforcement of Article 82 in conjunction with Article 86, and an increasing demand from European users for better and cheaper telecommunications services were the significant factors that led to the convergence.

In the first place, deregulation of the telecommunications industry in the US, Britain and Japan was spurring international competition (Thimm, 1992). Europe's protected telecommunications markets were expected to become a prime target of American efforts to remove barriers to international trade in telecommunications services, such as private virtual networks (PVN), because American 'Baby Bells' and new companies such as Microwave Communications Inc. (MCI) and Sprint wanted to have equal opportunities in European markets as European firms enjoyed in the American market (Thatcher, 2004b).

Member states realized that their individual efforts had largely failed (Sandholtz, 1993). For instance, in Germany, a consortium led by Siemens, which included both the Federal Post Office and the German government, had been working on a program to develop a more sophisticated analogue long-distance switching system known as EWS-A for the Bundespost since the mid-1960s. The consortium decided to use traditional analogue technology based on electro-mechanical switching components for transmitting sounds as a series of varying frequencies. Nevertheless, the international telecommunications industry moved to digital technology in the mid-1970s and deployed microelectronic circuits to perform all key functions in public switching or exchange equipment. The consortium's efforts became worthless as digital technology totally replaced its analog counterpart. Eventually, Siemens had to suspend its twelve-year EWS-A program in 1978 after a total investment of DM 1 billion (Fleming, 1982, p. 5).

At the national level in the early 1980s, diverse and mounting pressures were also beginning to stir new policy responses. Although this pressure was common to all European countries, there was a considerable divergence of response to it at the beginning. In the absence of a convergence of interests, member states took individual policy measures to cope with the domestic and international challenges to their existing telecommunications policy. For instance, West Germany set up a government committee to examine the Bundespost monopoly. Similarly, the Dutch Government launched an initiative to study proposals to curb the monopoly of its PTT and to give it more commercial independence. In France, the right-wing opposition favored reducing state control over the powerful Direction Generale des Telecommunication (DGT), and Italy considered injecting private capital into its main telephone company (De Jonquieres, 1985. p. 14).

EC member states were moving at varying speeds toward liberalization and adopting different solutions, making it hard to detect a clear overall direction for the future of a coordinated EC telecommunications policy.

There was an important reason behind such a divergence, according to De Jonquieres (1986):

> The confusion stems partly from the fact that European countries, in redefining their telecommunication policies, are seeking to pursue two separate goals. They want to stimulate more vigorous and innovative markets for telecommunication equipment and services while also building up internationally more competitive supplier industries. However, these objectives are not proving easy to reconcile. (p. iv)

At the beginning, it was difficult for member states to come together individually to adopt a common position. After several years of implementing separate national telecommunications policies proved ineffective, it became apparent that this approach to policy was not only wasteful, but also made them vulnerable to foreign intrusion in their markets. Member states had to find common ground to cooperate with each other against the US and Japan. The best solution to accomplish this objective would be the development of a common policy position at the European level.

Another factor was the rapid technological convergence of telecommunications, data processing and imaging technologies. It blurred the distinction between traditional industries such as telecommunications, computers and broadcasting (Hudson, 1997, p. 4; Carpentier, 1995, p. v). Similarly, a dramatic fall in the cost of long-distance telecommunications services, because of technological advances in fiber optic cables, satellite technologies and wireless networks, challenged many of the economic arguments for 'natural monopolies' in telecommunications by lowering barriers to new market entrants. Business customers, particularly American multinational companies, stepped up their demands for new types of telecommunications services and more say in how these were developed and operated. As a result, state-controlled monopolies, which had long dominated telecommunications in most European countries, were under growing pressure to adapt to competition and changing market needs in the mid-1980s (Elixmann, 1989, p. 4; Bruce, 1988, ch. 4).

The European Commission deployed Article 86 in 1982 for the first time in the history of EU competition law to enforce Article 82 in the telecommunications industry. As the next chapter analyzes the case in detail, the Commission, in *Telespeed Services Limited v. United Kingdom Post Office* (1983), informed British Telecom, a state-owned monopolistic service provider in the UK at the time of the decision, that it did not have a monopoly to offer telecommunications services, but only had a monopoly to build and run telecommunications networks (para. 15). The decision sent a strong signal to the member states that the services market would be open to competition soon. In response, the Italian government took the case to the ECJ and demanded the annulment of the Commission's decision, but the latter supported the Commission (*Italy v. EC Commission*, 1985, para. 30). The ECJ's decision left no other option for member states but to develop a common European policy. The Single European Act (SEA) also put additional pressures for abolishing market barriers in telecommunications in the mid-1980s.

In addition to the pressure from American multinationals and Brussels, there was also political pressure within many European countries for a change in the role and operating styles of the national telecommunications administrations (TAs). One source of pressure was mainly from domestic firms that were heavy users of telecommunications services (Humpreys, 1990, p. 201). Another source included European telecommunications equipment manufacturers that had increasingly become captives of their protected home markets and desired to expand and acquire the economies of scale necessary to cover soaring development costs (De Jonquieres, 1985, p. 14). As a result, they supported Europeanization of telecommunications.

Squeezed by protected national markets, tougher international competition, and rising costs, the telecommunications industry appeared ripe for rationalization. Initially, state-owned monopolistic PTT administrations were fiercely jealous of their independent roles, while smaller national telecommunications equipment makers were reluctant to lose their secure home markets. Nevertheless, this attitude soon changed, as the pressure of the domestic and international factors mentioned above increased, especially from large firms. For instance, a former executive vice-president of Alcatel—one of the biggest European telecommunications equipment producers—predicted that the most attractive aspect of the equipment market would be the amount of investment in the telecommunications industry in the order of ECU 500 to 1000 billion by the year 2000, and generating by then 7 percent of the EU's GNP compared to 2 percent in 1984 (Gluntz, 1989, p. 372). Since the problem for the European telecommunications equipment manufacturers was Europe's fragmented market, liberalization and deregulation were seen as an opportunity to create a pan-European telecommunications industry, which would facilitate Europeanization of the leading firms while avoiding political intervention from national authorities.

Despite their ardent support for liberalization, there was also a fear among the European telecommunications equipment vendors that fast and uncoordinated liberalization and deregulation would reduce their profitability for two reasons. The first was that the faster but uncoordinated opening of lucrative markets would attract non-European companies and allow them to reap the benefits quickly. Second, the faster and uncoordinated liberalization policy and freedom from state control would mean that European telecommunications operators might buy their equipment from non-European producers on a competitive basis, and the European telecommunications equipment producers might suddenly lose their customers. For Gluntz (1989): "This would occur if competing operators in those countries chose their suppliers on purely marginal commercial criteria where administration in other countries took national content or long-term policy into account in their sourcing" (p. 371).

To prevent such problems, as well as to keep profit margins for the European manufacturers higher, the former vice-president of Alcatel highlighted several solutions. In the first place, liberalization of markets, especially the basic and value-added services (VAS) that were the main revenue sources for the former monopolistic national operators, should be coordinated and orchestrated at the European level. Cooperation between the national telecommunications operators in their liberalization and deregulation policies would be essential for the success of European manufacturers. Controlled deregulation would provide national telecommunications operators with the profits to spend on new equipment in the process of developing an integrated telecommunications market:

> We need strong PTTs. Deregulation must not pressure their profitability if we want them to be able to create the new basic infrastructures for the future, without which there will be no possibility for the development of new liberalized services such as VANS [value-added networks] and VAS [value-added services], radio, telephone, and so on. (Quoted in Gluntz, 1989, pp. 372–3)

The second suggested solution was cooperation between national telecommunications administrations and European manufacturers. What was meant by cooperation was that TAs should not consider 'purely marginal commercial criteria' when they bought equipment. They should buy from the European manufacturers, even when their products were not the least expensive. The third and last solution offered was an industrial policy at the European level for supporting alliances, cooperation, mergers and acquisitions between European firms. Accordingly, a merger control regulation at the supranational level was proposed in the second half of the 1980s (Gluntz, 1989, pp. 369–70). As the subsequent section shall illustrate, Alcatel's policy proposals (as a reflection of the European telecommunications equipment manufacturers' policy preferences) could not be put into practice at the national level. But they found their expression in EC telecommunications policy at the supranational level.

In reaction to the changing global telecommunications industry conditions, 12 major European ICT equipment conglomerates wrote an urgent letter to the Council of Ministers in early 1983, stressing their concern about the 'weak position' of the European ICT industry.[4] At the same time, the leading European telecommunications firms established an organization called the Standards Promotion and Application Group (SPAG) in 1983 and submitted a proposal to the European Commission, as well as to the member states, for a European ICT standardization policy. These initiatives demonstrated that the largest European firms exerted a strong influence on the direction of EC telecommunications policy, after their perception about the evolution of the telecommunications industry changed in the early 1980s.

A central task for the supranational institutions was to reconcile all these divergent interests to satisfy various social forces as well as member states. The Commission attempted to persuade the member states to relax protectionist barriers and to sell telecommunications equipment to each other in the early 1980s. Accordingly, the EC launched a series of new policy initiatives in 1983. For instance, EC Industry Commissioner Etienne Davignon prepared a report for the President of the Council on June 15, 1983, proposing the creation of a common market in the telecommunications industry as well as the establishment of a European telecommunications agency. These measures were seen to facilitate the realization of the vast potential for growth in the industry, while increasing the international competitiveness of the European telecommunications firms. In the meantime, the Commission set out a list of fairly broad goals, including steps to coordinate national medium and long-term policy objectives, to achieve more technical standardization, adopt a common stand on external trade and, finally, to liberalize public procurement (Solomon, 1987, p. 220).

The Commission contended that harmonizing disparate regulations and opening national markets would speed up investment in modern telecommunications networks and stimulate the development of a technologically advanced industry vis-à-vis the American and Japanese firms. The Council of Ministers supported this view by setting up a special task force in 1983 to discuss further action, having acknowledged for the first time that telecommunications was too important to be left entirely in the hands of the national monopoly carriers. The creation of a new body called the Information Technologies and Telecommunication Task Force (ITT) within the Commission in 1983 was the first concrete action (Sauter, 1997, p. 174).

The ITT Task Force, in turn, created the Senior Officials Group on Telecommunication (SOGT) in 1983 that included representatives from different national institutions such as ministries of industry, economics and the PTTs. The SOGT agreed on the six-line Action Program proposed by the Commission to create a unified European telecommunications market. The Action Program became the basis for further Commission activities in subsequent years. These actions by the Commission included: initiating common research and development projects, liberalizing the terminal equipment market, helping the less-favored regions build their telecommunications infrastructure, developing a Community action towards the world at large and creating trans-European telecommunications networks (Neu, Neumann & Schnöring, 1987, p. 41).

The Commission was not blind to the danger that rapid liberalization would be harmful to the European equipment producers. Etienne Davignon stated that the Commission was aware of the fact that if Europe opened up public procurement quickly, European firms would lose market share to their American and Japanese counterparts ("Interview with Etienne Davignon," 1984, p. 110B). The interests of firms, and national and European levels of government agencies were, by and large, converging by the mid-1980s. In 1984, the Council of Ministers played a leading role by means of agreeing on the following plans and policies:

a. The creation of a European market for telecommunications equipment and terminals by means of a common standardization policy, procedures for mutual recognition of type approval (or certification) for terminals, and effective implementation of a European standardization policy;
b. Building advanced telecommunications services and networks through implementing infrastructure projects of common interest across national boundaries, launching a development program for the required technology and setting up video-communications links between the various political authorities in the EC; and
c. Building the advanced services and networks in the less-favored regions within the EC through the use of EC financial instruments. (Ungerer, 1990, p. 135)

Compared to the Council Recommendation of 1983, the new program was more concrete, specific and action-oriented in that it specified actions to be taken at the supranational level under the guidance of the member states.

In sum, the new action proposal by the Council of Ministers hinted at the emergence of a new strategy at the European level as part of an attempt to deal with international pressures, especially from American firms. This was noted by American *Business Week*:

> The strategy emerging in Europe for dealing with the rapid expansion of the US telecommunication industry is one of flexible monopoly. Where necessary, the Europeans will bend far to preserve their communications franchises. By doing so, they hope to thwart US competitors such as International Business Machines Corp. and AT&T before either giant secures a foothold in the European market. With hundreds of thousands of jobs and billions of dollars in revenue at stake, Europe's government-owned post, telephone, and telegraph companies (PTTs) are out to protect their turf at all costs. Toward that end, they are trying to learn to cooperate and compete at the same time. ("How Europe's Phone Monopolies," 1984, p. 110A)

This new two-pronged policy of cooperation and competition, essential for protecting the European manufacturers and services providers would be possible through common standards and gradual liberalization.

Common technical standards served as a common launch pad for EC telecommunications policy in the mid-1980s. In order to realize the standardization objective and to create common technical standards for new technologies at the European level, the Council adopted two projects. The first became known as the European Strategic Programme for Research and Development in Information Technology (ESPRIT), which arose out of discussions between the European Commission and Europe's 12 leading IT companies. It covered five sectors: advanced microelectronics, software technology, information- and knowledge-processing, office systems and computer-integrated manufacture. The objective of ESPRIT was to encourage transnational communications, common technical standards and collaborative approaches to information technology (CEC, 1987b). Some of the leading companies involved in ESPRIT in terms of total market value were Dutch Philips, German Siemens, British GEC and Plessey, French Thomson CSF, Bull Transac and IMAG, and Italian Olivetti (Shearman, 1986, p. 150). They were the largest ICT companies in Europe and influential in government policy circles.

The second project was called the Research and Development in Advanced Communications-technologies for Europe (RACE) program which commenced at the European level in 1985 (Council of Ministers, 1988; CEC, 1988b; Narjes, 1988; Council of Ministers, 1985). It covered areas such as mobile telecommunications, satellites and terrestrial networks, narrow-band networks, distribution networks of all kinds as well as specific broadband networks, including Integrated Broadband Communications networks (IBC) (CEC, 1988b, pp. 1–3). RACE aimed to establish the necessary technological base for the introduction of an EC-wide IBC network in three phases.

The first phase of RACE between 1985 and 1986 realized an IBC reference model and the identification of relevant research and development, design and pilot work. The purpose was to develop a consensus on the functional and techno-economic characteristics of the IBC network itself, the terminal environment as well as the applications and/or services made possible by their interaction (Council of Ministers, 1988). The second phase of RACE from 1987 to 1992 focused on the development of the technological base for IBC. This meant support for the formulation of common proposals for specifications, and standards, and for carrying out the necessary pre-competitive developments to provide trial equipment and services for IBC demonstrations. The third phase from 1992 to 1997 was intended to develop the technological base for enhanced IBC equipment and services (Shearman, 1986, p. 151).

The participating companies in RACE were the national telecommunications operators, and Alcatel, Philips, Ericsson, Bosch Telekom, GEC, Siemens, STC, Plessey, AT&T-NSI, IBM and Matra (Schnöring, 1994, p. 153). The European Commission expressed its opinion about the program as follows: "The programme is turning out to be a major factor in the formation of the Community's future industry and research structure in the sector" (CEC, 1988a, p. 29). As a catalyst in key areas of high technology development, RACE promoted the European telecommunications industry by reducing uncertainties and investment risk. By bringing the European manufacturers, service providers and operators together to determine the future direction of the industry, the EC facilitated collaboration, concentration and consensus formation between telecommunications equipment manufacturers and service providers.

In 1984, the Council of Ministers recommended that member states implement harmonization of standards in the field of telecommunications. Indeed, it called for the introduction of services based on a common harmonized approach in the telecommunications field. Harmonization was meant to realize two objectives: creating a range of harmonized telematic services by offering users a chance to communicate efficiently, and creating "a dynamic Community market for telecommunications equipment" (Council of Ministers, 1984, pp. 49–50). Complementing these projects, the Council also recommended the opening up of access to public communications contracts in November 1984.

Moreover, the Council adopted two common technical standards in its decision of 1986. The first one was in the field of information technology, and the second in the functional specifications for services especially offered over public telecommunications networks for exchange of information and data between information technology systems. The aim was to contribute to the process of internal market integration in the ICT industry, while improving "the international competitiveness of Community manufacturers by allowing for greater market uptake in the Community of equipment manufactured to recognized European and international standards" (Council of Ministers, 1987, pp. 31–7). To assist the project, the Council issued another Directive and asked member states to "implement the mutual recognition of the results of tests of conformity with common conformity specifications for mass-produced telecommunications terminal equipment" (Council of Ministers, 1986a, p. 21). Complementing the previous initiatives in the field of common technical standards, the Council further recommended that the telecommunications administrations in the member states introduce integrated services digital networks (ISDN). Again, the objective of this recommendation was "to maintain the Community's worldwide competitiveness in the light of the rapid pace of development in the telecommunication sector", while increasing the European telecommunications share in the world market (Council of Ministers, 1986b, pp. 36–41).

In sum, adopting common technical standards at the European level was the first tangible step in creating pan-European telecommunications equipment and services markets. New technical standards were difficult to realize because most European firms preferred to collaborate with their technologically advanced American counterparts rather than their European peers. In addition to the standardization attempts, the European Commission also launched a number of projects financed by the EC, besides ESPRIT and RACE, to create new market outlets for European telecommunications equipment manufacturers.

Some of these were the Special Telecommunication Actions for the Regions (STAR), the IT Education Technology (DELTA), and the IT Technology for the Financial Services (DIME), as well as the IT Technology for the Automobile and Road Traffic Industry (DRIVE) after the mid-1980s (Narjes, 1988, pp. 119–20). The one most widely taken up was STAR, which had been approved by the Council in October 1986. The underlying objective of STAR was to assist the development of certain rural areas of Greece, Ireland, Portugal, Italy (Mezzogiorno), the United Kingdom (Northern Ireland), France (Corsica and overseas departments), and regions of Spain by improving access to advanced telecommunications services (Hudson, 1987, p. 166; Lauder, 1987, p. 99). An unusual aspect of STAR was that it excluded investment in basic telephony and telex in those regions that needed such basic services urgently at the time, since investment costs for basic telephony would be very high and less profitable for the participating firms (Lalor, 1987, p. 119).

Overall, since 1984, the EC/EU adopted six framework programs and increased its financing of research activities from 2 percent of its total budget to 4.5 percent of the total EU budget between 1984 and 2006, as Graph 4.2 shows. Those multi-year Framework Programs from 1984 to 2006 were aimed at supporting research activities and technological development in

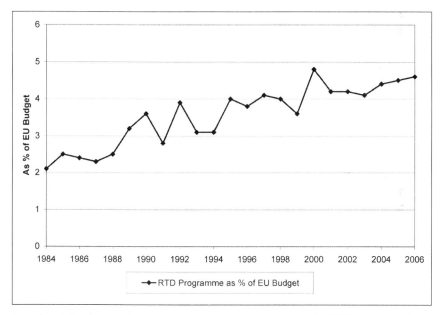

Graph 4.2 European Research and Development Framework (RTD) program budgets (as % of Total EU Budget): 1984–2006.[5]

areas such as information technologies (IT) and telecommunications, transportation, energy, environment, life sciences, industrial and materials technology, and others. Information technologies and communications have had the largest share in R&D spending, hovering around 25 percent or one-fourth of the total R&D budget between 1984 and 2006. Second, the IT and communications' share increased to more than 35 percent in the second half of the 1980s and early 1990s, before decreasing to 25 percent in subsequent years (CEC, 2004b, p. 27). It is not hard to explain this sharp rise if one remembers the number of projects launched in the second half of the 1980s to encourage cooperation between the European manufacturers.

After laying the ground for a European telecommunications policy, the next step was a roadmap for liberalization. The European Commission published the Green Paper, *Towards a Dynamic European Economy: Green Paper on the Development of the Common Market for Telecommunication Services and Equipment*, in 1987 (CEC, 1987c, p. 1). Understanding the rationale behind the Green Paper is crucial in comprehending the process of liberalization as well as privatization for subsequent years. Figure 4.1 explains the dynamics behind the first and subsequent Green Papers. The Green Paper of 1987, as the first and most important in the series, outlined a broad strategy for "the full development of the supply of services and equipment." Consistent with the theory of effective competition, the Green Paper's primary concern was supply-side stability, i.e. ensuring stable returns for both European equipment manufacturers and service providers (CEC, 1987c, p. 20). Certainly, consumers would benefit from such policies too, but they were left to the mercy of a few pan-European giant firms without any firm assurances.

European manufacturers needed large and lucrative markets to finance research and development for new products, recover their costs, and make profits. The discourse of international competitiveness was used to justify the policy initiative. The Commission suggested a two-pronged telecommunications policy in the Green Paper. The first was to create a pan-European equipment and services market through progressive market deregulation and liberalization. Gradual deregulation would allow the European manufacturers the needed time to adjust, as their profitability was in any case dependent on the profitability of telecommunications service providers. The Commission commented: "At the same time, the financial viability of the network infrastructure providers must be assured if they are to engage in the massive front-loaded investment needed to prepare the infrastructure of tomorrow's service economy" (CEC, 1987c, p. 49). It was clear to the Commission that profitability of European telecommunications equipment manufacturers was dependent on that of service providers.

The rationale for gradual deregulation and liberalization at the national level was obvious to the Commission: "[U]nless investments by the main network infrastructure provider(s) are carried out on the requisite scale

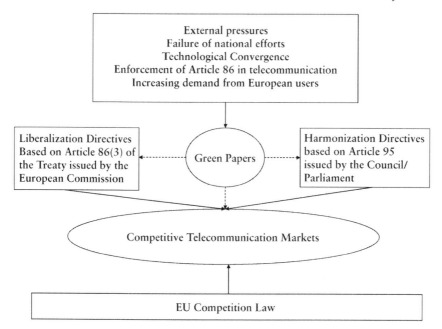

External pressures
Failure of national efforts
Technological Convergence
Enforcement of Article 86 in telecommunication
Increasing demand from European users

Liberalization Directives
Based on Article 86(3) of
the Treaty issued by the
European Commission

Green Papers

Harmonization Directives
based on Article 95
issued by the Council/
Parliament

Competitive Telecommunication Markets

EU Competition Law

Figure 4.1 Liberalization of EU telecom markets.[6]

now, manufacturers of terminals and service providers will not have the
security and incentive to engage in the necessary R&D and capital investment in their turn" (CEC, 1987c, p. 50). Commission officials were happy
with the resulting degree of support they received for the Green Paper of
1987 from the telecommunications administrations as well as the equipment manufacturers (Thomas, 1987, p. 4).

The second prong of the policy was re-regulation of the industry at the
European level to protect the European telecommunications markets against
firms from non-European countries in the aftermath of deregulation. Re-
regulation was accomplished by implementing two different strategies.
First, European competition policy replaced asymmetric, sector-specific
regulations at the national level. Second, re-regulation appeared in the form
of adopting common technical standards at the European level. Council
Directive 91/263/EEC on the approximation of the laws of the member
states concerning telecommunications terminal equipment, including the
mutual recognition of their conformity, was a policy instrument to realize
this objective (Council of Ministers, 1993a). The Directive asked the participating member states to take all measures to assure that terminal equipment
sold on the market and put into service complied with the requirements. As
a supplement to Directive 91/263/EEC, the Council issued another directive
in 1993 to bring satellite earth station equipment under coverage (Council
of Ministers, 1993b). By using Council Directive 91/263/EEC as a basis, the

European Commission issued more than fifty decisions to establish common technical regulations covering the European level (Bartle, 2006, p. 64). Deregulation did not result in less regulation, but the EU assumed more regulatory powers, compared to the member states.

European re-regulation of the telecommunications industry after its national deregulation seemed to be a conundrum for some observers such as Dawkins (1989): "The paradox is that the Commission had found it necessary to regulate at the same time as carrying out its liberalizing zeal" (p. 12). In fact, there was no contradiction for the European Commission:

> To ensure that this costly investment task is carried out, re-regulation of the telecommunication sector must safeguard the revenue-earning capacity of the central network infrastructure provider(s). This includes reasonable protection against excessive 'cream-skimming': exploitation by competitors of the most profitable parts of the market (i.e., high-density business traffic). (CEC, 1987c, p. 51)

Re-regulation was not only beneficial for the dominant operators, but also for the manufacturers, in that non-European producers and service providers were forced to accept the new European standards, while their European counterparts were given enough time to establish themselves firmly in the newly liberalized markets. Otherwise, intense competition between non-European and European firms would have reduced the profit rate for the latter. Put another way, the objective of re-regulation was to solve the problem of an excessively restricted national structure of supply by creating larger markets with higher profit rates at the European level. In the meantime, the former monopolies would have enough time to adjust themselves to new market conditions.

The Green Paper also suggested the reinforcement of rapid development and deployment of EU standards and specifications at the national as well as the European levels through the establishment of a new European Telecommunication Standards Institute (ETSI), which came into being in 1988, only a year after the publication of the Green Paper—lightning speed in Community terms. The new institute would set standards for telecommunications and broadcasting. It would cooperate with the Technical Center of the European Broadcasting Union in adopting technical standards in broadcasting through a Joint Technical Committee. The new institute would also represent the EC/EU in international negotiations. In principle, it adopts international standards where they exist, creates new European standards in areas where there are no international standards, and promotes European standards at the International Telecommunication Union (ITU) committees to make them international whenever there is an opportunity (Besen, 1990, p. 552).

Many PTTs in the CEPT did not want to hand over the power to determine European standards in the telecommunications industry to the ETSI.

Instead, they preferred the CEPT to retain ultimate authority over standards, while offering the ETSI the status of a mere research facility providing inputs to the CEPT. However, the European Commission, through the Green Paper, demanded that standardization be controlled by a broader cross-section of the industry (Drake, 1994, pp. 87–8). Telecommunications equipment manufacturers expanded their power at the expense of national PTTs. This outcome was in line with broader EC industrial policy in that it assigned a greater role for the private sector in the standard-setting process to further their interests (CEC, 1990, pp. 12–3).

The ETSI would help stabilize the market for the dominant telecommunications firms because they needed to consolidate and maintain their power in a new and highly fluid technical and political environment through changes in the regulatory framework (Hawkins, 1992, p. 341). The establishment of the ETSI allowed for the inclusion of big European manufacturers in the processes of standard-setting, unlike the CEPT, which had been designed as an exclusive club of the national PTTs (Drake, 1994, p. 240). With the establishment of the ETSI, decision-making power in setting technical standards for the telecommunications industry moved from the public to the private sector.

The foundation of the ETSI was a good example of the regionalization of standards development. The EC chose criteria for technical specifications, going beyond user and network safety, to include additional requirements for determining conformity. In fact, these common technical standards would become a not-so-disguised tool to discriminate against non-European equipment suppliers (Rich, 1988, p. 5). Wallenstein (1990) argued that "disagreement about the particular choice of standard characteristics was a necessary ploy for safeguarding European commercial interests" (p. 21). Not surprisingly, the American Computer and Business Equipment Manufacturers Association opposed the EC's standardization attempts (Delcourt, 1991, pp. 20–1). The US government wanted American manufacturers to be included in the ETSI's work in setting European standards. However, ETSI rules gave non-EC companies only observer status, meaning that they could not play an active role in the process of adopting new standards (Taylor, 1989, p. 355).

In sum, the Green Paper was a 'producer-driven' endeavor to increase the profitability of the European manufacturers (Solomon, 1987, p. 324). Luis Solana, Telefonica's former chairperson, criticized the European Commission's position in the Green Paper in the following way: "The Commission was giving too much emphasis to manufacturers of telecommunication equipment in its proposals" (Dixon, 1988, p. 4). The objectives of the Green Paper satisfied the needs of the biggest European manufacturers, alongside those of monopolistic national service providers, as EC policy makers promised to keep the former monopolistic service providers intact, while opting for progressive liberalization and deregulation at the national level coupled with re-regulation at the European level. Such a policy trajectory would also help the member states privatize the former monopolies successfully.

The Green Paper also favored multinational corporations at the expense of small business and residential users by recommending liberalization of most, if not all, of the services heavily used by large corporate users first. In other words, the Green Paper defined the public voice telephone service in such a way that the services used by small firms and residential users would not be liberalized immediately, while those needed most by multinationals would be opened up to market competition at the outset. Small business and residential users, therefore, had to wait another ten years for the regulatory model of the 1987 Green Paper that aimed to liberalize 'corporate services' without delay (Larouche, 2000, p. 13).

Following the Green Paper, progressive liberalization started with telecommunications services, which were either new or insignificant to the incumbents' revenues, but mostly needed by multinational corporations, while leaving untouched the main source of revenue, i.e. public voice communications. In this way, the damage to the former monopolies would be minimized, while corporate users' demands were satisfied. After the Green Paper and the adoption of the resolution in June 1988 on the development of the common market for telecommunications services and equipment over the next four years, the Council invited the European Commission to propose the necessary measures to bring this into being (Council of Ministers, 1988b, pp. 1–3).

Liberalization started in the telecommunications equipment market in 1988. The telecommunications equipment markets for a first telephone set, additional telephone sets, private automatic branch exchanges, modems, telex terminals, data-transmission terminals, mobile telephones, receive-only stations not reconnected to the public network of a member state, and other terminal equipment were opened up to market competition in May 1988 (CEC, 1988c, pp. 73–7). As a result, monopolistic service providers had to give up their exclusive or special rights to supply them.

In the field of telecommunications services, framework laws were put in place, in addition to opening up a few markets for competition to satisfy the immediate needs of European multinational companies. The Commission prohibited monopolies over advanced services, including fax services, e-mail, and data transmission and processing services through the Services Directive of 1990 (CEC, 1990c, pp. 10–6). A directive on the establishment of the internal market for telecommunications services through the implementation of open network provision (ONP) provided for the harmonization of conditions for open and efficient access to, and use of, public telecommunications networks and services. All member states could withdraw all special or exclusive rights for the supply of telecommunications services other than voice telephony, while taking the necessary measures to ensure that any operator was entitled to supply telecommunications services. But the directive did not cover telex, mobile, radiotelephony, paging and satellite services (Bernard, 1990, pp. 280–1).

A Council directive of June 1990, for the harmonization of conditions for open and efficient access to and the use of public telecommunications networks and services, covered leased lines, packet- and circuit-switched data services, integrated services digital network (ISDN), voice telephony service, telex service, mobile service, and, finally, access to the broadband network (Council of Ministers, 1990a, pp. 1–9). The Council issued a recommendation to create the conditions for the coordinated introduction of digital European cordless telecommunications into the Community (Council of Ministers, 1991, pp. 47–50). Another Council action was to advise that telecommunications administrations implement a detailed coordinated introduction of pan-European land-based radio paging in the Community by 1993 at the latest (Council of Ministers, 1990b, pp. 23–7). The Council subsequently adopted a directive for a coordinated introduction of pan-European land-based public radio paging in the Community by December 31, 1992, and hence, demanded that member states prepare plans and bring into force the necessary laws, regulations and administrative procedures (Council of Ministers, 1990c, pp. 28–9). All of these efforts demonstrate member states' determination to liberalize the telecommunications industry by using the institutional mechanisms provided by the EU.

Deregulation was simply not enough for new competitors. To ensure market competition in the liberalized market segment, a Council directive required member states to make available a minimum set of leased lines with harmonized technical characteristics throughout the EC to new entrants (Council of Ministers, 1992a, p. 27). Similarly, the Council, in its resolution of June 1992, asked member states to notify the telecommunications organizations in their territory to provide an ISDN with harmonized access arrangements and a minimum set of offerings together with adequate interoperability between ISDNs (Council of Ministers, 1992b, pp. 10–9; Council of Ministers, 1992c, pp. 1–2). Finally, in another recommendation, the Council requested that member states ensure the provision of a minimum set of packet-switched data services with harmonized technical characteristics in their respective territories by June 1992 (Council of Ministers, 1992d, pp. 1–9). The goal was to set up pan-European networks and facilitate the completion of the internal market.

The second period of forming a pan-European telecommunications market was thus about establishing a firm policy framework for further common action by setting out goals, bringing actors together and coordinating disparate individual national efforts at the European level. The EC telecommunications policy did not require the breaking up of national monopolistic telecommunications operators into several service providers for the reason that size would be essential for achieving economies of scale and selling telecommunications equipment and services inside the EC as well as internationally.

Common technical standards and a standardization policy for the EC telecommunications industry were seen as key for promoting European interests. These standards, such as the Global System for Mobile Communications (GSM) and the Universal Mobile Telecommunication System (UMTS), enabled Ericsson, Nokia, Alcatel and Siemens to dominate global mobile telecommunications markets. They were the products of the research projects financed by the European Commission. Besides standardization, ground rules for re-regulating the already liberalized markets were adopted in the second period. Even though there was a glimpse of what would come in the second period regarding market liberalization, full liberalization of the markets had to wait until the third period during which the most profitable market segments were gradually opened up for market competition.

4.3.3. Liberalization, Deregulation and Re-regulation: 1993–2004

As outlined in the second section, liberalization would start in the markets that contributed the least to revenues of the dominant telecommunications operators and would satisfy the immediate needs of European transnational firms. Progressive opening up of the major telecommunications services markets to competition was essential for the European firms to take advantage of liberalized markets. A striking feature of the third period was the rapid growth of the telecommunications industry as a whole in Europe, thanks to new services such as mobile phones and the Internet. The average growth rate for the market between 1993 and 2000 was 10 percent, whereas it declined to 3 percent on average between 2001 and 2004, as Graph 4.3 (below) demonstrates. Rapid growth encouraged EU institutions to complete the liberalization process as soon as possible.

The process of liberalization that had already started toward the end of the second period continued with accelerated speed in the third period. During this time, the first liberalization initiative occurred in the sphere of public procurement in 1993 (Council of Ministers, 1993c, p. 84–138; Council of Ministers, 1992e, pp. 14–22). The Council first recommended such action in the early 1980s, but member states dragged their feet for almost ten years before finally liberalizing it in 1993. The second initiative was in satellite communications services and equipment markets. In its 1991 Resolution, the Council indicated its desire to create a competitive common market for satellite telecommunications services and equipment (Council of Ministers, 1992f, p.1). It stressed the importance of developing a common EC policy with regard to satellite personal communications that would be based on the overarching EC telecommunications policy (Council of Ministers, 1993d, pp. 1–2). As a result, the European Commission issued a Directive to establish a common market

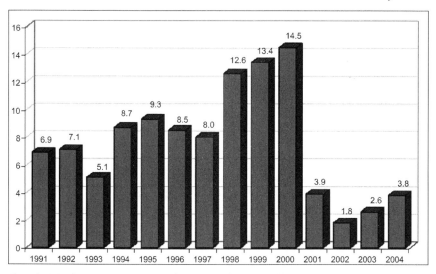

Graph 4.3 Western European Telecom market growth rate: 1991–2004.[7]

for satellite communications equipment and its services market in 1994 (CEC, 1994b, p. 15). These reforms satisfied the immediate needs of telecommunications equipment producers and business users, but not ordinary citizens. The producers would have a larger market, while big corporate users would be able to purchase cheaper satellite communications services.

The third initiative in the process of liberalization was in the sphere of mobile/personal communications, telecommunications infrastructure, cable TV networks, and public voice telephony services, as stated in the Council Resolution of June 1993 (Council of Ministers, 1993c, pp. 1–3). For the Commission, the policy objectives would be promoting the development of pan-European mobile telecommunications services, equipment and terminals; promoting the evolution of pan-European services markets; and facilitating the emergence of trans-European networks and services (CEC, 1994c). Commission Directive 96/2/EC of January 16, 1996 amending Directive 90/388/EEC included mobile and personal communications (CEC, 1996b, pp. 59–66). The European Parliament and the Council decided on the rapid introduction of compatible personal-communications services in accordance with the internal market principles in 1997 (European Parliament and Council of Ministers, 1997, pp. 4–12).

The fourth move was the liberalization of voice telephony. As a reaction to the Council's comments in 1993, the Commission published its Green Paper on the liberalization of telecommunications infrastructures and cable television networks in 1994 (CEC, 1994d). After that, the Council invited the Commission to take the necessary initiatives for the liberalization of telecommunications infrastructures by January 1, 1998 (Council of Ministers, 1994, pp. 4–5). In 1995, the Commission was called upon to present all legislative provisions to the Council and the Parliament for establishing the future European regulatory framework for telecommunications accompanying the full liberalization of the services market (Council of Ministers, 1995, p. 1–3).

The Council of Ministers and the Parliament also decided to set up trans-European networks in the area of telecommunications infrastructure to attain the following objectives: realization of the information society, improving the competitiveness of European firms while strengthening the internal market, reinforcing economic and social cohesion, and job creation. The strategy for accomplishing these objectives was based on the idea of giving support for projects of common interest, besides initiating actions aimed at providing the appropriate environment (European Parliament and Council of Ministers, 1997b, pp. 12–20). Accordingly, Parliament and the Council issued a directive to establish a regulatory framework for securing the interconnection of telecommunications networks and, in particular, the interoperability of services with regard to ensuring provision of service in an environment of open and effectively competitive markets in the EU. The directive was specifically concerned with the harmonization of conditions for open and efficient interconnection of and access to public telecommunications networks and publicly available telecommunications services (European Parliament and Council of Ministers, 1997c, pp. 32–52; European Parliament and Council of Ministers, 1998, pp. 3–38).

The final step in the field of liberalization was the opening up of local access networks to market competition as one of the building blocks of a new framework. The Commission requested that the National Regulatory Authorities (NRAs) adopt appropriate legal and regulatory measures for unbundled access to the copper local loop and associated facilities of public fixed network operators with significant market power under transparent, fair, and non-discriminatory conditions by December 2000 (CEC, 2000, pp. 44–50). To complete the project, the European Parliament and the Council jointly adopted a regulation on December 18, 2000, setting conditions for unbundled access to local loops and related facilities. The aim was to intensify competition, stimulate technological innovation on the local loop access market, and foster the competitive provision of a wide range of electronic communications services (European Parliament and Council of Ministers, 2000, pp. 4–8). However, the regulation, as well as the Commission recommendation, excluded new loops with high-capacity optical fiber from opening up to competition at the local level. This meant that the dominant operators would recover their investment costs and thereby make a profit, essential for their continuous spending on telecommunications equipment. Expressed differently, they would not be forced by the regulators to share their profits with competitors through the leasing of their state-of-the-art high-capacity fiber optic lines to their rivals at discounted wholesale rates while they were competing with them in the same market.

Having completed the liberalization process by 1998, the Commission reviewed the situation in the market as a basis for proposing a new framework for electronic communications infrastructures and associated services in 1999 (CEC, 1999b). The rationale was to create a common framework, replacing the previous patchy legal structures. The new framework would be general and horizontal to be applied to different networks and services, whether fixed or mobile, telecommunications or cable TV, satellite or terrestrial (CEC, 1997b).

On the basis of the proposals from the Commission, the Council of Ministers and the European Parliament adopted six directives in 2002 to establish a new framework to replace the old electronic communications laws, as Figure 4.2 below shows. As stated in Article 1, the Framework Directive "establishes a harmonized framework for the regulation of electronic communications services, electronic communications networks, associated facilities and associated services" (European Parliament and Council of Ministers, 2002a, pp. 33–50). Besides specifying the duties and responsibilities of NRAs, the new Directive provides a set of procedures for the harmonized application of the new structure throughout the EU. The Authorization Directive harmonizes as simplifies authorization rules and conditions for the provision of electronic communications networks and services in order to facilitate their provision throughout the EU (European Parliament and Council of Ministers, 2002b, pp. 21–32).

Similarly, the Access Directive harmonizes the way in which member states regulate access to, and interconnection of, electronic communications networks and associated facilities by establishing rights and obligations for both operators and firms seeking interconnection and/or access to their networks or associated facilities (European Parliament and Council of Ministers, 2002c, pp. 7–20). In contrast to the Access Directive, which deals with relations between telecommunications service providers, the Universal Service Directive regulates the relationship between service providers and end users by establishing "the rights of end-users and the corresponding obligations on undertakings providing publicly available communications networks and services", as Article 1 states (European Parliament and Council of Ministers, 2002d, pp. 51–77). The Directive on privacy and electronic communications protects the fundamental rights and freedoms of users, and in particular the right to privacy with respect to the processing of personal data in the telecommunications industry (European Parliament and Council of Ministers, 2002e, pp. 37–47). Finally, the Directive on competition in markets for electronic communications services regulates member states' actions by asking them to treat all firms equally in the areas of granting rights, radio frequencies, numbering, directory services, universal service

Article 86 Directives

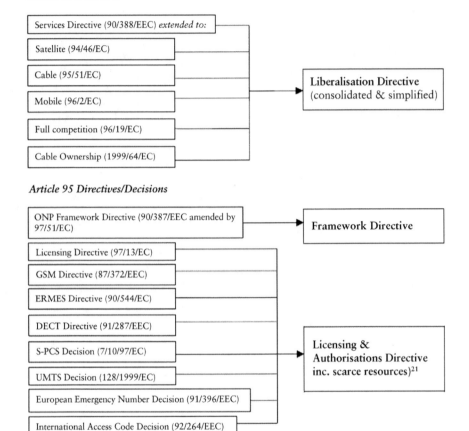

Article 95 Directives/Decisions

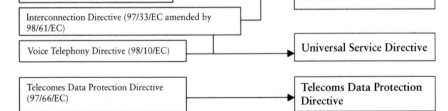

Figure 4.2 EU e-communications framework.[8]

obligations, accounting separation, matters relating to satellites, cable networks and mobile communications (CEC, 2002a, 21–6).

Briefly, both EU institutions and member states created market conditions conducive to effective competition in order to assure profitability of the European telecommunications firms. To accomplish this objective, the EU pursued a three-pronged telecommunications policy. While the first was adopting new common telecommunications standards, the second was progressive and facilitated the gradual liberalization of equipment and services markets. The next section discusses the third part of the plan: the gradual privatization of state-owned telecommunications service providers.

4.4. THE POLITICAL ECONOMY OF TELECOMMUNICATIONS PRIVATIZATION

Progressive privatization was another cornerstone of the telecommunications policy in assuring the profitability of the European manufacturers, as the member states protected their interests through gradual liberalization and deregulation. In principle, the EEC/EU is neutral to the ownership of private property in the member states, as stated in Article 295 (ex-Article 222): "This Treaty shall in no way prejudice the rules in Member States governing the system of property ownership." The choice with regard to the status and ownership of the national telecommunications operators remains at the national level. Nevertheless, the EU forced the member states indirectly to sell publicly-owned enterprises by putting a brake on government deficit as part of monetary integration. In fact, effective competition envisages a lesser role for the state in the market, restricted mainly to regulative functions.

As part of the initiative to establish and maintain effective competition in telecommunications, the member states have privatized the former monopolies gradually. Progressive privatization created an opportunity for member states to have new sources of revenue, without immediately giving up their power to influence investment decisions of the dominant telecommunications operators (Zaharidis, 2003, ch. 2). Privatization and liberalization were intrinsically linked to one another. Privatization was slow or more gradual because the member states did not want to lose their grip on the national telecommunications operators suddenly. Moreover, progressive liberalization helped member states sell their stakes in former monopolies at high prices, since market protection, especially in core market segments, was necessary for attracting private investors before privatization (Kok, 1992, p. 702). Golob commented: "This favorable image of telecommunications, essentially a belief in attractive earnings growth relative to the local markets and therefore attractive returns for investors, led to a major industry in telecommunication privatizations" (Golob, 1992, p. 739). While gradual privatization ensured the profitability of the manufacturers, as member states influenced the national telecommunications operators' decision to buy their equipment from national or European manufacturers, progressive liberalization helped the member states to privatize the operators successfully.

Gradual privatization also assured their smooth financial transition. As *The Economist* noted, when the states launched privatization, they were aware that the "less competition the state-owned giant must face, the more attractive its shares will look, and the more money a government may hope to raise" ("Ready, Steady . . . Whoops," 1997, p. 5). This was also the rationale behind slow liberalization of the services market. The regulatory regimes installed by the governments as well as by Brussels were tilting towards former monopolies with the purpose of securing their financial advantage, given the flexible attitude towards the incumbents displayed by Brussels until liberalization (Price, 1997, p. 12).

Telecommunications regulators had to carry out their jobs under often contradictory legal obligations. One obligation was to secure better value for consumers. For consumers, this was about less cost for services. However, complications arose from the other aim imposed on the regulators in that they had to encourage new entrants to build networks that could compete with monopolistic operators. The incentive for the new entrants to invest was that, as nimble and efficient firms, they could undercut the dominant operators and could still make a handsome profit. Nevertheless, the dominant operators became more efficient at the same time, which weakened the new entrants' ability to undercut them. In short, if the overall telecommunications market became less profitable in the short term, there would be fewer new entrants and thus, less competition against the dominant operators in the long term ("The Great Telephone," 1996, p. 70).

The EU institutions as well as the member states were mainly concerned about creating a profitable market for the European manufacturers. They realized this objective in two ways. First, market liberalization was progressive, starting with the market segments, which contributed least to dominant service providers' revenues, but were mostly needed by corporate users, leaving the highly profitable services used mostly by small firms and residents to the last moment. Second, privatization of the national operators was progressive to maintain the member states' final say on procurement policies. Undoubtedly, the member states wanted ultimate control over their national telephone companies by retaining either 51 percent or a golden share, essential for playing an influential role in policy decision-making. They still owned a considerable portion of their national telecommunications carriers even after their so-called privatization. For instance, the German state (43 percent of Deutsche Telekom), the Norwegian state (53.2 percent of Telenor), the French state (53.1 percent France Telecom) the Greek state (33.8 percent of OTE), the state of the Netherlands (19.1

percent in KPN) and the Belgian and Finnish states (45.3 and 19.1 percent of TeliaSonera respectively) were major telecommunications shareholders as of August 2004.[9]

Overall, both the EU institutions and the member states have worked together to increase the profitability of EU telecommunications manufacturers and service providers, in the hope of sustaining employment and promoting exports to non-EU countries. Since European telecommunications policy was aimed at creating a profitable 'level playing field' for the manufacturers and telecommunications operators by creating oligopolistic equipment, infrastructure and services markets respectively, EC/EU decisions were made behind closed doors with the participation of a small number of groups. Shearman (1986) observed:

> In all the European initiatives the policy process leaves little room for public debate. Decisions are made by small groups of industrialists, politicians and civil servants with vested interests; little opportunity is provided to voice the opinions of, for instance, the small company or trade unions. Major policy questions remain undebated. (p. 158)

What the supranational institutions did was protect the interests of the largest players at the expense of other interests, including those of workers and EU citizens.

4.5. CONCLUSIONS

This chapter has demonstrated that the primary objective of EU telecommunications policy put forward in the 1980s was to ensure stable rates of return for the European telecommunications firms under the name of improving 'international competitiveness' of the EU telecommunications industry. In that sense, EU telecommunications policy is a subset of EU competition policy. External pressures, failure of national efforts, technological convergence, application of Article 86 in telecommunications, and increasing demand from European users were the factors behind the formation of a unified EU competition policy.

Adopting common technical standards, progressive liberalization, re-regulation, and gradual privatization were the four major components of EU competition policy. The supranational institutions, together with the member states, perceived adopting common technical standards as central to realizing their target of improving profit margins by creating a larger market, whilst protecting it from non-European firms and enhancing the international competitiveness of the industry. Liberalization and deregulation were progressive, and started with the financially least significant markets to service providers but the most valuable markets to European multinationals. Privatization was also gradual, as the member states did not want to lose control over the investment decisions of former telecommunications monopolies suddenly.

To guarantee the profitability of the European telecommunications operators, the member states, as well as the European institutions, decided to keep the former monopolies intact, rather than creating several competitive service providers out of them to establish a genuinely competitive EU services market. This was done, paradoxically, in the name of enhancing the international competitiveness of the European firms in global markets. The next chapter will provide further evidence to the claims made in this chapter by focusing on the competition law decisions made by the European Commission, the CFI and the ECJ in the telecommunications industry since 1980, in addition to illustrating the flaws, deficiencies and weaknesses of EU competition law.

5 Implementing EU Competition Law in Telecommunications

The previous chapter established that EU competition policy was aimed at assuring the profitability and international competitiveness of European firms. After the sharp decline in profitability in the 1970s, these policy objectives were achieved through the opening of new areas to market competition by implementing Article 86, in the early 1980s, for the first time in the history of EU competition policy. This chapter elaborates on the implementation of Articles 81 (dealing with cartels), 82 (preventing the abuse of dominant position individually or collectively), 87 (controlling state aid), and the Merger Control Regulation (MCR) (regulating mergers, acquisitions and structural or merger-like joint ventures) in the telecommunications industry. The focus is on competition law decisions made pertaining to the industry by the European Commission between 1980 and 2004.

Implementation means deployment of the competition rules to regulate not only behavior of telecommunications firms in the relevant markets, but also financial relations between firms and the member states. The existing literature on the enforcement of EU competition law in the telecommunications industry has mainly tackled procedural questions related to the difficulties of enforcing the law given the convergence of the telecommunications, mass media and information technology industries (Larouche, 1998; Styliadou, 1997). According to Lang, convergence would create considerable challenges to EU competition law, especially when a dominant firm extended its power into other areas through a joint venture with another dominant firm (Lang, 1997). Under such circumstances, EU competition law would have limited conceptual capacity to measure conglomerate power (Just & Latzer, 2000; Lera, 2000; Latzer, 1998). Even if Articles 81 and 82, 87, and the MCR were fully applicable in telecommunications, mass media and information technology, they did not contain any telecommunications-specific or media-specific measures (Clements, 1998).

With respect to the problem of dealing with conglomerate power, the literature assumed that the trend of convergence—which had been discussed in official circles since the 1970s—was unknown to the EU institutions. In fact, the European Commission was aware of the issue in the Green Paper of 1987. One of the stated aims of EU telecommunications policy was to accommodate convergence among the communications, information technology and broadcasting industries. Similarly, the new electronic communications framework law, discussed in the previous chapter, was intended to accommodate convergence by being neutral to technology, i.e. treating all technologies equally. In addition, the Commission published several telecommunications industry-specific guidelines for applying the competition rules, as both the telecommunications markets and EU competition policy evolved over the past fourteen years (CEC, 2001b; "Notice," 1998; "Guidelines," 1991). In sum, the literature was correct in pointing out that EU competition law would have a problem with market power, but missed the intricate link between market power and profitability, on the one hand, and the source of the problem in EU competition law in identifying market power, on the other hand.

To fill the gap, this chapter has two aims. The first is to show that market power, in fact, was a critical element in EU competition law decisions in that firms needed market power for effective competition to exist in the market. These decisions in the telecommunications industry provide sufficient evidence to support this assertion. This chapter draws on the competition law rulings listed in Table 5.1 (below).

The second objective is to demonstrate the problems such as inconsistency, unpredictability and uncertainty in EU competition law in defining relevant product and geographical markets. In other words, this chapter provides empirical evidence of the two key theoretical claims made in the second chapter with respect to the model of effective competition's objectives and its contradictory foundations.

The first section explains the important role of strengthening the market power of the European telecommunications firms in EC/EU competition law decisions to restore their profitability by focusing on Articles 81 and 87. The second section demonstrates the existence of both dynamic and static visions of market competition in EU competition law judgments in the field of telecommunications. It also provides ample empirical evidence that the static view is predominant by drawing upon EU competition law cases in telecommunications under Articles 81–82 and the MCR, even though it is possible to identify a few cases where a dynamic vision of market competition prevailed. The third section illustrates problems such as inconsistency, arbitrariness and ambiguity in the definition of the relevant services market in mobile communications by drawing on cases related to mergers and acquisitions. To come full circle with the analysis, the last section of the chapter reconnects the notion of market power to profitability.

Table 5.1 Competition Law Decisions in Telecommunications: 1980–2004

Article 81 Cases	MCR Cases	Article 82 Cases	Article 87/88 Cases
GEC/ANT/Telettra/ SAT	Alcatel Cable/ AEG Kabel	Wanadoo Interactive	France Telecom
ATES/ANT	Siemens/Italtel	BT/AT&T	Mobilcom
Aerospatiale/Alcatel Espace	AT&T/Philips	Deutsche Telekom	
ECR 900	Nortel Networks/ Bay Networks		
Plessey/General Electric/Siemens	Solectron/Ericsson Switches		
STET/Italtel-SIT/ AT&T	Nortel Networks/ Bay Networks		
BT/Astra	Ericsson/Nokia/ Psion		
T-Mobile Deutschland/MM02	Cable & Wireless/ VEBA		
	Belgacom/Tele Danmark/Tulip		
	Enel/FT/DT		
	BT/Airtel		
	Viag/Orange UK		
	Mannesmann/ Orange		
	Vodafone Airtouch/ Mannesmann		
	France Télécom/ Orange		
	Vodafone/BT/Airtel		
	Vodafone/Airtel		
	KPN/E-Plus		
	Telia/Sonera		
	MCI Worldcom/ Sprint		

5.1. PROFITABILITY AND COMPETITIVENESS

As noted previously, EU competition policy became an important tool for industrial policy in the 1980s. The goal of ensuring profitability to boost the international competitiveness of European firms prevailed over other concerns, although EU institutions did not often mention it directly. Instead, they pointed to competitiveness with such words as 'increasing costs' in research and development, achieving 'economies of scale' and strengthening the 'international competitiveness' of the European firms vis-à-vis their American and Japanese counterparts. The European Commission deployed Article 81 to permit and encourage cooperation agreements and cartels, and relaxed the application of Article 87 to open the door for the member states to financially assist the European telecommunications firms, especially in times of low profit rates. The European Court of Justice and the Court of First Instance generally supported decisions made by the European Commission with the exception of a few cases.

In the case of Article 81, which deals with restrictive practices and cartels between firms, the rhetoric of cutting costs and boosting international competitiveness legitimized positive decisions that allowed alliances between firms. Knowing this, European firms often exploited the rhetoric in their applications as well. For example, General Electric Company plc (GEC), Ant Nachrichtentechnik GmbH (ANT), Telettra Telefonia Electronica E Radio (Telettra), and Societe Anonyme de Telecommunication (SAT) planned to cooperate in 1986. The collaboration would concentrate on transmission systems, equipment and technology for cable transmission, microwave transmission, earth stations, multiple broadband video transmission and integrated digital services networks (ISDNs), while excluding components such as optical fibers (GEC/ANT/Telettra/SAT, 1988, paras. 1–2).

GEC was a global British electronics conglomerate, manufacturing and selling all types of electrical and electronic equipment, while GEC Telecommunication Ltd was a wholly owned subsidiary of GEC, responsible for producing telecommunications equipment for public and private networks. ANT, owned by Robert Bosch GmbH (80 percent) and Allianz Versicherungs AG (20 percent), was a German telecommunications equipment maker specializing in a range of transmission equipment. Telettra, based in Milano, Italy, was a supplier of telecommunications systems and equipment. Finally, SAT was a French company, producing and distributing transmission systems for the telecommunications industry and navigation systems mainly for military use (GEC/ANT/Telettra/SAT, 1988, para. 3).

The parties sought negative clearance for their plans from the European Commission under Article 81(3). After considering the impact of the cooperation agreement in a particular product market, the Commission took into account such factors as the increase in development costs and the structure of the telecommunications market, the market share of the new entity, its contribution to longer-term European industrial development, European exports, employment and competitiveness. However, the major factor in this decision was a reduction in research and development costs and an increase in corporate profitability (GEC/ANT/Telettra/SAT, 1988, para. 7).

The three companies were the largest telecommunications equipment producers in their respective countries. After considering their global position, the Commission approved the demand for negative clearance for the reason that the collaboration would strengthen their financial and market power, which was deemed necessary for profitability. It is possible to see the same rationale in the *Alcatel Espace/ANT Nachrichtentechnik* case of 1990.

Alcatel Espace SA (ATES) and ANT Nachrichtentechnik GmbH notified the Commission of an agreement in July 1986 under Article 81. ATES, which was the wholly owned subsidiary of Alcatel NV, was responsible for manufacturing electronic space equipment carried on board satellites and/or space vehicles. Alcatel NV was the second-largest manufacturer of telecommunications equipment and systems in the world at the time of the agreement. As mentioned above, ANT was one of the leading firms in the field of telecommunications technology in Germany (ATES/ANT, 1990, paras. 4–5).

The agreement targeted the field of civil radio communications and broadcasting satellites. The parties would not only collaborate with each other in the research and development stage of satellite equipment that would make possible data transmission to, from and between satellites and/or space vehicles throughout the world, but also jointly produce and sell the equipment (ATES/ANT, 1990, para. 1). One of the objectives of the agreement was to cut research and development costs by avoiding duplication efforts, as well as to combine resources for the exploitation of the results through rationalizing manufacturing, servicing and testing. The Commission reasoned that:

> [T]here is thought to be a substantial 'learning curve' for all aspects of satellite production, so that the more similar space projects a firm is involved with, the more effectively it can develop and produce new satellites or their components. This effect particularly benefits the United States space industry, where the number of space projects is higher than in Europe. (ATES/ANT, 1990, para. 8)

The Commission permitted the parties to cooperate not only in research and development, and production, but also in marketing. This decision testified to the Commission's attitude toward a full-circuit cartel in the research, production and marketing stages of satellites and their components.

The ANT was also involved in two similar cooperative projects with other companies. In an already transparent oligopolistic market, creating overlapping cartels via coordinated research and development projects would definitely have negative implications. Permitting such agreements to cut costs not only in the research and production stages, but also in the marketing phase was against the spirit of competition, as the arrangements would discourage the firms concerned from making new product offerings on an individual basis. Nonetheless, the Commission did not mention this in its decision. Rather, it preferred to remain silent. The next case, *Aérospatiale and Alcatel Espace,* provides further evidence for this observation.

Aérospatiale and Alcatel Espace notified the European Commission on August 6, 1992 about a cooperation agreement that they had concluded in March 1991. The agreement initially covered civilian and military telecommunications satellites, with a possibility of broadening it later to cover observation, meteorological and scientific satellites. Again, Alcatel Espace was the principal player. Aérospatiale was a French firm operating in the aerospace industry and producing planes, military and civilian helicopters, missiles, and as far as space communications equipment was concerned, satellites and satellite launchers. According to the agreement, Aérospatiale would be the prime contractor of satellites, as well as providing satellite platforms and optical payloads. Alcatel Espace would be the main supplier of satellite communications systems and the supplier of telecommunications payloads, and other necessary sub-systems and related equipment (Aerospatiale/Alcatel Espace, 1994, pp. 705–6).

After considering the market position of the European satellite manufacturers in this case, the European Commission reasoned that there was a need for "large-scale undertakings with a very high degree of vertical integration" (Aerospatiale/Alcatel Espace, 1994, p. 708). Companies with economies of scale would reduce production costs through standardization and synergy. The alleged highly fragmented nature of the European satellite market due to the compartmentalization of national markets in Europe prevented the European firms from gaining adequate size, according to the Commission. Yet, growth was essential for competing against American firms. Using the official logic, the two largest French satellite makers could make a similar claim that their agreement aimed at improving their international competitiveness. As stated in the Agreement:

> The aims of the agreement are, firstly, to improve competitiveness through optimum verticalization and to cover satellite activities as widely as possible and, secondly, to *improve profitability* and increase market shares through close business collaboration between the parties. (Aerospatiale/Alcatel Espace, 1994, pp. 709–10, italics added)

To help the concerned firms enhance their market shares, market power and hence profitability, the Commission took a favorable view and granted a ten-year exemption from Article 81 that was renewable after the end of the period. In sum, Alcatel and ANT took part in two projects out of the three and served as a bridge among the three cooperation agreements mentioned above to control the relevant satellite market.

Alcatel was an active partner in another market segment as well. Research and development expenses for new technology were the key in the cooperation agreement between AEG AG, Alcatel NV and Oy Nokia AB, about which the parties notified the Commission in April 1988. It is not surprising to see Alcatel again because the telecommunications equipment market was rapidly consolidating in the late 1980s and early 1990s, as the next chapter shows. AEG AG, which was a German firm owned on a majority holding basis by the Daimler-Benz AG group, was a manufacturer of automation systems, electrical tools, energy distribution, and household equipment in addition to information and communications systems and technologies. Nokia was a Finnish firm specializing in information systems, telecommunications, mobile telephone handsets and consumer electronics (ECR 900, 1992, paras. 2–4).

According to the agreement, the parties would form a consortium to develop, manufacture, and distribute a pan-European digital cellular mobile telephone system. However, the agreement did not include mobile phone sets (ECR 900, 1992, para. 1). The Commission granted negative clearance or permission to the consortium for three main reasons. First, the parties did not have enough time to develop, manufacture and distribute the system individually. If they had not collaborated, non-European firms might have become leaders in the concerned market segment. Second, the companies argued that they did not have enough financial and human resources to accomplish the project individually because of their 'small size'. In fact, these firms were the leading equipment makers. Third, the parties contended that they could not bear the financial risk involved in the project independently, as the demand was limited to the Global System for Mobile Communications (GSM) system at that time:

> The relevant market is characterized by narrowly limited demand. At present, the only potential customers are 15 national network operators in the CEPT countries, or the undertakings acting for them, with the result that the suppliers' prospects of achieving a bid award are limited. Only if they achieve a bid award will the suppliers be able to amortize the extremely high development costs, since the results of the development work will have only limited use outside the field covered by the invitations to tender. This *real and serious economic risk* can be borne only if the parties to the agreement bear the costs jointly. (ECR 900, 1992, para. 29, italics added)

That the financial and economic risks of not recovering research and development expenses would reduce the future profitability of the concerned companies led the Commission to grant an exemption so that the parties could reduce the risk by forming a cartel.

In a similar, but somewhat different case, the Commission's attitude outraged both a national competition authority and one of the market players involved in the case. In 1988, GEC and Siemens AG formed a jointly owned company, GEC-Siemens plc, to acquire Plessey Company plc and to reorganize Plessey's activities. In this case, GEC and Siemens—the two biggest European electrical and electronic conglomerates—were attacking GEC's junior competitor in the UK, a collective abuse of a dominant market position, according to EU competition law. The acquisition of Plessey would result in further market concentration. Before this attack, GEC had offered Plessey a merger proposal in late 1985. However, Plessey wanted to remain independent and fought back (De Jonquieres & Barber, 1985, p. 1). In 1986, the UK's Monopolies and Mergers Commission (MMC) rejected the proposed merger claiming that it would diminish competition ("GEC-Plessey," 1986, p. 51). Eventually, the firms only merged their telecommunications activities to create GEC/Plessey Telecommunication (GPT).

When the two dominant German and British firms planned to acquire their British competitor collectively, the European Commission applied only Article 81 (dealing with cartels) without carrying out any market analysis. Surprisingly and in contrast to its normal procedure in other cases, the Commission did not even introduce the parties involved in this case by providing a brief description of their activities. The analysis was rather limited to the description of Plessey's activities and it was difficult to find any overall picture of the telecommunications equipment market in the decision either before or after the acquisition.

Plessey contended that the parties were violating both Articles 81 and 82 because their action would substantially eliminate competition in private switching and transmission systems market segments (Plessey/General Electric/Siemens, 1992, para. 25). Even though the deal resulted in market concentration, the Commission preferred not to apply Article 82. In addition to Article 81, it could have applied Article 82 (which controls abuse of a dominant position) to prevent market concentration, as it had done in the *Continental Can* case in the early 1970s. The justification for a positive decision was that expenditure on research and development of new telecommunications products was very high and that there were many small telecommunications firms in the EU compared to the US and Japan. Therefore, market concentration was essential for reducing the number of players and strengthening the market power of the remaining firms (Plessey/General Electric/Siemens, 1992, para. 19). As stated in the decision:

> The Commission considers that the agreement in question will enable GPT and Siemens, through joint research programmes and, in due course joint product lines, *to amortize research and development costs over greater turnover*, thereby enabling them to maintain the level of leading-edge technology necessary to compete internationally. (Plessey/General Electric/Siemens, 1992, para. 21, italics added)

This decision demonstrates how the Commission, in contrast to the British competition authority, encouraged market concentration in its efforts to improve profitability through a supportive attitude towards mergers and acquisitions in the European telecommunications industry in the late 1980s and early 1990s.

It is not difficult to see the same intention in another decision. The Commission received a notification of commercial cooperation from Societá Finanziaria Telefonica per Azioni (STET), Societá Italiana Telecommunicazione SPA (Italtel-SIT), American Telephone and Telegraph Company (AT&T) and AT&T Network Systems International BV (AT&T-NSI) in July 1989 for their agreement. STET was a holding company of the Italian public group, IRI, and specialized in the manufacture and installation of telecommunications products and systems. Being a wholly owned subsidiary of STET prior to the cooperation agreement, Italtel was designing, producing and marketing systems and equipment for public and private telecommunications, especially public switching and transmission systems. Finally, AT&T was the world's biggest telecommunications company. As a vertically integrated company at the time of the agreement, AT&T was operating both as a telecommunications network operator (providing international network and domestic long-distance services) and as a manufacturer of telecommunications equipment such as public and private switching and transmission systems and terminal equipment (STET/Italtel-SIT/AT&T, 1993, paras. 5–11).

Aiming at joint development of telecommunications equipment for public and private switching systems, operations systems, public transmission systems, and private terminal equipment, the notification sought individual exemption pursuant to Article 81(3). In general terms, the exemption allows cartels, if their benefits are more than their impact on competition and if consumers also benefit from the agreement. The parties wanted to establish technological and commercial cooperation in the field of telecommunications equipment, notably public and private switching transmission systems and some terminal equipment.

The Commission granted an exemption following the reasoning of the previous cases and allowed commercial cooperation:

> In general, *research and development accounts for a very substantial and ever-growing share of the costs of the telecoms equipment industry,* largely because of the very short life of the products and the preponderance of software in their design. Thus, manufacturers of telecommunication equipment are compelled to invest heavily if they are to retain their positions on the market. (STET/Italtel-SIT/AT&T, 1993, para. 12, italics added)

The parties promised not to cross-subsidize, discriminate against others or limit territorial coverage of the area for the distribution of public network products, except for licensed products, in addition to assuring that they would sell products to one another only based on the cost of product. The rationale for such protection was that the scale of investment necessary to place a product on the market was too high. In other words, protection was necessary for a limited period for the parties to be profitable. Not unlike previously mentioned decisions, the Commission did not hesitate to endorse the agreement between the two leading Italian equipment makers in cooperation with a dominant American firm that reduced competition in the Italian equipment market substantially.

The only decision where the European Commission did not grant an exemption to a joint venture agreement under Article 81(3) was the *British Telecom(BT)/Astra SA* case. The issue at hand in this case, however, was not the profitability of the parties to the agreement, but the profitability of a European telecommunications organization, Eutelsat (European Telecommunication Satellite Organization). While BT was a former monopoly entitled to carry out telecommunications activities in the UK, Société Européenne des Satellites SA (SES) was a Luxembourg firm established in 1985 to operate satellites (BT/Astra, 1994, paras. 2–3).

The two firms decided to set up an equal ownership joint venture company, BT Astra SA, on December 17, 1987. SES would lease transponders to Astra for a minimum of nine and a maximum of 11 out of 16 transponders of its Astra IA satellite. Astra, in turn, would dispose of them via a UK licensed operator, but not necessarily through BT. Nevertheless, SES agreed that the joint venture would grant BT options over nine transponders. In short, the Luxembourg firm would lease transponders to Astra or further disposal to customers in a package deal contract that included the uplink (BT/Astra, 1994, para. 6).

The Commission did not grant an exemption to the joint venture agreement under Article 81(3) (which exempts agreements, if the benefits outweigh the damaging effects on competitors) for two reasons. The first was that all broadcasters in the UK were obliged to use the uplinking services of BT when they leased space on SES's satellite. Second, BT had to consult SES on prices and was not to charge lower prices for uplinking services to other satellites at its disposal. In turn, the latter would not offer uplink services or satellite capacity in the UK on preferential terms. The joint venture would mean, according to the European Commission, the foreclosure of the uplink market (BT/Astra, 1994, para. 17). As a result, it perceived that BT and SES were competitors in providing space segment capacity for the transmission of television channels in the EC. In fact, BT had been offering space segment capacity on Eutelsat (and Intelsat) satellites to program providers since 1983 (BT/Astra, 1994, para. 11).

Beyond this apparent reasoning for the foreclosure of the uplink market, there was a hidden, but crucial, motivation behind the Commission's refusal to grant an exemption to the joint venture agreement in that the joint venture would have the adverse effect of reducing Eutelsat's profits.

Eutelsat was established in 1982 by the European governments, with each member country designating one signatory, usually the telecommunications operator of the member country. BT was a Eutelsat signatory. According to the Eutelsat agreement, the operation of non-Eutelsat satellites should not 'cause the Eutelsat system significant economic harm.' The Eutelsat Assembly decided that the joint venture would not cause significant competitive damage provided that "Astra would be used for one-way television transmission only" and "no more than four Eutelsat channels switched from Eutelsat's satellites to Astra" (BT/Astra, 1994, para. 5). The Eutelsat's interests were at stake with the entrance of a new competitor to the market.

Given that BT was the largest user at that time and had over nine transponder options to dispose, the joint venture would do 'significant economic harm' to the Eutelsat system by reallocating customers from Eutelsat's satellites to Astra's satellite. The Commission reasoned that:

> BT's involvement in the sale of transponders on the Astra satellite admittedly facilitated the transfer of BT's Eutelsat and Intelsat customers to Astra thanks to the joint venture agreement provisions on double-illumination and early termination of existing customer contracts. (BT/Astra, 1994, para. 28)

As a result, the parties did not get permission under Article 81(3) to the joint venture agreement. This case, along with the previous cases, indicate that profitability exerted a significant influence on EU competition law decisions. The next case backs this observation.

The last action to come from the Commission under Article 81 was permission for network-sharing agreements between European mobile phone operators. After the sudden downturn in the telecommunications industry in 2002, due to a sharp decline in profitability, the operators wanted to share infrastructure networks for the third generation (3G) of mobile phones. T-Mobile Deutschland GmbH and MMO2 plc (formerly known as BT Cellnet) agreed on sharing the 3G infrastructure, as well as national roaming, in February 2002.[1] While MMO2 was a leading provider of mobile communications services with complete ownership of mobile network operators in three countries—the UK, Germany and Ireland—as well as a leading mobile internet portal, T-Mobile Deutschland was a subsidiary of Deutsche Telekom AG, the largest telecommunications service provider in Europe.

The parties were permitted to cooperate because of a number of factors such as faster rolling-out of networks that would lead to increased services competition, while limiting the new network's environmental impact, as the parties would deploy less equipment for infrastructure (CEC, 2002b). In fact, the negative effects of the agreement outweighed its benefits for the reason that network sharing would have an adverse impact on national roaming, which would "limit network-based competition with respect to coverage, retail prices, quality and transmission speeds" (CEC, 2003a). Despite these, the Commission allowed the firms to share their networks because of the concern about profitability in the aftermath of the slowdown in the telecommunications industry, rather than any environmental or other incidental concerns.

Based on the case law analysis of Article 81 decisions, it is possible to observe three common patterns. First, Article 81 was deployed to strengthen the market power of European telecommunications firms by permitting them to form alliances. Second, factors such as increasing research and development expenditures, high market risks, and serious threats from American and Japanese firms were used to justify the positive decisions that resulted in enhanced market power of the firms, especially in times of low profitability. Third, the common characteristic of all of these cooperation agreements and positive decisions was that they took place in a particular historical period, i.e. in the late 1980s and early 2000s. Profitability was the lowest in these two particular time periods compared to others, and market actors had to cooperate to restore profitability, as the next chapter will show in a detailed analysis of the telecommunications equipment and services markets.

Another public policy tool to deal with profitability is Article 87. The European Commission followed the same rationale in state aid cases dealing with production, showing a very favorable attitude toward the largest European telecommunications firms in implementing Article 87, which regulates state aid to firms. Thompson Telecommunication, the leading French telecommunications equipment manufacturer, received aid from the French Government in 1987 to finance its product innovation and the Commission did not object to the aid (CEC, 1987a, p. 158).

In a similar vein, Philips and Siemens were granted state aids by the Dutch and German Governments for a collaborative research and development project in 1983. Both Philips and Siemens were the largest electrical and electronic conglomerates in Europe at the time of the agreement. The project was to develop the submicron C-MOS technology and the tools for designing integrated circuits incorporating memories of a complexity equal to or greater than one megabit. These integrated circuits were thought to be crucial for the development of the computer and telecommunications industries (CEC, 1987a, p. 171). The Commission approved the aid, as it did in the case of the state aid granted by the Belgian government to the subsidiary of Siemens AG in Belgium, Siemens SA. The objective of the aid was to extend a research center and obtain new data processing material for research and development on operating systems software (CEC, 1989).

In another case, the Commission approved a state aid to SGS Thomson Microelectronics srl, Finmeccamica SpA, BULL HN and Italtel SpA for their participation in a Eureka research project under the name of Jessi in May 1995 under Article 87(3)b. According to the Commission, the project was designed to meet 'specific objectives' of the EU: "The common European interest also consists in the necessity to reach a strategic position within the Community as regards *American and Japanese competition* in the area of microelectronics" (CEC, 1996a, p. 238, italics added). In sum, the discourse of international competitiveness was often deployed to rationalize state aids to the largest firms.

In another case, profitability underlined the Commission's decision. The German federal government granted EUR 50 million in aid to MobilCom AG and MobilCom Holding GmbH in September 2002. The German fixed line, mobile, and Internet service provider received an additional EUR 112 million in aid from the federal and land government authorities in November 2002 in order to escape from bankruptcy. Pursuant to Article 87(3)(c) of the EC Treaty, the Commission approved the first aid as a rescue aid (Mobilcom AG, 2005, p. 6). Concerning the second aid provision, the European Commission characterized it as 'restructuring aid' and justified its approval as follows:

> The Commission is accordingly satisfied that the package of measures financed by the State-guaranteed loan had effects that were primarily structural, being aimed at ensuring the *long-term profitability* of the service provider division and of the company, and not merely at keeping the firm in operation until a restructuring plan was drawn up. (para. 140, italics added)

This reasoning indicated that the long-term profitability of firms in the market played a key role in the European Commission's decisions.

However, a state guarantee to Hermes Europe Railtel (HER) to be given by the Belgian Government under Article 88(2) was rejected in 1999. HER was a small joint venture company owned by the Dutch HIT Rail BV and GTS, an American telecommunications services company. HER planned to supply a wide range of high-technology trans-frontier telecommunications services via its network by means of setting up and operating a trans-European fiber-optic network. The Commission did not approve the aid for the reason that the region of the country to be served was not depressed, nor was it an area of high unemployment (CEC, 1999a, p. 251). There was no mention, in contrast to other similar cases, of the project's contribution to the building of a trans-European telecommunications network or to the formation of a competitive European services market. This decision suggests that the Commission's concern and objective was to support the profitability of the existing service providers by preventing a market glut in transmission capacity with the entrance of a small competitor in the EU in the late 1990s, during which market competition was very intense.

In January 2003, the Commission opened a formal investigation procedure under Article 88(2) of the EC Treaty in respect of the business tax scheme applicable to France Telecom between 1994 and 2002. The French government did not provide an explanation with respect to the purpose of the aid. As a result, the Commission concluded that the aid was illegal because FT paid less taxes compared with its competitors under the specific business tax scheme applicable to it. The French government was asked to take the necessary measures to recover the aid from FT around €800 million to €1.1 billion with interest in 2004 (France Telecom, 2005, para. 52).

In another incident, the Commission also found that a promised €9 billion credit line to FT and statements of support by Francis Mer, the former French finance minister, were illegal in that the Commission could not classify the aid as either rescue or restructuring. Nor did the French government make any statement with respect to the nature of the aid (France Telecom, 2006, paras. 253–6). Given that France Telecom did not use the credit line, the Commission did not ask for repayment (Buck, Johnson & Minder, 2004, p. 27; Matlack & Reinhardt, 2003, p. 26). In the meantime, the aid served its purpose and FT made good progress in restructuring its debt without facing bankruptcy. This episode indicates the strong link between the former monopoly and the state, and more especially, the impact of gradual privatization on market competition ("France Telecom," 2003, p. 20).

Briefly, Article 87 shared similar concerns with Article 81 in comparable historical times. Whenever European telecommunications firms were weak and needed help, Article 87 was relaxed, especially in the second half of the 1980s, as was broadly stated in Chapter 3. Nonetheless, it was strictly applied during the periods of healthy profitability like the 1990s. Again, the rhetoric of augmenting research and development costs and enhancing international competitiveness played a crucial role in justifying state aid to the largest European telecommunications firms under Article 87.

Across these decisions three underlying common points can be highlighted. First, the firms involved in the above-mentioned cases were more or less the same and they were the leading industry players. Second, the rhetoric of international competitiveness and research and development provided the needed justification for less stringent enforcement of Article 81 and 87 decisions. Third, the nature and the timing of these agreements and decisions reveal another concern: the aim was to strengthen market power and restore the profitability of the firms in times of low profitability, especially in the second half of the 1980s and early 2000s, for which the next chapter provides ample evidence. Articles 81 and 87 served as a public policy tool to cut firms' costs and improve profit margins. Article 81 functioned as a public policy tool to allow the firms to restore their market power to become profitable again, while Article 87 provided the member states with an opportunity to intervene directly to provide financial assistance.

Given that market power was a key factor behind profitability, the question to be raised here is: How was market power measured in EU competition law decisions? Answering this question requires an understanding of how the EU institutions that were responsible for applying and interpreting EU competition law perceived market competition. The vision of market competition is critical for defining the relevant product and geographical markets as part of an attempt to figure out whether a firm or firms have 'significant market power' in the concerned market. The next section elaborates on the vision of market competition in EU competition law decisions in the telecommunications industry.

5.2. THE VISION OF MARKET COMPETITION IN TELECOMMUNICATIONS DECISIONS

Determining whether a firm or firms have significant market power (under Article 82) or will have significant market power in the aftermath of a merger, acquisition or cooperation agreement (under the Merger Control Regulation and Article 81 respectively) has to do with the perception of market competition. The second chapter revealed that the model of effective competition was a synthesis of the static and dynamic theories of market competition. In fact, dynamic elements from the Classical and Austrian Schools were incorporated into the static neoclassical framework. The end result was the predominance of the static vision of market competition over the dynamic view. This section provides empirical evidence to this assertion from EU case law in telecommunications, before analyzing the problems that these two visions created in identifying significant market power, the subject of the next part.

The static view of competition in EU competition case law in both the telecommunications equipment and services markets prevailed over the dynamic vision, which only appeared in a few cases. Next, several cases illustrate the European Commission's static market analysis in the equipment market. The *Alcatel Cable/AEG Kabel* case where the former acquired a 96.8 percent share of the latter from AEG AG serves as a case in point. Alcatel Cable SA was 66.66 percent owned by Alcatel NV and represented 28 percent of the total activities of the latter. Alcatel Alsthom was the ultimate parent company of Alcatel NV and the world's largest firm in the telecommunications equipment and power cable markets at the time of the agreement. AEG Kabel was the cable business subsidiary of AEG AG, which had been bought by Daimler-Benz AG in the 1980s, with principal businesses in the design, manufacture and sale of power and telecommunications cables and general and specialty wiring (Alcatel Cable/AEG Kabel, 1991, paras. 3 and 6).

In this particular case, there was no analysis of the rationale behind Alcatel's decision to acquire AEG Kabel and AEG AG's exit from the market by selling its telecommunications business at that time. It was also hard to see any clear picture of the state of the telecommunications equipment market or the evolution of the demand and supply conditions in the public switching equipment market, together with their impact on the transmission equipment market as well as the strategies of the firms. The German competition authority, not unlike the British competition authority in *GEC-Siemens*, warned the European Commission that the power cable market would become more concentrated and tightly oligopolistic in Germany. This would make for conscious parallel behavior by the main manufacturers easier. After considering the market shares of the combined entities and the processes of market liberalization and standardization, the Commission ignored the German competition authority's warning and accepted the acquisition of AEG Kabel by Alcatel (Alcatel Cable/AEG Kabel, 1991, para. 20).

In a similar case, Siemens AG and STET decided to create a European telecommunications group by combining their assets in Italy, i.e. Siemens Telecomunicazioni and Italtel in 1994 (Siemens/Italtel, 1995, paras. 4–5). The aim of the agreement between Italtel and Siemens was to jointly develop, manufacture and sell public switching and transmission equipment and provide after-sale services. In evaluating the markets for telecommunications equipment, the Commission considered technological developments, public procurement rules, trends in liberalization, and vertical aspects (the impact of joint development, manufacturing, selling and servicing activities on market competition) of the merger and the market position of the parties (Siemens/Italtel, 1995, para. 24).

Nonetheless, the Commission overlooked factors such as the trends in the market, supply and demand conditions, market growth, maturity, and the stage and intensity of competition. These factors were essential for contextualizing a particular firm's conduct by carefully picturing past as well as future trends. Although the combined market shares of Siemens and Italtel were respectively 60 and 50 percent in public switching and transmission in 1993, the Commission accepted such a high level of concentration as a requirement of the technology of public switching (Siemens/Italtel, 1995, paras. 38–44).

Not unlike the previous cases, American Telephone and Telegraph (AT&T) acquired transmission networks, microwave transmission, access and cellular systems from Philips in 1996. AT&T was one of the largest American telecommunications companies, providing a broad range of voice and data communications services and international long-distance carrier services. In contrast to AT&T's specialization in telecommunications services, Philips, the Dutch company, was one of the world's largest electronics companies, active in lighting, industrial and consumer electronics, recorded music, components, semiconductors, medical systems, and communications systems. AT&T acquired transmission networks, microwave transmission and access, and cellular infrastructure systems from

Philips. It was hard to find any reasonable explanation for the rationale behind Philips' move to sell its communications businesses in the decision (AT&T/Philips, 1996).

The *Nortel Networks/Bay Networks* case strengthened the observation. When Nortel Networks acquired Bay Networks in 1998, it was hard to find an analysis of the evolution of the market in the Commission's decision. Nortel was the leading North American telecommunications company, manufacturing telecommunications and data-networking products, systems and services. Bay was a specialist in producing data networking products and services which were distributed directly or through its subsidiaries. The European Commission only mentioned the competitors of Nortel Networks, but failed to present any substantial market analysis to locate this particular move within a broader global telecommunications market picture (Nortel Networks/Bay Networks, 1998, paras. 3–4 and 19).

In the *Solectron/Ericsson Switches* case in 2000, Ericsson decided to sell its manufacturing units for the production of hardware for telecommunications switching systems, located in Sweden and France, along with certain assets in Sweden, to Solectron, a Singapore-based global firm in the electronics industry providing manufacturing solutions to original equipment manufacturers, most particularly in the telecommunications and computer industries. Ericsson was a global telecommunications firm and a market leader in mobile communications infrastructure (Solectron/Ericsson Switches, 2000, paras. 5–6).

The European Commission explained the rationale behind the move as follows: "The present operation is described as constituting an expansion by Ericsson of that outsourcing strategy, so as to allow it to focus on its core activity of developing new telecom products and systems" (Solectron/Ericsson Switches, 2000, para. 11). There was, however, no clarification as to why Ericsson decided to extend its policy in 2000 in particular and to sell its manufacturing units for the production of hardware for telecommunications switching systems. The Commission's analysis fell short of explaining the broader trends and growth prospects in the telecommunications switching systems, essential for understanding the rationale behind Ericsson's decision as well as the implications of its decision for the telecommunications industry. Since the business strategies of firms, as well as competitive trends in the relevant markets, were not clarified, it was difficult to understand the rationale behind individual firm behavior correctly.

BT/MCI is a case in point. British Telecom (BT) and Microwave Communications, Inc. (MCI) formed a joint venture (Newco) for the provision of enhanced and value-added global telecommunications services to multinational or large regional companies in 1993. BT was the former UK monopolist telecommunications services provider, active in all market segments. MCI was the second-largest long-distance operator in the US after AT&T, at the time of the agreement, and provided a broad range of US and international voice and data communications services, including long distance telephone, record

communications and electronic mail services to and from the US. In this decision, the dynamics of the relevant market were not analyzed properly to grasp
the motivation behind the firms' decision (BT/MCI, 1994, paras. 1–12). In
fact, BT and AT&T were not alone. Deutsche Telekom and France Telecom
bought stakes in Sprint and formed a joint venture company to protect their
core markets against new entrants, while expanding into adjacent markets
swiftly by forming alliances and joint ventures, in response to liberalization
in the 1990s, as the next chapter analyzes in detail.[2] This trend was missing
in the European Commission's analysis.

Due to the static framework of competition, the Commission incorrectly
speculated on the pricing behavior of firms in the case of *Ericsson/Nokia/
Psion* as well. In 1998, Ericsson, Nokia, a global market leader in cellular
phones, and Psion plc, a UK firm that was developing, manufacturing and
marketing handheld portable computers and software, decided to form a
joint venture company, Symbian Limited, for the development of an operating system for use in wireless information devices. The purpose was to
offer a new industry standard based on the so-called EPOC32 software
platform for mobile digital data systems, as the product market was just
emerging (Ericsson/Nokia/Psion, 1998).

This case was important for understanding the perception of the pricing behavior of firms by the Commission that deployed the following
reasoning:

> In addition, if the parties were to attempt to raise the price of the op-
> erating system in the short term as a means of co-ordinating prices on
> the equipment market, this would risk damaging the prospects of the
> operating system becoming a successful product used by third parties.
> (Ericsson/Nokia/Psion, 1998, para. 31)

This statement suggested that the Commission used a short term analysis, as informed by the static neoclassical framework, in assessing the
impact of a new operating platform. Additionally, the European competition authority's view about the pricing behavior of firms was not right,
as firms usually cut prices in the short term, driving their competitors
out of the market, after which they raise prices. As discussed earlier,
Ericsson/Nokia/Psion was a typical case of systems competition, but it
seemed that the Commission had a reasoning based on the static vision
of competition.

A clear manifestation of the impact of this static vision in the implementation process can be seen in the minimal use of Article 82 in pun-
ishing dominant firms that were abusing their position. It was applied
only three times in the telecommunications industry between 1980 and
2004. Whereas the abused parties informed the Commission about the
first two cases, the Commission discovered the third case through its
own investigation. Former competition Commissioner, Karel Van Miert

acknowledged the difficulties of implementing the competition rules in telecommunications services, especially Article 82 on the abuse of dominant positions. According to Van Miert, firms—small and large—did not want to lodge formal complaints against telecommunications operators for fear of suffering reprisals (Adonis, 1994, p. 4). This might be a partial explanation for the rarity of Article 82 cases. Another reason might be owing to the fact that its clauses also excluded many abusive behaviors that are carried out by non-dominant firms.[3] However, the most important factor might be because the static vision of competition did not equip the European Commission to capture abusive behavior when it did occur.

As noted, firms tend to abuse their power in the stage of destructive or hyper competition. The static framework of competition did not take the dynamics of competition into account. Naturally, the Commission had difficulty in detecting abusive market conduct unless abused parties complained to the Commission. For example, two initial Article 82 cases were brought to the attention of the Commission by the abused parties, but the Commission discovered the third one on its own initiative. The first case was the *British Telecommunication* (BT) case in 1982. Article 82 was applied in conjunction with Article 86 in this case for the first time in the history of EU competition policy. Telespeed Services Ltd. lodged an application on June 22, 1979 against the UK Post Office. It maintained that BT prohibited retransmission of messages originating outside the UK to destinations outside the UK (Telespeed Services Limited/United Kingdom Post Office, 1983, para. 15).

As a public corporation with a statutory monopoly for the provision of telecommunications services in the UK, BT abused its dominant position on three occasions, according to the Commission. In the first place, BT refused to allow UK message-forwarding agencies to receive telex messages from outside the UK and to forward them by telex to receivers outside the UK. Secondly, it put a condition on international message-forwarding agencies that the prices charged would not undercut the cost of a direct telex message bypassing the UK. Finally, BT refused to allow UK message-forwarding agencies to send or receive international telephone messages intended for ultimate reception in visual form, such as telex, facsimile or computer terminal. The European Commission asked BT to terminate any restrictions it had put on the UK message-forwarding agencies within two months, but did not impose any fine (Telespeed Services Limited/United Kingdom Post Office, 1983, para. 41).

The second case took place in May 2003. Upon complaints by Mannesmann Arcor, and local and regional carriers in Germany, the Commission initiated an investigation and discovered that Deutsche Telekom AG (DT), a former monopoly and incumbent telecommunications services provider in Germany, abused its dominant position by charging higher prices for the provision of local access to its fixed telecommunications network (local loop) in May 2002. Indeed, it charged new entrants higher fees for wholesale access to the local loop than what DT's subscribers paid for retail access. The Commission concluded that DT abused its dominant position by practicing a 'margin squeeze' in charging more to its competitors (CEC, 2002c). In particular, its fee rate was higher for new entrants for wholesale access to the local loop than what DT's subscribers were paying for the fixed-line subscriptions for the period 1998 through 2001, since in Germany, unbundling was mandated by national law as of 1998. As a result, the Commission fined Deutsche Telekom AG €12.6 million for abusing its dominant position under Article 82 in 2003.[4]

Article 82 was applied for the third time in the telecommunications industry in July 2003. The European Commission discovered in 2001 that Wanadoo Interactive, a 99-percent-owned subsidiary of the firm SA, which was itself a 72-percent-owned subsidiary of former monopoly and market leader France Telecom. Wanadoo Interactive abused its dominant position under Article 82 by charging rates below cost for eXtense and Wanadoo ADSL products marketed by Wanadoo. Indeed, Wanadoo charged below-average costs for services known as Wanadoo ADSL and eXtense until August 2001. It also charged significantly below total costs up until October 2002. Accordingly, the Commission imposed a fine of €10.35 million (Wanadoo Interactive, 2003). By and large, the existence of only three cases under Article 82 between 1980 and 2004, as well as the fact that two of them were brought to light by the abused parties, indicates that EU institutions had difficulty uncovering abusive firm behavior under Article 82 because of the dominance of the static foundations in the model of effective competition. That the Commission discovered one of the cases through its own investigation was indicative of the effects of the dynamic vision of competition.

The following two cases illustrate the existence of the dynamic vision in the European Commission's decisions, even though it was less influential than the static vision. In the *BT/AT&T* case, British Telecom (BT) was the largest telecommunications firm and former monopoly in the UK, offering a full range of telecommunications services to both business and residential customers. American Telephone & Telegraph (AT&T) was also the largest long-distance firm in the US, mainly serving business users. In this case, the Commission drew attention to long-term industry trends:

> In the last decade, the telecommunication sector has seen a dramatic evolution in all respects with regard to the means of supply of telecommunication services, the demand for such services both in nature and quantity, the nature of telecommunication services, the technologies involved, the industry's structure, the applicable regulatory framework and the size, number and structure of market players. (BT/ATT, 1999, para. 17)

This illustrates that the Commission considered the evolution of markets in this particular case by pointing out the decline in the cost of telecommunications equipment, but not the price of services (BT/AT&T, 1999, para. 38). The *BT-AT&T* case indicated that the European Commission could occasionally provide a clear picture of the overall market to contextualize individual firm market conduct.

There was recognition of the impact of market competition on the behavior of firms in pricing in the *France Telecom/Orange* case in August 2000. France Telecom was the incumbent telecommunications operator in France, providing a full range of telecommunications services to residential, professional and large business customers, primarily in France, while being active through mobile joint ventures in Belgium, Denmark, the Netherlands, Italy, Portugal and Greece, at the time of the agreement. In contrast to France Telecom, Orange plc. was a UK-based mobile telecommunications operator, offering mobile communications services in a number of European countries (France Telecom/Orange, 2000, para. 27).

In this decision, there was an acknowledgement of the impact of market competition on pricing, reminiscent of the Classical School's vision of competition as a mechanism to discipline firms on the market: "For Proximus and Mobistar the price reduction from 1997 to 2000 is around 33% and 50%, which is an indicator of an increased degree of competition in this market" (France Telecom/Orange, 2000, para. 27). Nonetheless, such analysis of the dynamic aspect of market competition is not a regular occurrence.

On the whole, these cases under Article 82 and the MCR share several similar features. First, they perceive market competition in static terms (except for two cases), providing a picture of market competition at one point in time, whilst failing to offer a dynamic analysis of the relevant markets over time. Second, related to the first, a large number of cases took place in the late 1990s, during which competition was very intense in the services market and the rationale behind the mergers, acquisitions, and merger-like joint ventures was to restore profit margins eaten up by destructive competition. Even the earlier cases, such as the *Alcatel Cable/AEG Kabel* of 1990, the *Siemens AG/STET* of 1994 and the *Philips/AT&T* case of 1996, were a response by the concerned firms to restore profitability through market consolidation in the traditional public switching and transmission equipment market segments. The next chapter will provide a detailed analysis of the industry as well as the business strategies of firms. Third, the European Commission did not object to any of these agreements and underestimated the long-term effects of market power by permitting mergers, acquisitions, and cooperation agreements.

The next section demonstrates that the existence of the two visions created inconsistencies and ambiguities in defining relevant product and geographic markets, critical for deciding whether a firm or firms have significant market power. It draws on merger control regulation cases in the mobile communications market segment to illustrate these problems by analyzing the line of reasoning the European Commission followed to delineate relevant product markets in its decisions in the process of implementing the merger control regulation.

5.3. INCONSISTENCIES AND CONTRADICTIONS IN DEFINING RELEVANT MARKETS

Defining relevant markets is the key for deciding whether a firm or firms have significant market power. In European competition law, *significant market power* refers to a position of economic strength that affords a single firm, either individually or jointly with others, the power to act independently of competitors, wholesale customers and, ultimately, consumers to an appreciable extent (Landes & Posner, 1981, p. 937; Kolasky, 2001). EU competition law points to two forms of market power: an individual firm's market power and collective market power of dominant firms. In measuring market power in the telecommunications services market, a 50 percent market share is a sufficient criterion to demonstrate market dominance, but it is not the only factor considered. Other factors such as the existence of other network providers in the relevant geographic area, privileged access to facilities and the scope of the rights the telecommunications operators receive from the member states' authorities also play an important role in determining market power ("Notice," 1998, p. 12).

The first step in analyzing whether a firm or firms hold a dominant position and have 'significant market power' is the delineation of the relevant product or service as well as the geographic markets. "A relevant product market comprises all those products and/or services which are regarded as interchangeable or substitutable by the consumer, by reason of the products' characteristics, their prices and their intended use ("Commission Notice," 1997, para. 7). Complementing the relevant product or service market definition, relevant geographic markets are delineated on the basis of supply-side factors and conditions of competition, in addition to demand, side issues, as the following description depicts:

> The relevant geographic market comprises the area in which the undertakings concerned are involved in the supply and demand of products or services, in which the conditions of competition are sufficiently homogeneous and which can be distinguished from neighboring areas because the conditions of competition are appreciably different in those areas. ("Commission Notice," 1997, para. 8)

While characteristics of products or services are considered from the customers' point of view in defining the relevant product or service market, supply, demand, and conditions of competition are taken into account in delineating the relevant geographic market.

Defining the relevant markets is not merely a technical issue or a neutral process. As one European Commission competition policy document indicates: "The concept of relevant market is closely related to the objectives pursued under Community competition policy" ("Commission Notice," 1997, para. 10). The goals of competition policy—as informed by the model of effective competition—determine the definition of the relevant market and hence, the existence or absence of significant market power. As Camesasca and Van Der Bergh (2002) put it:

> Rather, it appears that the European regulators had resolved the markets of relevance in a pragmatic manner, leading to allegations that the outcome of the market definition exercise had been predetermined by a desire to prohibit (or, alternatively, allow) business behavior rated as potentially distortive (or supportive) of the competitive process. (p. 144)

This partially explains the rationale behind the approval of all mergers, acquisitions and cooperation agreements mentioned above, despite their long-term deleterious effects on market competition.

Another explanation may be that defining the markets in the real world is not free from random problems. Goyder (1998) explained the problem as follows: "The definition of product markets is, if anything, even more elusive. There are few products for which there are no substitutes of some kind, and the interrelationship of quality, price, and availability is in nearly all cases difficult to analyze with exactness" (p. 326). It is not surprising that delineating the relevant product and geographic markets contains an element of arbitrariness (Kauper, 1997, p. 1697). These are unavoidable random errors.

Without denying the influence of these two factors (goal-oriented market definition and random errors) on market definition, this section argues that there are systematic inconsistencies in the definition of the relevant markets in EU case law because of the existence of the static and dynamic visions of competition and the predominance of the former over the latter. It is possible to see the tensions between these two views in official documents both in EU guidelines for implementing the competition rules and relevant case law.

For instance, one of the guidelines stated that competition law does not perceive the relevant product and geographic markets in static terms, as the following excerpt clearly indicates:

> Market definition is not a mechanical or abstract process but requires an analysis of any available evidence of past market behavior and an overall understanding of the mechanics of a given sector. In particular, a dynamic rather than a static approach is required when carrying

out a prospective, or forward-looking market analysis. (CEC, 2001b, p. 8)

The other guideline simply refutes this statement: "In assessing relevant markets it is necessary to look at developments in the market in the short term" ("Notice," 1998, p. 9). The existence of this tension between the short term and long term as a reference period in defining the relevant markets reveals the contradiction between the static and the dynamic visions of competition in European competition law. Additionally, the problem of a short term reference period is compounded in the absence of any clarification of what 'short-term' means, in contrast to the US merger guidelines for which 'short-term' covers one or two years (Korah, 2000, p. 90).

To illustrate the problem of inconsistency and arbitrariness in EU competition law decisions in the telecommunications field, the market for the provision of mobile telecommunications services is selected. There are two reasons for making this choice. First, all decisions are in the field of the MCR, which makes it easier to compare them. Second, there are many similar cases to compare and illustrate the inconsistencies in the definition of relevant markets. The cases that cover the time span of four years between 1995 and 1999 depict how the tension between the static and dynamic views of competition created serious inconsistencies in the definition of the relevant service market in mobile communications.

In the *Cable & Wireless/VEBA* case of 1995, there were two actors. Cable and Wireless plc. (C&W), a British international provider of telecommunications services based in the UK, and VEBA AG, a German holding company for subsidiaries with activities in electricity, chemicals, oil trade, transport and telecommunications, decided to establish two joint venture companies, named VEBACOM and Cable & Wireless Europe. Their objective was to provide telecommunications services such as national and international fixed terrestrial telephone networks, satellite telecom services, mobile PCN networks, paging, cable TV, corporate networks, managed bandwidth and value-added services to the German and other European markets (Cable & Wireless/VEBA, 1995).

In this case, the European Commission contended that mobile telephone networks formed a distinct market from fixed telephony networks. It went one step further and distinguished personal communication networks (PCN) from global systems for mobile communications (GSM) networks. Frequencies (900 MHz for GSM and 1710–1880 MHz for PCN), network structures (a PCN network requires a denser system of transmitters), subscribers (local or regional users), interoperability between two networks, international roaming agreements (not existing) and national coverage (not reached yet) served as the basis for distinction (Cable & Wireless/VEBA, 1995, paras. 16–24).

The Commission eventually concluded: "Due to these characteristics of PCN, there are strong indications that PCN forms a separate product market which is different from GSM and has to be considered as a national market" (Cable & Wireless/VEBA, 1995, para. 18). Although the functions of the two mobile communications networks were more or less the same, the Commission preferred to identify two separate markets on the basis of technical characteristics of the two networks, rather than how consumers perceived the services offered through the networks (Cable & Wireless/VEBA, 1995, para. 27).

In May 1998, in the *Belgacom/Tele Danmark/Tulip* case, Belgacom and Tele Danmark challenged the market definition deployed in the *Cable & Wireless-VEBA* case. Belgacom was the former monopoly, offering domestic and international telecommunications services in Belgium. Similar to Belgacom, Tele Danmark was the leading provider of domestic and international telecommunications services in Denmark. The parties decided to create a joint venture to operate mobile communications networks and provide communications services in the Netherlands (Belgacom/Tele Danmark/Tulip, 1998, paras. 3–7).

Both Belgacom and Tele Danmark contended that analogue mobile telephony and digital mobile telephony (including both DCS 1800 and GSM) formed one and the same product market based on technological evolution and the characteristics of customer demand. Nonetheless, the Commission did not comment on the parties' contention and preferred to remain silent (Belgacom/Tele Danmark/Tulip, 1998, para. 15). This shows that it tended to ignore both the technological and market developments over the past three years. This was surprising, especially given the fast pace of technological developments in the telecommunications industry as well as the Commission's insistence on the delineation of the market on the basis of technology in the previous case.

Because of the dominant static view, the Commission overlooked the proposed definition in the *Belgacom/Tele Danmark/Tulip* case and followed the market definition it had deployed in *C&W/VEBA* three years ago in the *Enel/FT/DT* case. Enel, FT and DT formed the Wind joint venture to offer fixed line and mobile communications services in Italy in June 1998. Both France Telecom and Deutsche Telekom were former monopolies in France and Germany, providing a full range of telecommunications services respectively. Enel was the leading provider of electricity in Italy. Enel STC was the division within Enel, responsible for installing, maintaining and operating Enel's internal communications network in addition to providing telecommunications services to Enel (Enel/FT/DT, 1998, paras. 3–6).

The Commission defined two main product markets as relevant, fixed line and mobile telephony respectively. In the mobile communications market, Wind would use the DCS 1800 standard to offer mobile communications. The European Commission applied similar reasoning to that applied in *C&W-VEBA* in 1995, while overlooking the *Belgacom/ Tele Danmark/Tulip* decision made a month earlier. It also used two new criteria to distinguish the DCS 1800 market from that of GSM. In the first place, the price for a DCS 1800 subscription in comparison to that of the high-priced GSM subscription was considered. Secondly, the total number of subscribers of GSM and DCS 1800 networks in Western Europe was taken into account (Enel/FT/DT, 1998, paras. 21–2). Overall, the European Commission ignored both the empirical evidence provided by Belgacom and Tele Danmark as well as market developments over the past three years.

There was a reversal in the European Commission's reasoning in defining the relevant services markets in mobile communications only three weeks after the *Enel/FT/DT* decision. In justifying the tension between the static and dynamic views of market competition and the impact of the definition of the relevant markets on the determination of 'significant market power', the *BT/Airtel* case of July 1998 is very interesting. Three parties were involved in the case. BT was the incumbent telecommunications provider in the UK, in addition to its international activities through its joint ventures in France, Germany, Ireland, Italy, the Netherlands, and Spain. Grupo Acciona SA was a Spanish financial investment company, which was acting through its subsidiary Inversiones Europa SA. Airtel Movil SA was the second GSM mobile operator in Spain and had 13 shareholders, the biggest of which were AirTouch and BT. Airtel Móviles SA was a full function joint venture that had provided mobile telecommunications services in Spain since October 1995. According to the agreement, BT, AirTouch and Grupo Acciona would acquire joint control over Airtel (BT/Airtel, 1998, paras. 1–4).

In this case, the Commission did not insist on the same reasoning followed in the *Enel/FT/DT* case three weeks ago that the DCS 1800 and GSM constituted separate product markets. Rather, it agreed with the new services market definition in mobile communications put forward by BT and Airtel. The parties contended that dual-band handsets that made it possible to roam between DCS1800 and GSM networks, and the allocations of 1800 MHz spectrum to GSM operators, rendered the distinction meaningless as the following excerpt from the decision indicates:

> In the past the Commission has considered (as, e.g. in its decision in 1995 in the Cable & Wireless/VEBA case) that there were indications that systems such as DCS 1800 are used to operate on a market which is different from the one on which GSM services are provided. In the present case the parties submit that, nowadays, the product market is made up of mobile telecommunication services, notwithstanding the standard they use (analogue, GSM, DCS 1800). The parties sustain their claim by pointing out the increasing availability of GSM/DCS 1800 dual-band handsets, which interface both systems, as well as a number of market factors, such as customer demand to be able to roam between DCS 1800 and GSM networks and the allocation of 1800

MHz spectrum to GSM operators (for example to Airtel and Telefónica in Spain), that indicate that those dual handsets will become the norm. This expected convergence of the two systems has been confirmed by third parties' comments. (BT/Airtel, 1998, paras. 15–6)

This decision was surprising because of such a dramatic shift in the Commission's interpretation of technology and market conditions in just three weeks. It is astonishing to note that the *Cable & Wireless/VEBA* case was cited in the decision, but not the *Enel/FT/DT* case. Nor was the *Belgacom/Tele Danmark/Tulip* case used to strengthen the argument made in the *Airtel* ruling.

The *Viag/Orange UK* case of August 1998 reinforced the BT-Airtel case. Orange Overseas Holding Limited and VIAG AG, created a joint venture company Orange Communications S.A within the meaning of Article 3(1)(b) of the Merger Regulation. VIAG AG was the main parent company of the VIAG Group, an internationally active diversified group having businesses in the area of energy, chemical products, packaging, logistic and telecommunications (through VIAG Interkom GmbH &Co). Orange plc was the ultimate parent of the Orange Group that was providing communications services. Its core activity was the operation of the Orange DCS 1800 network in the UK and the sale of Orange network services (Viag/Orange UK, 1998, paras. 1–4). The Commission concluded that the DCS 1800 networks and the GSM networks were part of the same relevant product (Viag/Orange UK, 1998, paras. 19–22).

A year later, the Commission followed a very different path in demarcating the relevant product market for mobile communications in the *Mannesmann/Orange* case in December 1999. Rather than using mobile communications systems technology as a basis for market delineation, it adopted the consumers' viewpoint. Mannesmann AG acquired sole control over Orange plc within the meaning of Article 3(1)(b) of the Merger Control Regulation. Mannesmann AG was a German-based engineering and telecommunications company, providing mobile and fixed-line telephony services, as far as the telecommunications industry was concerned (Mannesmann/Orange, 1999, paras. 1–4). For the first time, the relevant services markets were divided into three: the carrier market for mobile telephony, the distribution market for mobile communications services, and the market for distribution of mobile telephony including the sale of mobile telephone handsets. The Commission defined them as follows: "The carrier market means the market for operating a mobile telephony network whereas the distribution market refers to the sale of complete packages of mobile telephony products to end-customers" (Mannesmann/Orange, 1999, para. 7). The reason for the separation was that these two markets involved different activities and German law recognized the difference between carriers and distributors. It was necessary to obtain a license to operate a mobile telephony network, yet distributors did not have such an obligation (Mannesmann/Orange, 1999, para. 8). In addition to these two markets, the Commission maintained that the sale of handsets could be considered as a separate product market (Mannesmann/Orange, 1999, para. 9).

On the whole, this market demarcation became the basis for defining relevant services markets in subsequent decisions. There was not a significant shift in the Commission's line of reasoning other than clarifying the definitions of already delineated services markets, while adding new sub-markets. One might argue that the sudden shifts and inconsistencies in the Commission's line of reasoning was because of the dynamic nature of the relevant market. However, this does not explain such a dramatic shift within the short time span of three weeks. The Commission left the market definitions open because of its affirmative decisions in all referred cases. Nevertheless, frequent change in its definition of the relevant markets clearly supported the previous theoretical assertion of the inconsistency, contradiction and ambiguity in the definition of the relevant services markets.

The only merger case the Commission ever rejected in the telecommunications industry was the one proposed by MCI WorldCom and Sprint in 2000. Although it happened in a different market segment, it is worth mentioning the *MCI WorldCom-Sprint* case, as the dominant static view played a significant role in the decision. It involved two American companies. In October 1999, MCI WorldCom and Sprint decided to merge their activities. While MCI WorldCom provided services to companies and consumers, such as facilities-based local, long distance and international freephone, calling card, debit card and Internet services, Sprint offered telecommunications services, including local, long-distance, and wireless communications and Internet services in the US. It also had a joint venture with Deutsche Telekom and France Telecom in Europe, called Global One (MCI Worldcom/Sprint, 2000, para. 2).

The Commission did not permit the merger. It reasoned that the Internet was a hierarchical structure and that there was a tier of top-level network providers. The latter achieved their connectivity entirely by 'peering agreements' between the top level networks or internally. Accordingly, the Commission concluded that there was a distinct market for the provision of top level or universal Internet connectivity ((MCI Worldcom/Sprint, 2000, para. 60). The merged entity of WorldCom and Sprint would create a dominant position in this market segment:

> The merger between MCI WorldCom and Sprint will lead to the creation of a top level network provider that through its sheer size would be able to behave to an appreciable extent independently of its competitors and customers. Given the global scope of the market, this will impact consumers in Europe as much as any other consumers. (MCI Worldcom/Sprint, 2000, para. 145)

According to the Commission, the merged entity would be in a position to discipline the market either by the mere threat of selectively degrading the connectivity of its competitors or by raising prices (MCI Worldcom/ Sprint, 2000, paras. 152–3). For the parties, the Commission defined the relevant product market very narrowly. In their reply to the European Commission's reasoning, the parties contended that the market was growing rapidly and demand was sensitive to price changes. Moreover, the pace of technological change was very fast in the market (MCI Worldcom/Sprint, 2000, para. 300). Nevertheless, the Commission did not take into account the evolution of the market. The focus was mainly on the market structure and competitors in the relevant market. The merging parties promised to divest some of their overlapping assets, but the Commission did not see enough promise. Before the official decision, the parties abandoned the initiative. Nonetheless, when the two former monopolies in Sweden and Finland (Telia and Sonera) merged in 2002, the Commission was jubilant (Telia/Sonera, 2002). This case recalls the *Continental Can* case of the 1970s and the Commission's differential attitude toward European and non-European firms, besides the predominance of the static view.

5.4. CONCLUSIONS

This chapter has demonstrated that market power was critical in the process of applying the EU competition rules in the telecommunications industry. Regarding the crucial role of market power in competition, it is possible to identify three patterns based on the practice between 1980 and 2004. First, EU competition policy was concerned about the market power of firms as the key tool for profitability. As the cited cases under Articles 81 and 87 made clear above, getting permission for cooperation agreements was easier, especially in times of economic downturn. Firms could restore their market power collectively and control their respective markets, rather than being squeezed under market competition.

The Commission rationalized its supportive stance by using the discourse of cutting costs, achieving synergies and economies of scale, and enhancing the international competitiveness of the European firms against their American and Japanese competitors, besides citing profitability. Relaxing Article 81 was a method for finding a solution to the problem of profitability within the 'boundaries' of the market. If firms were in a critical situation financially because of economic stagnation, state aids were usually deployed to help them. In other words, the member states intervened directly in urgent situations where the 'market solution' was not enough. In line with the argument made in the third chapter, the implementation of Article 87 was relaxed to encourage member states to provide financial help in times of low profitability. The rationale behind the permission will become clear, as the next chapter provides an in-depth analysis of the telecommunications industry from the market perspective.

The second feature regarding market power was the way the European Commission conceptualized and measured it. This chapter has provided empirical evidence for the existence of static and dynamic perspectives of competition in EU competition law cases. As Article 81 and 82 and MCR cases demonstrated, it was possible to see the imprint of these two views of market competition in EU competition law cases. Nonetheless, while the static view prevailed over the dynamic view, the dynamic vision of market competition was not completely absent.

Moreover, this chapter has illustrated the problems of inconsistency, ambiguity and arbitrariness in measuring market power because of the existence of the two views of market competition in EU competition law. The last section of the chapter focused on the relevant services market in mobile communications to demonstrate the inconsistency and erratic behavior in the Commission's line of reasoning in defining this market segment. Ultimately, the problems at the crucial stage of defining the relevant markets, together with the predominance of the static view of competition, confirmed that EU institutions had difficulty understanding the complex and dynamic processes of market competition and hence, in dealing with market power at the implementation stage. Accordingly, the boundaries of relevant product/service and geographic markets were narrowly drawn in most cases, resulting in the underestimation of the market power of large firms.

Finally, the European Commission often failed to carry out detailed market analyses to outline the general picture of the concerned markets before dealing with the details of products and services in different geographical areas. In particular, Commission decisions were not very clear about the rationale behind the intense merger, acquisition, and alliance formation activity in the equipment market between 1986 and 1992 as well as in the late 1990s. The situation was not very different in the case of the services market in that the Commission was optimistic about alliances between the dominant players in the mid-1990s and acquisition and merger activity between the dominant mobile phone companies in the second half of the 1990s. Instead of understanding the broader forces behind similar activities, the Commission preferred to deal with products and services, rather than with the firms themselves. Losing the forest for the trees resulted in the disappearance of market power from the analysis. The next chapter provides a detailed analysis of competition in the telecommunications equipment and services markets respectively between 1980 and 2004, from the market point of view, to explain how the factor of profitability drove competitors to seek alliances, acquisitions or mergers.

6   EU Telecommunications Equipment and Services Market Analysis

This chapter analyzes the evolution, dynamics, and outcomes of market competition in the telecommunications equipment and services markets between 1980 and 2004. In particular, it examines the structural characteristics of the concerned markets, and the impact of profitability on the business strategies of firms, and on market outcomes. The goal is to provide an analysis of competition from the market's point of view. It is argued that market concentration substantially increased in the telecommunications equipment market at the EU level because of the decline in the number of major firms from around 19 in 1980 to only four by 2004. The creation of competitive services markets had yet to be realized, as the incumbents still controlled more than fifty percent of the market in many member states as of 2005. Large European business users benefited most from price cuts in services, compared to households and small business users. Service quality indicators gave mixed signals, and employment in the industry as a percentage of total labor force declined considerably in contrast to the initial assertions of creating more jobs in telecommunications.   ·

The first half of this chapter analyzes the evolution of competition in the EU telecommunications equipment market by focusing on four leading European firms—Alcatel, Ericsson, Siemens and Nokia. The purpose is to investigate the complex processes of competing and monopolizing in the relevant market as well as the evolution of the whole market over time. The second half concentrates on three main European telecommunications operators—British Telecom (BT), Deutsche Telekom (DT) and France Telecom (FT)—around which the European telecommunications services market analysis is conducted, followed by a policy analysis in the third section.[1] The last section states findings.

6.1. STRUCTURAL CHARACTERISTICS OF THE EQUIPMENT MARKET

In analyzing the dynamics of the telecommunications equipment market, it is necessary to bear in mind its structural features at the outset. This market has three major attributes. The first is that it is dynamic in that major technological innovations shake the foundations of the market from time to time (Coy and Levine, 1991, p. 138). The second is the long-term technological dependency of purchasers of telecommunications equipment. Once a telecommunications operator or service provider buys a system from a producer, the former becomes dependent, in the long term, for after-sales services and upgrading equipment. As Crisp (1983) observed: "Once a system is established in a country the company which supplies it is in a much stronger position to win further orders in that country for many years" (p. 6).

Finally, the size of firms plays a crucial role in competition for a number of reasons. In the first place, telecommunications equipment supply is a cyclical business, such that the demand is intermittent. Principal telecommunications operators buy equipment from time to time in order to establish their networks or upgrade existing ones, after which they stop spending on infrastructure for some time. Equipment makers must be financially powerful enough to stay in business in 'tough' times. Alternatively, they may adopt a conglomerate structure to weather market downturns with profits from other industries. Second, telecommunications equipment prices fall sharply with the advance of new technology. Firms must be financially strong enough to endure intense competition (Cane, 1995a, p. 8).[2] Third, the equipment is technologically-intensive, requiring huge expenditures on research and development, and large cash flows to sustain such initiatives. Fourth, telecommunications operators depend on powerful firms after buying their initial equipment for after-sales services and upgrading, given that these systems often last more than a decade (Keller, et al., 1989, p. 138). Finally, it is essential to get recognition and financial support from the state in the form of research subsidies ("A Market Where the US Lacks," 1980, p. 73). As a result, market structure based upon large firm size constitutes a serious market entry barrier in the long term, if not in the short run.

6.1.1. The Panorama of the Telecommunications Equipment Market in the 1980s

Germany, Britain, France, Sweden, Finland, and Italy were the five countries hosting the major telecommunications equipment firms in the beginning of the 1980s. American International Telephone and Telegraph (ITT) was the only outsider with subsidiaries in several European countries. There were three main players in France. These were CIT-Alcatel, a subsidiary of Compagnie Générale d'Electricité (CGE), Compagnie Générale Constructions Téléphoniques (CGCT), a subsidiary of ITT, and Thomson-Brandt. Thomson-Brandt's telecommunications division, Thomson-CSF, was formed after Thomson-Brandt bought the French subsidiaries of ITT (LMT) and Ericsson (SFT) in 1976, when successive French governments forced foreign companies to sell their French assets. Alcatel, a subsidiary of Compagnie Générale d'Electricité (CGE), was in a strong position in transmission systems and optical fibers (Lorenz, 1983, p. 12).

Siemens and Standard Electric Lorenz (SEL), a subsidiary of ITT, dominated the German telecommunications equipment industry, accounting for 90 percent of domestic equipment sales. AEG, owned by Daimler-Benz, was the third major player in the West German market. Werner von Siemens established the Siemens & Halske Telegraph Company in 1847 to build the first telegraph line between Berlin and the parliament in Frankfurt. Prior to the 1980s, Siemens benefited from a steady flow of income in its position as a quasi-monopoly supplier of telecommunications equipment and power plants in Germany. The Swedish enterprise, L.M. Ericsson was a highly successful European player with a long history, like Alcatel and Siemens. Ericsson grew out of an electrical engineering workshop set up in 1876 ("Ericsson Milestones, 1997, p. 2). Compared to Alcatel and Siemens, however, Ericsson was purely a telecommunications company before the 1980s.

In Finland, Nokia, an octopus-like conglomerate in the late 1970s, was producing small digital public exchanges and telephone cables. With its origins in forest products, Nokia began operations in a small, inland town in 1865 from which it took its name. It moved into rubber and cables and began to develop an electronics business in the 1960s (Carnegy, 1995a, p. 11). Nokia and the combined Finnish Rubber & Cable Works merged to form Nokia Group in 1967. The world oil crisis played a vital role in this diversification as well as the internationalization of Nokia in the mid-1970s. These twin processes found their expression in Nokia's focus on the newly expanding mobile communications market during the rest of the century.

There were three significant players in the UK: Plessey, General Electric Company (GEC), and Standard Telephones and Cables (STC), an ITT subsidiary. Established in 1917, Plessey was a profitable electronics conglomerate in the early 1980s. Like Plessey, GEC also had a long history in that it was formed in 1886 as a wholesaler of electrical products and quickly moved into manufacturing. Finally, GEC was incorporated as General Electric Company Limited in 1900. In Italy, there were two small firms, Italtel, owned by the Italian state and Telettra, part of Fiat, an Italian auto-maker. While the former focused on public exchanges, the latter specialized in transmission equipment. They were relatively small and technologically backward, in comparison to their larger European counterparts (Buxton, 1982, p. 6).

Because of the separation of national markets by legal factors, there were around 19 major equipment producers in Europe at the beginning of the 1980s and the number of effective players decreased to four by 2004. In other words, market concentration moved from the national to the European level over the past quarter century. Alcatel, Ericsson, Nokia and

Siemens, each of which had the longest corporate history, could survive market deregulation and the accompanying intense competition. By contrast, ITT, Plessey and GEC disappeared. The question to be raised here is: how could these four big firms endure stiff competition and swallow their competitors? Answering this question entails analysis of the different stages of market competition and market outcomes. It is possible to identify two significant full cycles in the equipment market between 1980 and 2004, with the first full cycle occurring between 1980 and 1992, and the second, between 1993 and 2004. The next section explicates the complex processes of competing and monopolizing that brought on the high degree of market concentration.

6.1.2. Public Switching and Transmission: 1980–1992

The most significant telecommunications invention between 1980 and 1992 was digital public switching equipment, the brain of a telecommunications network, as noted by Williams (1982a):

> Coupled with the evolution in the office is the increased demand for telecommunications, resulting in another growth sector for electronic components. The western world is now going through a transition from outdated electromechanical telephone systems to completely electronic ones. (p. 1)

Digital public switching equipment was critical in that it comprised 50 percent of the total market, besides being "the key to unlocking orders for related products, such as transmission gear and cables" (Peterson et al., 1987, p. 98). Gradual market liberalization and market saturation intensified competition in the digital public switching and transmission market segments in the second half of the 1980s.

6.1.2.1. Increasing Competition and Exaltation: 1980–1982

Demand was high, whereas supply was limited for digital public switching equipment in the late 1970s and early 1980s, because all competitors could not bring their equipment to the market at the same time. Therefore, competition was weak and profit opportunities were high for the few. Moreover, growing demand for digital public switching stimulated consumption of transmission as well as terminal equipment. In other words, several markets were on the rise at the same time until 1983, as Graph 6.1 below demonstrates, with a decrease in expenditures by public telecommunications operators in the EU15 from around 44.60 percent of their revenue in 1980 to 13.68 percent in 2003. Although there was a clear trend of decline, fluctuations definitely matched the oscillations in the profitability of the equipment makers, as the previous section indicated.

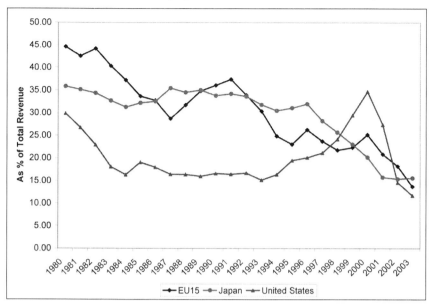

Graph 6.1 Public Telecommunication Operator (PTO) investment as % of total revenue: 1980–2003[3]

Many telecommunications firms attempted to produce digital central public switching equipment, but some of them failed. For instance, in Sweden, the telecommunications administration, Televerket, was producing about three-quarters of its equipment requirements in its own manufacturing branch Teli, which brought Teli and Ericsson together to produce new digital switch exchanges in the early seventies. The result was a highly successful new digital public exchange, called AXE. Ericsson brought it to the market in 1977, one of the earliest offerings. Together with Nokia, Ericsson also established the first and most advanced working mobile telecommunications network in the Scandinavian countries in 1981, called the Nordic Mobile Telephone System (NMT). In other words, Ericsson was ahead of their competitors in both fixed and mobile telecommunications equipment market segments.

While ITT sold its first digital switch (System 12) in the market in 1978, Siemens, as a latecomer, offered its first digital public exchange (EWS-D) for sale in 1980. Both Alcatel and Thomson brought their digital switching equipment to the market in 1979 (models E 10, MT 20 / 25).[4] The latter also ran into technical troubles with its digital switching equipment. Overall, Ericsson, ITT, Alcatel, and Siemens were the main suppliers of digital exchanges by 1980. Owing to the troubles their competitors were having, these four firms could establish themselves firmly in the concerned market segments. However, they were not immune from the pressures of market competition as their competitors solved technical problems and brought their switching equipment to the market in the early 1980s, intensifying competition.

In addition to the impact of latecomers like Nokia, GEC and Plessey on market competition, growing demand, short supply and higher profit margins attracted new entrants from the US (AT&T, GTE) and from other industries such as the auto, steel and consumer electronics (Bosch, Mannessman and Philips). Nokia sold its first fully digitalized exchange in Finland in 1982. Besides, its focus on niche markets with its DX 200 digital exchange, suited to small exchanges with as few as 400 or 500 subscribers with an upper limit of about 10,000, Nokia, together with Ericsson, took part in the development of the NMT mobile communications network and was responsible for producing mobile phones (Barnes, 1983, p. 17). Two leading producers, Plessey and GEC, together with an ITT subsidiary, Standard Telephones and Cables PLC (STC), developed a new digital exchange system or digital switch called System X in the early 1970s under the leadership of the British telecommunications administration, but could not sell their products until 1983 due to development and delivery delays (OECD, 1988, p. 73).

In addition to the industry players that were late in entering into competition, there were newcomers that intensified the rivalry. For instance, Bosch, the German car component maker, decided to enter into the telecommunications equipment market in 1981 with the purpose of reducing its dependency for revenue on manufacturing car parts at around 60 percent at the beginning of the 1980s. The rationale behind the move was that Bosch was worried about the ailing European car industry. The telecommunications equipment market was a growth business. AEG, which was in poor financial health and in urgent need of fresh capital, sold some parts of its profitable telecommunications and office equipment business in the early 1980s, to save itself from bankruptcy. Bosch and Mannesmann, the steel pipes and engineering groups respectively, acquired AEG's telecommunications activities in December 1981 ("AEG/Robert Bosch," 1981, p. 82). Nonetheless, Mannesmann moved into the telecommunications services market later, after selling its stake to Bosch.

In a similar way, Philips, the Dutch electronics conglomerate, tried to develop its own digital exchange in the early 1980s, but abandoned the project by 1983, after losing several hundred million dollars. It then joined AT&T internationally to market the latter's digital public exchanges (Betts & Ellis, 1983, p. 1). In sum, the European equipment market was growing in the early 1980s; profit margins were healthy; new firms were entering the market; and market competition was intensifying. Philips's sudden withdrawal was because of its direct attack on the core markets of the established firms. Bosch targeted newly opening markets that made it possible for the company to stay in the market successfully for almost twenty years.

6.1.2.2. Intense Competition and Prosperity: 1983–1985

Profitability showed signs of decline around 1983 for several reasons. First, new and advanced models of digital public switching were coming to the market from Siemens, GEC, Plessey, and STC. Second, formerly isolated national markets were opening up to competition with cautious liberalization in the EC and around the world. Third, research and development costs were increasing rapidly. European firms followed two major business strategies to respond these challenges. The first was moving into closely related production markets, e.g. office automation equipment. The second strategy was geographical market expansion, mainly into the US market.

The logic behind expansion into office equipment was to be able to package different equipment around the central switch. Dodshworth (1982) pointed out that "[o]nce the company has won an order for the switching apparatus, it is argued, it has the base on which to sell the rest of its range, from screens, to memories, to copiers" (p. 6). Four firms followed comparable aspirations under the pressure of market competition. For instance, Ericsson decided to move into the office equipment market after realizing that it had become too dependent on its public switching systems because 50 percent of its total sales was coming from these systems in the late 1970s (Williams, 1982b, p. 14). Ericsson's entrance was not through internal growth, but through external acquisitions such as Datasaab, the AXXA word-processing system and Facit, together with its agreement with American computer maker Digital Equipment to design and sell computers for retail banking systems. This meant that it could provide full telecommunications and data systems to its customers (Field, 1986, p. 86).

Siemens followed a similar strategy as well. In response to its declining profitability, Siemens developed an advanced office communications system, Hicom, and merged its computer and private telecommunications equipment businesses in 1984 in an effort to expand into office automation (Muchau, 1995, p. 25). Plessey's strategy, like that of all other European electronics conglomerates, was to provide telecommunications and office automation systems simultaneously (Cane, 1982, p. 20). As part of the plan, Plessey decided to bundle its public and private telecommunications businesses into a new division, while divesting its four non-core capacitor manufacturing businesses (Campbell-Smith, 1982, p. 28). Alcatel preferred controlled expansion into office automation from its base in telephone switching systems by adding a range of compatible peripherals around its private telephone exchange systems. Alcatel's business strategy was comprised of a series of acquisitions, including a US automated mailing company, Frieden, the office equipment division of Vickers Ltd, a London firm,

Italian Olivetti, and STC Data Systems, a computer services group run by the ICL computer company (Mars, 1983, p. 1). Finally, Nokia bought the formerly state-owned Swedish Luxor group to add consumer electronics to its data processing and information systems base and to broaden its market presence in Sweden (Barnes, 1982, p. 5).

Geographical expansion, especially to the liberalized American market, was aimed at lessening the impact of intense competition on profitability. Ericsson set up an equally owned joint venture company with American Honeywell to research and develop advanced digital switching products in 1983. This would increase Ericsson's distribution channels in the American market, while giving Honeywell access to Ericsson's digital private exchange technology. Such a decision was a response to the linkages between American AT&T and Dutch Philips, and American IBM and American private exchange maker Rolm Corp ("Americanization of L.M. Ericsson," 1983, p. 63).

Likewise, Siemens preferred the US as well and based its expansion strategy on agreements and acquisitions, especially in the technology areas of semiconductors and communications, as its joint venture company with the American GTE illustrated (Keller & Miller, 1986, p. 62). In the same way, Alcatel opted for expansion into the US market, besides its pan-European growth ("CGE/Thomson," 1985, p. 72; Betts, 1984, p. 14). The French government approved Alcatel's acquisition of Thomson, despite the Ministry of Posts and Telecommunications' opposition due to its concerns about the increasing market power of Alcatel ("Thomson and CGE," 1983, p. 1). After the rapid expansion, CIT-Alcatel became a dominant force in the French telecommunications equipment market with a 90 percent market share. In its attempt to expand into the US market, Nokia established a joint venture company with the Tandy Corporation of the US through its subsidiary Mobira for manufacturing mobile cellular phone handsets in the Far East ("A Mobile Phone Maker," 1984, p. 10). Together with diversification into the office equipment market, the leading European manufacturers expanded geographically to improve their profitability.

It became apparent by the mid-1980s that the widely practiced plan of expanding into the office equipment market and geographical expansion had not solved the problem of profitability. Market consolidation through mergers and acquisitions, and concentrating on core areas through divesting non-core businesses were the two strategies followed by the industry players to restore profitability in the third period.

6.1.2.3. Destructive Competition and Crisis: 1986–1990

The period between 1985 and 1990 witnessed the largest consolidation movement in the traditional public switching and transmission markets in Europe. Alcatel was the principal winner. Its acquisition of International Telephone & Telegraph (ITT) in 1986 shook the edifice of the European equipment market. Registered in Amsterdam and headquartered in Brussels after the acquisition, Alcatel would control all the public telecommunications and business systems activities of ITT worldwide, except for Standard Telephones & Cables (STC), ITT's UK subsidiary, which was not included in the deal ("Alcatel-Alsthom," 1991, p. 65; "Alcatel," 1987, pp. 146–7). The last major acquisition Alcatel added to its holdings was Telettra, the telecommunications division of Italian Fiat in 1990 (Dawkins, 1990, p. 28).[5]

GEC attempted to acquire Plessey in 1986, but the Monopolies and Mergers Commission (MMC), the British competition authority, rejected the deal. Then GEC and Plessey combined their telecommunications activities and created GEC-Plessey Telecommunications (GPT) in early 1988. Siemens teamed up with GEC to launch a joint bid for Plessey in November 1988 ("European Electronics," 1988, p. 78). Despite Plessey's and the MMC's opposition to the hostile takeover in the UK, the European Commission blessed the deal, showing its true intention of helping big business in Europe. After the successful bid, Siemens took a 40 percent stake in GPT, while the remaining 60 percent went to GEC in 1989 (Dodsworth and Dixon, 1989. p. 22). Siemens also bought Rolm Systems from IBM to bolster its position in the US (Kehoe, 1992, p. 24 ; Oram & Fisher, 1988, p. 23). Siemens' final acquisition during the first period was Nixdorf Computer, a leading German computer and telecommunications firm (Fisher, 1990, p. 1).

Similarly, Ericsson took over France's CGCT in April 1987. AT&T and Siemens were also vying to buy CGCT. The American and German governments lobbied intensively on behalf of their respective companies and put heavy pressure on the French government from the beginning. Facing such pressure, the powerful Finance Minister Edouard Balladur resigned in late 1986, as he wanted a 'European solution'. The French government's attempt to placate its allies was the reason behind selling CGCT to Ericsson as a 'neutral' decision (Betts & Housego, 1987, p. 1). Ericsson also became the full owner of Intelsa, the Spanish telecommunications manufacturer that was making Ericsson equipment for the Spanish market (Web, 1987a, p. 34).

Nokia was not very selective in its acquisition strategy, but increased its presence in the telecommunications and office automation markets. Nokia made numerous acquisitions in 1987 and 1988 in various fields, with a special focus on office equipment and mobile communications. Some of these were a 25 percent stake in the UK concern Shaye Communications, US paging operator Diversicom Cue, Ericsson's data systems business (Web, 1987b, 37; Virtanen, 1987, p. 29). With the acquisition of Technophone of the UK, Nokia became the world's second-largest cellular phone manufacturer after American Motorola and the largest cellular mobile phone manufacturer in Europe (Owen, 1991, p. 26).

Graph 6.2 illustrates the results of the business strategies of the four leading telecommunications equipment producers between 1980 and 1990. The average rate of return improved in the second half of the 1980s, parallel to industry consolidation. Because of differences in business strategies,

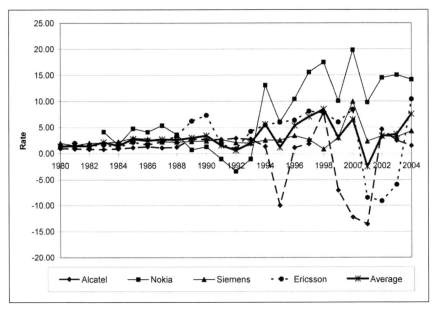

Graph 6.2 Net rate of return on total assets, 1980–2004.[6]

there was a wide variation among the four firms. Market concentration in Europe with the decline of the effective number of firms from 19 in 1980 to only 8 by the end of 1992 solved the problem of profitability for Alcatel and Siemens for a while through raising their market share in the traditional digital switching and transmission markets.

Selling non-core businesses to focus on telecommunications was the second part of the business strategy followed by these four major players. For instance, Ericsson abandoned its office equipment strategy and divested all of its activities in this market segment (Done, 1987, p. 31). Siemens, not unlike Ericsson, sold US$2 billion in non-core businesses (Miller, 1995, p.52). Similarly, Alcatel also made business disposals, including some software companies in France, a manufacturing business in Sweden, and the consumer electronics division of SEL, the West German arm of the former ITT business, to Nokia, besides its postal franking and folding machine businesses (Dawkins, 1992, p. 22). Solutions adopted to deal with Nokia's problems included internal restructuring, refocusing on telecommunications, computers, and consumer electronics as long-term growth sectors, and divesting some of the non-core businesses (Virtanen, 1989, p. 22). Overall, market concentration and deconcentration went hand in hand in the equipment market in the second half of the 1980s. Simultaneous mergers and mass divestures indicated that market concentration was not a simple or unilinear process.

What the analysis so far indicates is that profitability determined the form and intensity of market competition that, in turn, shaped the business strategy, organizational structure and market behavior of these firms. Contextualizing the aggressive acquisition of Plessey by Siemens and GEC revealed the fact that the objective behind the mergers and acquisitions in the second half of the 1980s was to eliminate a strong competitor and restore profitability. The European Commission's rationalization, as analyzed in the previous chapter, as stimulating technical development or enhancing international competitiveness, did not have a substantive basis. Most, if not all, of the cooperation agreements between the European manufacturers approved by the European Commission between 1985 and 1992 had the objective of restoring 'peace' by restricting competition in the relevant market, even though it was difficult. As Graph 6.2 above demonstrates, this industry consolidation stopped the decline in average profitability toward the end of the 1980s temporarily, but the economic stagnation in Europe in the early 1990s, coupled with the decline in the demand for traditional switching and transmission equipment, resulted in temporary depression in the equipment market.

6.1.2.4. Waning Competition and Depression: 1991–1992

The declining investment by PTOs in traditional digital public switching and transmission, as well as the economic stagnation in 1991–1992, hit the European traditional telecommunications equipment producers hard. Firms turned inward rather than focusing on their competitors, and restructured their operations to prepare for another cycle of competition during the depression period. The rate of profit for each firm determined the degree of internal focus. Whereas Ericsson and Nokia were early reformers, Alcatel and Siemens were slow to adapt themselves to the changing markets.

Ericsson underwent a major restructuring in the early 1990s to make sure that its fractious business units worked as a team (Taylor, 1990, p. 34). While centralizing sales of all products in each country unit, Ericsson introduced a matrix system with unit managers reporting to both product divisions and corporate headquarters. The new structure would facilitate effective information sharing among the firm's 40 research and development labs around the world as well as moving products to the market quickly (Flynn, 1994, p. 88). Ericsson also made heavy R&D investments in its core product areas of telecommunications switching equipment and mobile telephones, approaching 15 per cent of its 1990 sales. Its estimated research budget in 1991 would amount to almost 20 per cent of its sales and greatly exceed its profits. Ericsson believed that such a large R&D commitment was necessary to safeguard its market position (Burton, 1991, p. 18).

Having faced a significant drop in its profit margins, Nokia underwent a significant restructuring as well. After a major divestment in the late 1980s, the company decided to concentrate on consumer electronics, mobile phones and telecommunications (Tessieri, 1991a, p. 30). Nokia subsidiaries of consumer electronics, mobile phones and telecommunications accounted for 61 per cent, its cables and machinery for 29 per cent and the basic industries division for 10 per cent of net sales respectively toward the end of 1991 (Tessieri, 1991b, p. 35). Compared to Ericsson and Nokia, Siemens was not in a hurry, but reorganized its management board in the late 1980s (Simonian, 1989, p. 30). After the far-reaching reorganization of their corporate structure, Siemens also decided to decentralize its research and development policy. A new chief executive put more emphasis on market requirements than Siemens' traditional policy of perfectionism and high quality, while reducing the workforce by 7.5 percent through early retirement and selling $2 billion in non-core businesses to bring focus to the company (Parkes & Fisher, 1992, p. 32).

Alcatel was the least threatened firm with respect to profit margins, and restructured itself in 1991 to digest its acquisitions and focus on four worldwide product groups. These were network systems, radio-communications, space and defense, and business systems and cable ("Alcatel Goes," 1991, p. 13). Surprisingly, it continued its acquisitions, buying the transmission equipment division of US Rockwell International Corporation in 1991, the cable business of AEG, Vacha in eastern Germany and Orbitec in France in 1992 (Rawsthorn, 1992, p. 28). After these small-scale acquisitions in the traditional switching and transmission equipment markets, Alcatel became the world's largest equipment manufacturer. Its strength would become its weakness in the next full cycle of competition.

Different company experiences have indicated that firms usually focused their internal affairs and restructured themselves during the period of waning competition to get ready for the next cycle. The degree of focus depended on profit margins: the larger the decline, the deeper the restructuring the firm undertook. Compared to Siemens and Alcatel, Ericsson and Nokia underwent a major reorganization to increase their strength in mobile phones. By contrast, Alcatel and Siemens restored their profitability by acquiring their competitors. Their expansion in the traditional markets would become their main drawback in the next cycle.

6.1.3. Mobile/Data Communication Equipment, Bubble, and Burst: 1993–2004

During the second cycle of competition, mobile communications systems and mobile phones, as well as data communications equipment became the epicenter of the business strategies of telecommunications equipment producers around the world, stimulated by the rise of the Internet in the second half of the 1990s. To adapt themselves to the powerful idea of the convergence of telecommunications and computers with the spread of Internet usage, European firms, like their North American counterparts, readjusted their business strategies around mobile communications and data equipment market segments.

Compared to data communication networks equipment that was relatively new, mobile communications had been around for some time. Ericsson and Nokia had a head-start in the competition owing to their success in building the first generation systems in Northern Europe in the 1980s. Additionally, both companies, especially Ericsson, invested heavily in second generation mobile phones in the late 1980s and early 1990s. Put another way, they positioned themselves very well, whereas Alcatel and Siemens amplified their exposure to the declining traditional public switching and transmission equipment through mergers and acquisitions. As with the evolution of competition in the first cycle, it is possible to see similar trends in the second full cycle.

6.1.3.1. Increasing Competition and Exaltation: 1993–1995

After the period of depression in the equipment markets, market competition was weak in 1993 and 1994 for two critical reasons. The first was that market consolidation in the digital public switching and transmission markets had decreased the intensity of competition in the industry. The second factor was that newly opened second-generation mobile communications and terminal equipment markets relieved some of the pressure of competition. New products in mobile and data communications markets attracted competitors' attention and they concentrated their efforts in those markets.

While Ericsson dominated the second-generation mobile phone (GSM) networks, Nokia was the leading European mobile handset maker. Ericsson was the first company to install a GSM network successfully for Mannesmann Mobilfunk in Germany in 1992. After this success, it gained as much as 60 percent of the world market in digital cellular equipment by 1993, compared to its leading 40 percent share of the world market for the first-generation analogue cellular transmission equipment (Carnegy, 1993a, p. 32). Not unlike Ericsson, Nokia became the largest cellular mobile phone supplier in Europe, and the second in the world, with its 20 percent world market share (Motorola had a 30 percent share by July 1993) (Carnegy, 1993b, p. 26).

Because of their success in mobile communications equipment, both Ericsson and Nokia aimed to strengthen their position in data communications markets, while still maintaining their leadership in mobile communications infrastructures and phones. In addition to cutting staff numbers in its public telecoms division by up to 6,000 from 30,000, Ericsson divested component manufacturing operations such as plastic parts, cabling, mechanical parts, relays and printed circuit boards in the same division (Carnegy, 1995, p. 17). After this, developing new digital multimedia switches that could handle a mixture of voice, video, data, and high-speed transmission systems, was the next target (Levine, 1993, p. 106). Similarly, Nokia divested all of its non-core businesses between 1993 and 1996 (Carnegy, 1996a, p.

16). Nokia's expansion strategy included forging a strategic alliance with the US electronics group, Hewlett-Packard, to develop the next generation of telecommunications infrastructure or intelligent network systems that would use advanced electronics to provide new services such as free-phone, personal numbering and call forwarding (Adonis, 1994, p. 9). Overall, Ericsson and Nokia prioritized mobile and data communications markets.

Unlike Ericsson and Nokia, Alcatel and Siemens were in disarray, after their traditional digital switching and transmission markets reached maturity in 1994, as the percent of digital lines reached 80 percent, resulting in low PTO investment (see Graph 6.1 above). Moreover, a wave of privatizations among European telephone companies was loosening the once-tight supplier-customer ties that Alcatel had enjoyed in Germany, France, Belgium, Italy, and other affluent West European markets (Newman, 1994, p. 8). Furthermore, European operators decided to clean up their balance sheets before the industry's deregulation in 1998 and therefore, cut their investment spending (Ridding, 1995, p. 26).

As Graph 6.2 above indicates, Alcatel was the most vulnerable to the decline in the traditional market segment because of its product and geographical market specialization. Unlike Ericsson or Nokia, Alcatel was also very weak in mobile communications equipment to offset the decline in the fixed-line telecommunications equipment (Truell & Hudson, 1994, A14). To compensate for the loss, Alcatel attempted to increase its market share in developing countries such as China, but this was not enough (Toy, 1996, p. 17). That Alcatel's chairman was under investigation, in the second half of 1994, in a case alleging overbilling of France Telecom and using corporate money for private gain worsened Alcatel's problems (Buchan & Ridding, 1995, p. 21).

To restore profitability, Alcatel cut jobs, divested unprofitable businesses, restructured its internal organization and diversified into the telecommunications services market in 1994 (Rawstyorn, 1993, p. 16; Ridding, 1995, p. 26; Jack, 1995, p. 27). Nevertheless, the new strategy did not produce immediate positive results and hence, restructuring efforts continued in 1995. New strategies included the reorganization of Alcatel into eight new business divisions, job cuts, centralization of financial controls, asset write-downs and divesting of some non-core businesses worth about $2 billion, and withdrawing from the telecommunications services market (Lavin, 1995, p. A10). Alcatel now accelerated the move into the mobile communications and multimedia businesses where it had lagged behind its international rivals (Edmondson, 1998, p. 20).

Siemens also followed suit by restructuring itself. Its efforts included changes in corporate culture and strategies in research, development and marketing, cutting its workforce by 7.5 percent through early retirement, and selling off $2 billion in non-core businesses (Miller, 1995, p. 52). Siemens also shifted its focus to mobile communications and data systems. Besides establishing a joint venture company with Italtel, it formed an alliance with the US Scientific Atlanta and Sun Microsystems to develop a design or architecture for multimedia networks for the emerging multimedia market in 1994. Siemens had already developed the basic multimedia software, called IMMXpress (Cane, 1994, p. 24).

Overall, Ericsson and Nokia successfully expanded their market shares in mobile communications equipment markets, while, at the same time, entering into data communication markets in the first stage of competition. Alcatel and Siemens turned inward to complete their restructuring attempts and shifted their focus to mobile communications and data equipment markets. This new business strategy of the largest two firms hinted at the intensification of market competition that was soon to come.

6.1.3.2. Intense Competition and Prosperity: 1996–1997

After the big players turned their attention to mobile and data communication equipment in the second half of the 1990s, competition became intense. Swedish Ericsson and American Cisco Systems were the market leaders in these two segments respectively. Steep growth in mobile and data communications traffic and, hence, in revenues, attracted manufacturers that had no significant business in these areas in the mid-1990s. With the increasing intensity of competition, firms followed similar business strategies, i.e. alliances and cooperative agreements with American and Japanese firms.

To rectify the grave mistake of cutting back research and development spending to so-called broadband technology that was carried out in the first half of the 1990s, Ericsson made an agreement with US-based Bay Networks to sell the latter's full range of data communications products in 1997 ("Ericsson Deal," 1997, p. 11). Similarly, Nokia signed a deal with Computer Sciences Corporation, a leading US information technology group. The global alliance would provide customers for Nokia's telecoms products, which included the world's largest fixed and mobile telecoms operators, with the information systems necessary to underpin the rapid introduction of new and innovative services (Cane, 1998a, p. 36). Nokia also launched the Nokia 9000 in August 1996, a new 'personal communicator' device that combined a telephone, personal organizer, notepad and built-in messaging, e-mail and Internet connections (Carnegy, 1996b, p. 11).

In March 1996, to catch up with Nokia and Ericsson, Alcatel formed a partnership with Sharp, the Japanese electronics group, for the development of the next generation of portable telephones (Jack, 1996, p. 30). In response to the rapid convergence of voice, data and video traffic, which reflected a demand from customers for a single access point to telecommunications networks, Alcatel also made an agreement with Cisco Systems, for developing the equipment through which users access telecommunications networks, as well as the wider networks, themselves. The main goal for Alcatel was to again access to Cisco Systems' expertise in this new area, since the latter was dominating the market for the routers that controlled traffic on the Internet (Waters, 1997, p. 22).

Siemens and GEC were latecomers in that they were busy restructuring themselves. For instance, Siemens sold its high-performance printing division in 1996 in addition to its TV network, defense electronics activities, and dental equipment business, as part of an attempt to be ready for the liberalization of the German telecommunications market in 1998 (Studemann, 1997, p. 26). As well as organizational restructuring, GEC sold its GEC-Plessey Semiconductors (Wagstyl, 1998, p. 21).

In addition to the existing firms' growing attention to mobile communications equipment, the high growth rates in mobile and data communications markets attracted new entrants. For instance, Philips launched a cell phone joint venture with Lucent Technologies of the US to reap the benefits of the growing demand for mobile phones (Baker & Echikson, 1998, p. 26). In summary, major firms narrowed their activities and focused on mobile and data communications markets between 1996 and 1997. Market competition was intense, but not yet, destructive. Cooperation agreements were the dominant approach to catching up with the market leaders.

6.1.3.3. Destructive Competition and Crisis: 1998–2000

Market competition became destructive between 1998 and 2000 for several reasons. Major equipment producers wanted to become major players to cash in on the sharp rise in global wireless and Internet traffic. As Graph 6.4 below indicates, global mobile cellular and Internet subscribers doubled in number between 1996 and 2002. Deteriorating profit margins also heightened the intensity of competition and forced competitors to speed up their efforts to move into mobile and data communication equipment markets. Given that traditional telecommunications equipment manufacturers did not have enough time and technology, especially to produce data communications equipment, they opted for acquiring American start-ups, in the main, between 1998 and 2000, while divesting their 'non-core' businesses. Nevertheless, there were some variations between firms, depending on their business history and strategy.

For instance, Ericsson bought American start-ups such as Advanced Computer Communication, Torrent Networking Technologies and the telecommunications infrastructure business of US-based Qualcomm (Cane, 1999a, p. 8). Moreover, it set up a joint venture company with Microsoft in December 1999 to collaborate on developing software for the wireless Internet, besides signing a licensing agreement with Sun Microsystems to use the latter's Java computer programming language as a platform for the development of its 'third generation' cellular handsets (Taylor, 1999, p. 1; "Ericsson in Java Deal," 1998, p. 22). Ericsson also sped up its efforts to develop the so-called Third Generation (3G) mobile phone infrastructure equipment (Reed, 2000, p. 48).

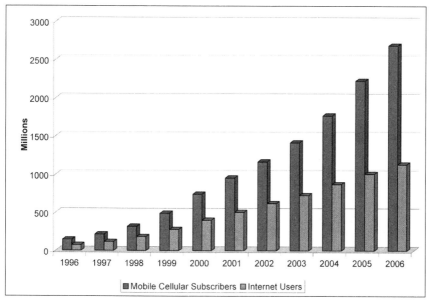

Graph 6.3 Number of global mobile cellular and internet subscribers.[7]

Similarly, Siemens acquired Argon Networks, Castle Networks, an equity stake in Accelerated Networks, and a new company, Unisphere Solutions, between 1998 and 2000, while expanding its joint venture with 3Com, a Silicon Valley networking powerhouse (Baker, 1999, p. 20). In its attempt to strengthen its mobile communications business, Siemens also bought Robert Bosch's mobile phone interests in addition to the wireless technology and systems activities of Italtel (Simonian, 1999, p. 11; Betts, 2000, p. 18). After a series of acquisitions, Siemens consolidated its strategy of making the Internet mobile and formed a new division, called the Information and Communications (IC) division, in April 2000 by bringing its Business Services together with IC Networks and IC Mobile divisions (Daniel, 2000, p. 10).

Alcatel followed a similar business strategy, but went even further than Siemens. Stiff market competition and the economic stagnation of 1998 put heavy pressure on the firm to become a specialized telecommunications equipment maker with an emphasis on transmission equipment. In implementing its new business strategy of expanding into data-networking equipment, Alcatel followed the trend and acquired a number of firms between 1998 and 2000 (Crawford & Owen, 2000a, p. 30). Overall, Alcatel spent more on acquisitions compared to its European counterparts.

Nokia's business strategy was somewhat different. Instead of competing with the North American giants head-to-head in the data communications market, it decided to carve out a wireless niche and build up a software portfolio in mobile systems with two consistent business strategies. The first was to collaborate with the leading American firms to develop new software for mobile phones, and the second was to develop the company's skills through internal growth, while acquiring small firms that fit Nokia's new strategy, if necessary (Cane, 2000a, p. 15; Larsen, 2000, p. 23; Burt, 1999, p. 24). Offering new innovative products, such as the world's first 'lap phone' with Internet browsing and imaging functions in the summer of 1999, boosted Nokia's market, which increased from 28 percent in 1999 to 30 percent in 2000 (Brown-Humes, 2000, p. 27).

GEC carried out the most dramatic transformation. After buying a 40 percent stake in GPT from Siemens in 1998, GEC concentrated on its core defense, aerospace and US industrial electronics businesses (Cane, 1999b, p. 24). GEC's Marconi Communications owned impressive technology such as wave division multiplexing, which was essential for Internet data traffic, but its product portfolio was not complete and it was weak in wireless networking systems ("GEC," 1999, p. 4). Accordingly, it acquired the very costly American Reltec Corp and Fore Systems and expanded into the wireless telecommunications business as well (Bogler, 1999, p. 23; Cane, 2000b, p. 21). After changing its name to Marconi in October 2000, the radical transformation was complete, but it was too late (Cane, 2000c, p. 23).

A detailed description of the business strategies of the leading European telecommunications equipment producers made it clear that destructive competition, as a consequence of declining profit rates in the relevant market after 1998, worked as a mechanism to discipline and force firms to follow similar business strategies to restore profitability. The merger and acquisition frenzy by the dominant firms in the late 1990s was part of their business strategy of entering into newly opened mobile and data communications markets to improve their profitability.

6.1.3.4. *Waning Competition and Depression: 2001–2004*

Expensive acquisitions purchased during the stock market peak deteriorated the financial situation of the incumbents as well as the new entrants, pushing financially fragile players into bankruptcy, when the telecommunications bubble burst in 2001. Destructive competition resulted in the eruption of the crisis. Demand for telecommunications equipment declined whereas supply increased, which depressed profit margins mainly because European clients were impoverished after paying hefty third generation mobile communication (3G) spectrum fees to the states. For instance, the British state earned $35.3 billion from five licenses, while its German counterpart collected $45.8 billion from six licenses ("Equipment Lex," 2000, p. 24).

The world economy was slowing down as well. Firms were competing with each other destructively to restore profitability, paradoxically depressing their products' prices and, hence, their profit margins. The crisis that initially emerged in the US market hit the European firms in varying degrees, depending on their amount of exposure to the US market and areas of specialization (Roberts, 2001, p. 30; "Alcatel Lex," 2001, p. 22). The financial sector, in turn, became reluctant to lend to the telecommunications industry immediately by mid-2000. The share and asset prices of these telecommunications equipment producers and operators collapsed. Between 2001 and 2004, the telecommunications equipment producers sold many of their businesses, shed thousands of their workers, closed plants and outsourced their production.

The only European telecommunications equipment firm that went bankrupt was Marconi or the former GEC. The severe crisis in the telecommunications industry hit Marconi toward the end of the summer 2000. Deteriorating conditions in the telecommunications market because of declining demand and intense competition led to a 22 percent fall in its sales and, therefore, a sharp rise in its net debt in early 2002. Marconi was losing market share very fast (Hunt, 2002a, p. 19). To increase its cash flow, it tried to sell its 'non-core assets' (Hunt & Kapner, 2002, p. 21). Low asset prices meant that the firm could not raise enough cash to reduce its debt or to finance its day-to-day operations. Job cutting was another leg of Marconi's business strategy to reduce operating costs and working capital, but it was not successful in escaping bankruptcy in 2002 ("Marconi to Cut," 2002, p. 1; Hunt, 2002b, p. 21).

Ericsson revealed that it would lose $1.6 billion on mobile phones in 2000, while its arch-rival Nokia was making a profit (George, 2000a, p. 21). A glut in the handset market as well as the decision by telecommunications operators to delay the rollout of new third-generation services worsened Ericsson's profitability problem (George, 2000b, p. 34). Laying off 20,000 workers in 2001, ceasing handset production at sites in Sweden and the US, and subcontracting the task of actual production to contract-manufacturing Flextronics International in Singapore, were part of the general business strategy of cutting cash outflow. In addition, Ericsson established a London-based equally owned joint venture company, SonyEricsson Mobile Communications, with Japanese Sony in 2001 for developing and producing 3G or multimedia phones (Brown-Humes, 2001, p. 26). Disposal of a large part of its stake in Juniper Networks, the US maker of high-speed Internet routers, provided financing for product development and research in third generation mobile communications (Brown-Humes & Waters, 2000, p. 34). Overall, Ericsson's specialization in telecommunications made it vulnerable to the economic slowdown.

Siemens' conglomerate structure, with products ranging from power turbines to light bulbs, had a smoothing effect on its profits, as the range of products were subject to different economic cycles (Benoit, 2001a, p. 29). Nevertheless, it was not immune to the crisis that pushed Siemens' margins in network and mobile businesses down in the summer of 2000 ("He's Putting," 2002, p. 16B). As a response to the falling demand in mobile handsets, Siemens, the world's fourth-largest producer of mobile phones in 2001, shut down four handset production plants in April 2001, withdrawing totally from mobile phone production in October 2005 ("No One Said," 2005; "Simenes to Cut," 2001, p. 25). Siemens also cut employment by more than 10,000, sold its US subsidiary Unisphere Networks and unloaded seven non-core businesses (Barber, Benoit & Calusen, 2002, p. 31; Benoit, 2001b, p. 20). Overall, Siemens also implemented similar measures in response to the crisis.

Alcatel, like its peers, sold or reduced its holdings to concentrate on third generation wireless infrastructure (Minder, 2002, p. 26). Along with cutting its workforce by 10,000, Alcatel scaled down its undersea-cable and optical-fiber operations in the US, France, Britain and Australia, and outsourced the manufacturing of its European-standard mobile handsets to Flextronics International of Singapore (Arnold, 2002a, p. 28; Mallet, 2001, p. 26). It also formed a joint venture company with Japan's Fujitsu in mobile communications systems in an attempt to strengthen its position in markets for third-generation phones (Nakamoto & Owen, 2000, p. 33). Briefly, Alcatel, similar to Ericsson, initiated a series of measures to cut costs and clean its balance sheet, actions essential for avoiding bankruptcy.

The crisis in the telecommunications industry also hit Nokia in the summer of 2000 (George, 2000c, p. 32). Competition was destructive for the reason that Siemens, Samsung and Motorola each brought new mobile handset models to the market, while demand for this product declined (Baker, Resch & Crockett, 2000, p. 42). In March 2001, Nokia cut its costs by outsourcing more of its network infrastructure manufacturing business to SCI Systems of the US (Brown-Humes & Heavens, 2001, p. 36). Finally, it bought the US concerns Ramp Networks and Amber Networks to strengthen its capacity to supply data over the mobile network. Taken as a whole, Nokia was one of few telecommunications equipment makers that not only survived the crisis successfully, but also benefited from it by increasing its market share in Europe to 50 percent and to 36 percent in the world by the end of 2002 (Brown-Humes, Budden, & Gowers, 2002, p. 21).

In sum, the downturn in telecommunications affected market players in varying degrees. Depending on the decline of their profitability, the firms undertook a number of measures to restore their profit margins. Common to all of them was the sale of 'non-core' businesses, reducing the number of employees, and re-focusing their business strategies to profitable areas, reminiscent of the depression in 1991 and 1992. In other words, internal and external dimensions of restructuring were essential for understanding the dynamics of market competition. Is it possible to observe similar trends in the telecommunications services markets as well?

6.2. EU TELECOMMUNICATIONS
SERVICES MARKET ANALYSIS

This section analyzes the impact of deregulation, liberalization and privatization policies on the EU telecommunications services market. The findings are not as conclusive as the ones for the equipment market due to the recent completion of full liberalization of the market. Nevertheless, three general trends can be observed. For one, the concerned markets remained concentrated, despite the entrance of many new competitors. European telecommunications services firms have stabilized prices and prices have shown upward trends in some countries recently, in contrast to expectations of further price cuts. Large business users benefited from price drops most. Complaints increased about service quality, and job loss in the industry rose significantly.

The focus in this section is on three main European telecommunications operators—British Telecom (BT), Deutsche Telekom (DT) and France Telecom (FT)—around which the European telecommunications services market analysis is carried out. The first section summarizes the structural characteristics of the market, followed by an analysis of market competition between 1993 and 2004 in the second section.

6.2.1. The Structural Characteristics of the Services Market

The structure of the telecommunications services market was different from that of the equipment market. A stated-owned telecommunications operator (PTO) or Posts, Telephones and Telegraphs (PTT) operated as a monopoly in each member country in the EC before 1980. With the exception of the UK and Finland, many of the member states, including France and Germany, for example, opened their markets to competition only in the 1990s. The holdings of the state-owned monopolies included comprehensive national telecommunications networks that had largely been paid for by public funds and modernized in the 1980s ("The Short Arm," 1997, p. 14). Their networks included the latest digital technology in public exchanges and fiber optic transmission cables in backbone networks.

Comprehensive and already paid networks gave the former national monopolies such as BT, DT and FT several advantages over their competitors. As vertically integrated firms with the capability to offer multiple services, the incumbents had enormous amounts of cash flow and could control the pricing ability of their new competitors through interconnection fees, and finally by obstructing their competitors' traffic on their networks because of their knowledge of the networks. The former monopolies had extensive customer information, collected over many years, plus years of market experience, even if they did not compete (Price, 1997, p. 12; "Ready . . . Steady," 1997, p. 5; Edmondson et al., 1995, p. 20). Besides, they each had a well-recognized brand in the market and strong brand loyalty ("To

Keep on," 1995, p. 25). Furthermore, they had long years of experience in the industry, especially in establishing and maintaining telecommunications infrastructure ("Surviving," 1998, p. 13). They also had easy access to scarce resources, such as spectrum, property and public finance in difficult times because they were still owned by the member states with the exception of a few cases (Manner, 2002, p. 134). Finally, strong connections between the former telephone monopolies and the member states due to ownership and historical ties played a significant role in gradual market liberalization ("The Short Arm," 1997, p. 14).

This does not mean that new competitors did not have any advantages. First, they started without the legacy of established networks and inefficiencies. They could design their systems to easily meet the fast-changing pattern of demand for low-cost wireless, data services and bandwidth ("In the Shark Pond," 1998, p. 59). Second, their costs were minimal, as their new networks had the latest technology and were cheaper to run compared to the old networks of the former monopolists. Nevertheless, new entrants preferred to share the incumbents' networks rather than build their own in most cases. Third, they did not have any solidified bureaucratic institutional structures, slow decision-making mechanisms or risk-averse shareholders. Instead, they had an entrepreneurial spirit with a market-focused culture. Finally, they did not have unions to placate and their sales force was slim. In all these respects, they differed from the established firms ("Surviving," 1998, p. 13; "Ready . . . Steady," 1997, p. 5). Despite their competitive strengths, they could not compete head-to-head with the incumbents. EU-wide reforms in the services markets started in the early 1990s and therefore market analysis is limited to the period between 1993 and 2004 in the next section.

6.2.2. The Period of Bubble and Burst: 1993–2004

The EU issued the first services liberalization directive in 1991, but it was not the last one. The acceleration of market deregulation and liberalization at the EU, as well as at the national levels in the early 1990s, created the impetus for the incumbents to adapt themselves to competitive pressures as well as to protect their home markets against new entrants. Moreover, the sudden economic slowdown in 1992–3 forced the former monopolies to restore their profit margins, while liberalization gave them the freedom to expand into new geographic and product markets (Fransman, 2002). Privatization provided them with the financial sources they needed in the 1990s for growth.

6.2.2.1. Increasing Competition and Exaltation: 1993–1995

Due to the economic recovery after the slowdown in 1992–93, market competition was less intense, but continued to increase until 1995.

Gradual liberalization was not touching the core markets of the dominant operators, at least not until the second half of the 1990s, except in the UK and Finland. Despite the fact that the British government brought its duopoly policy to the telecommunications services market in the first half of the 1990s, BT and Cable & Wireless (C&W), Mercury's parent company, persuaded the government not to grant licenses to others immediately (Dixon, 1992, p. 9).

BT concentrated on the core business of providing telecommunications services after withdrawing from the office and telecommunications equipment markets. BT and C&W became a global company by taking advantage of liberalization around the world to make up the loss of their domestic market shares through EU services liberalization directives in the 1990s (Leadbeater, 1990, p. 8). Similarly, DT repositioned itself in many areas to achieve three strategic objectives: safeguarding key business activities, offering new services such as in multimedia, and internationalization (Sommer, 1995, p. 39). Influenced by similar developments, FT had two aims: defending its local loop dominance and expanding into high growth/high margin businesses (such as wireless and value-added network services) outside France to replace the inevitable loss of revenue in its increasingly competitive domestic market (Taylor, 1996a, p. 15). Gradual EU deregulation policy forced the dominant firms to follow similar strategies.

In anticipating increasing competition, BT, DT and FT expanded geographically not only in Europe, but also in international markets through acquisitions, joint ventures and cooperation agreements. For instance, in June 1993, BT decided to take a 20 percent stake in MCI, the second-largest US international carrier, and set up a joint venture company with it to exploit the fast-growing market for multinational companies in international voice and data transmission services (Adonis & Tait, 1993, p. 1). As part of a further push into Europe's liberalizing telecommunications market, BT formed a joint venture company with Grupo Santander in September 1993 to sell data communications services in Spain (Adonis, 1993a, p. 28). BT also boosted its international ambitions by signing a partnership agreement with three of Scandinavia's four national telecommunications operators, including Norwegian Telecom, Telecom Finland and Tele Danmark, in September 1994 (Adonis, 1994c, p. 21).

Establishing a joint venture company in Germany, called Viag Interkom with the German industrial group Viag to provide data services and intra-company private voice and data networks, was another major step for BT, in addition to forming Albacom, an alliance with Banca Nazionale del Lavoro, to offer similar types of services to the largest firms in Europe (Cane, 1995b, p. 3). Finally, BT formed a strategic alliance with the French utility, Compagnie Générale des Eaux, and acquired a 25 percent stake in Cegetel, CGE's telecommunications subsidiary, offering a range of fixed and mobile services in France (Cane & Owen, 1996a, p. 1).

DT followed a comparable path with FT, a strong partner. In December 1993, DT and FT extended their existing Eunetcom alliance further by building a European 'backbone' network offering multinational companies enhanced services, including data services and value-added business services (Adonis, 1993b, p. 23). Their alliance was largely defensive, stemming from the fear that BT and AT&T could erode their monopoly bases in Germany and France respectively. DT and FT planned to withstand stiff competition by forming a united front ("Euro Telecom," 1993, p. 23). In their effort to expand geographically, they bought a 20 percent stake in Sprint, thus establishing a joint venture company with the third-biggest US international carrier. Indeed, they aimed to carve out a leading share in the market that targeted the outsourcing telecommunications needs of multinational companies (Adonis & Dickson, 1994, p. 31).

FT and DT formed their European joint venture, known as Atlas. The tie-up of Atlas with Sprint—known as Phoenix (became Global One in 1996)—offered corporate clients around the world a new range of services through a single global network (Lindemann, 1996a, p. 27; Jackson & Cane, 1995, p. 22). Besides its activities with FT, DT expanded internationally by acquiring stakes in developing countries (Lindemann, 1996b, p. 29). FT followed a similar strategy of international expansion by acquiring shareholdings of telephone companies in Argentina, Mexico, Czechoslovakia, Poland, the UK and the US (Williamson, 1991b, p. 26). FT also formed a joint venture company with US West to sell mass-market electronic information services (Ridding & Kehoe, 1994, p. 32).

In general, the former monopolies expanded in international markets through acquisitions to make up for losses in their respective domestic markets from increasing competition. The true intention behind the joint ventures and alliances, nevertheless, was to defend their growing home markets, as Cane (1995c) observed:

> Much of what is happening in telecoms today is *preparation for that inevitable squeeze on profits*. The big operators are seeking to protect their home markets while finding ways into new markets—chiefly through their alliances. They are also hoping to stimulate demand for new services to offset declines in revenues from traditional telephony. (p. 15, italics added)

The alliances and joint ventures that became so popular in the first half of the 1990s were defensive, as well as offensive, in motivation (Adonis, 1994d, p. 13). This brief account of market competition reveals the fact that the European Commission's analysis of market competition in the early 1990s was partial in that it underestimated the main motivation behind the alliances, as Chapter 5 demonstrated. The incumbents, in fact, joined forces to form defensive cartels and protect their home markets from new entrants, while agreeing not to enter each other's markets.

6.2.2.2. Intense Competition and Prosperity: 1996–1997

Liberalization of the markets, the ready availability and falling cost of new technologies, and rapidly growing data traffic with the Internet attracted new entrants in the mid-1990s. The date set for the full liberalization of the services market in January 1998 was approaching fast as well. These three factors accelerated market competition. The dominant firms in general, and BT, DT as well as FT in particular, deployed three main strategies. While the first was offering new and innovative products, the second was defensive pricing to deter entry (Cane, 1995c, p. 15). Finally, they deployed 'dirty tricks' such as blocking their competitors' business by deliberately disconnecting their networks or tarnishing their public image by providing misinformation.

As for the first strategy of offering new and better services, DT expanded its agreement with Netscape, the US Internet software group, for the distribution, marketing and system integration of Intranet and Extranet solutions in February 1997. DT's T-Online unit had about 1.4 million subscribers after a 40 percent increase in growth in 1996, making T-Online the largest European Internet access provider ("New Telekom, 1997, p. 22). DT also launched a 'VIP' service for high-spending private customers in March 1997. The aim was to protect DT's market share against encroachment by new competitors, once the country's public service telecommunications market opened up for competition (Atkins, 1997, p. 25).

FT also offered new services to protect its core market segments in the second period. One part of the overall strategy was revealing in January 1996 that it would launch itself fully on the Internet and revitalize its Minitel telephone-based information service that dated back to the early 1980s. From March 1996, FT provided access to the Internet from anywhere in France for the cost of a local telephone call. It would also provide its own services on the Internet through a new subsidiary (Buchan, 1996, p. 2). To fight against its competitors in the mobile communications market segment, FT launched a package called Declic at the start of May 1996 (Owen, 1996, p. 31).

Likewise, BT set up a global public server service in partnership with Hewlett Packard in 1996. Instead of building a wide area network independently, multinational corporations would be able to support business processes using BT's global network to integrate with suppliers and customers around the world, using applications located on public servers (Newing, 1996, p. 18). BT also launched a virtual private network (VPN) service in Hong Kong in 1997 (Lucas, 1997, p. 26). Together with British Sky Broadcasting (BSkyB), Midland Bank, and Matsushita Electric, BT decided to form a new company, British Interactive Broadcasting (BIB) in July 1997 to offer interactive services such as shopping, banking, holiday booking, education, computer games, and Internet access in 1998 (Stewart, 1997, p. 6). In short, offering new services and bundling them helped the incumbents keep their customers, while attracting new ones.

Pricing, which was 'harmful' for all competitors as it was eating up profit margins, was a deadly weapon in the arsenals of the big three during the phase of increasing market competition, although it worked like a double-edged sword. The incumbents did not use pricing for offensive purposes at this stage of competition, since it would hurt their profit margins. On the contrary, being a significant tool for all players, pricing was pre-emptive and defensive. In August 1996, BT cut the prices of its high-speed data service, ISDN2, which was designed to appeal to small and medium sized-businesses or branch offices of larger organizations. This move came just before a number of the UK's cable operators entered the ISDN (integrated services digital network) market. ISDN was a high-speed service in which information—voice, data and images—was transmitted in digital form (Cane, 1996a, p. 8).

Likewise, DT used its market power in local phone services to increase local call prices in the process of compensating for its losses on international calls where it was facing stiff competition (Lindemann, 1996c, p. 2). The 1996 tariff reform sought to offset big cuts in long-distance rates by raising charges for some local calls, as mentioned above. DT gave high discounts (up to 43 percent) to corporate customers in 1997. DT's new German competitors, Thyssen, Viag, and Mannesmann, brought the aggressive price cuts to the European Commission's attention. Wolfgang Botsch, then Germany's minister for Post and Telecommunications, and a senior DT executive went to Brussels in October 1996 to lobby Karel Van Miert, then competition commissioner, not to do anything that might delay the introduction of discounts that DT had planned to offer to its corporate clients as of November 1, 1997. Any cut in the discounts would upset the sales and profit forecast made by DT, just weeks away from its partial privatization. Van Miert was under pressure and did not have any other choice but to accept DT's plan with some conditions ("Brussels Clears," 1996, p. 2).

Likewise, FT deployed its deadly weapon, price manipulation, to protect its core markets against new entrants, just prior to the full liberalization of the telecommunications services market in January 1998. Initially, FT raised line rentals, while cutting international call charges in early March 1996 (Cane, 1996b, p. 2). Then, in July 1996, it reduced national and international telephone call prices by 13 percent—the second reduction since the start of 1996. In March, 1997, it raised its standard monthly telephone subscription price by 28 percent again, besides cutting the cost of national and international calls several times in 1997 (Owen, 1997, p. 38). Finally, like its British and German counterparts, FT attempted to pre-empt the effects of full liberalization in advance by reducing its fixed-line charges three times in 1996–97, which resulted in steep cuts in international and national long-distance call rates over this period. The new pricing benefited businesses at the expense of residential users. Aggressive price-cutting by the big three was a defensive tactic used to deter entry to their core markets.

The last strategy employed by the big three was to use 'dirty tricks' to harm their competitors. For instance, BT misled customers about its rivals, according to a report prepared for *Which?,* the British Consumers' Association magazine. Researchers, who made twenty-three telephone inquiries and three personal visits to BT, received advice ranging from misleading to incorrect (Taylor, 1996b, p. 7). Additionally, BT Cellnet, a subsidiary of BT, restricted free access to the Internet, by reprogramming its most recent mobile handset to prevent customers from selecting a rival Internet portal (Roberts, 2000a, p. 1). Similarly, DT tried to worry quality-conscious Germans about the newcomers' technical standards by spreading false information about its competitors. Aiming to protect its core markets, DT, like BT, disseminated misleading and false information about its competitors in desperation ("Deutsche Telekom," 1998, p. 68). This shows that market competition was not limited to price competition or product competition. Sabotage was a dominant feature, especially in times of intense competition.

Taken as a whole, dominant market players offered new and improved services to their customers, cut some prices while increasing others as a pre-emptive measure, and used dirty tricks to defend their central markets from new entrants. Their historical ties with the member states were a positive asset. They were successful, to some extent, but they were unable to deter all new entrants.

6.2.2.3. Destructive Competition and Crisis: 1998–2000

After the full liberalization of the European telecommunications industry in 1998, the telecommunications service providers enjoyed a successful year, as the overall size of the European market grew at about 8 percent a year. Their success was fuelled by the explosive growth of mobile, Internet and other data services as an effect of declining prices. One of the main problems for the incumbents was the rate at which they were losing market share (McCartney, 1999, p. 13). New entrants had an unexpected effect of stimulating demand by sharply reducing prices, thus, triggering competition. Technological innovations also helped reduce costs. Investment in packet-switching technologies cut operators' cost bases by 80 to 90 percent and triggered a fundamental shift (Cane, 1999c, p. 32). Many operators had to rethink their strategies seriously, as the wholesale price of bandwidth continued to tumble at alarming rates of up to 60 percent a year on competitive routes (Parkes, 2000, p. 6). The negative outcome of more efficient technologies was excess capacity.

Two prevalent strategies for the leading firms during this stage of competition were aggressive mergers and acquisitions, and price cuts with the purpose of maintaining their market share. Failing to acquire MCI Communications, BT formed a wide-reaching international joint venture with AT&T in 1998 to provide seamless, one-stop shopping for all the telecommunications needs of multinational companies in key markets around the world (Cane, 1998b, p. 19). In September 1999, BT and AT&T agreed on a strategic alliance to link their wireless telecommunications businesses, spanning 150 countries worldwide, in response to British carrier Vodafone's acquisition of Airtouch, the biggest purely wireless operator in the US (Waters & Taylor, 1999, p. 1). BT also made a number of acquisitions around the world, as part of the general strategy of concentrating on the fast-moving, high-growth areas of mobile, Internet and data communications (Cane, 1999d, p. 22; Cane, 1999e, p. 22).

In a similar way, DT planned to reinvent itself as a *Systemhaus*. It would sell multimedia and electronic commerce and build an impressive business as an Internet service provider between 1998 and 2000 ("Deutsche Telekom," 1998, p. 68). In April 1999, DT initiated negotiations to merge with Telecom Italia, the former Italian national telecommunications monopoly ("Telecoms Groups," 1999, p. 23). However, it lost Telecom Italia to Olivetti, the Italian personal computer and office equipment maker, in May 1999, owing to the Italian state's implicit policy of protecting its national telecommunications operator from foreign ownership. In the process, DT alienated relations with FT, and its key alliance with FT and Sprint, Global One, imploded in September 1999 (Edmondson et al., 1999, p. 26). In addition to acquiring one British and two American mobile phone operators (One-2-One, Voice-Stream and Powertel), DT bought mobile communications stakes in Croatia, Austria, Poland, Hungary, Russia, and the Czech Republic (Benoit, 2000a, p. 21). Finally, DT pushed itself into the global information technology services industry with its acquisition of DaimlerChrysler's IT arm, Debis Systemhaus (Benoit & Waters, 2000, p. 34).

After DT had breached the contract between them, FT gave up its collaborative efforts with DT, deciding to move forward internationally on its own, with a special focus on European markets. Similar to its peers, FT adopted a strategy of becoming an international player with a concentration on wireless, data and the Internet in the new century (Owen, 2000a, p. 38). Accordingly, it purchased stakes in mobile communications, cable and network firms located mainly in Europe. (Roberts, 2000b, p. 25; Barket, 2000, p. 27). The rationale behind FT's strategic move was to offset the declining profits from French fixed-line services by growing in new areas, especially in mobile communications in France and international expansion (Owen, 2000b, p. 34).

Besides geographical expansion, pricing played a crucial role in this period of destructive competition. It was the last weapon firms could use against one another to protect their markets and gain market share. For example, in September 1999, BT cut call charges for residential customers in response to intense competition from cable communications groups and mobile phone operators. In an attempt to raise its UK Internet market share, it also slashed subscription charges in March 2000 (Cane, 2000d, p. 4).

Germany's telephone price war escalated, as new competitors to DT unveiled tariff rates pitched at snatching market share from the former monopoly carrier. In June 1998, DT's mobile telephone subsidiary cut the price of calls to a specified area by up to 64 percent. In response, Mannesmann D2 declared that some of its rates would fall by up to 30 percent. A week before this announcement, E-Plus, the mobile telephone sister company to O.tel.o., announced price reductions up to 67 percent for specified calls. After this move, DT considered further tariff cutbacks in fixed-net and mobile services. Mannesmann Arcor, the fixed-line business operated by Mannesmann, observed the market closely and dropped its rates accordingly (Atkins, 1998, p. 16). In January 1999, DT lowered its long-distance prices by up to 62 percent, besides cutting its mobile telephony service charges considerably (Atkins, 1999a, p. 30). Finally, DT slashed prices for its Internet services substantially in October 1999 in an attempt to head off an aggressive pricing challenge from AOL Europe (Atkins, 1999b, p, 44).

FT followed the pace and cut the price of long-distance and international phone calls for the third time in two years in February 1999 by reducing the price of international calls by 10 percent on average and rates for long-distance national calls by 12 percent from March 1999. The chief beneficiaries of FT's reductions, however, were its business customers because FT increased residential subscription charges by 15 percent, as it rebalanced income from calls and line rentals (Owen, 1999, p. 32).

The three incumbents (BT, DT and FT) not only weathered the storm with less damage than expected, but they also became one of the main beneficiaries of increasing Internet usage (Benoit, 2000b, p. 15). The acquisitions, falling prices in core voice telephony, heavy investments on networks and expensive third-generation mobile phone licenses augmented the debt burden, and aggravated the problem of profitability, as Graph 6.4 (below) illustrates. BT's debt soared from almost nil to an estimated £28 billion as investment spending stretched the balance sheet between late 1999 and August 2000 (Ratner & Roberts, 2000, p. 20). FT spent €88 billion on acquisitions between 1999 and 2000 and owed around €60 billion (Johnson, 2002, p. 25; "Telecommunications Lex," 2001, p. 20). In a similar way, DT's debt mountain was standing around €67.2 billion thanks to its acquisitions and investments in third-generation mobile communications. On the whole, price cuts, acquisitions and huge piles of debt meant a crisis of profitability. The average rate of return for the big three went down from around 7 percent in 1998 to approximately -5 percent at the end of 2000.

Toward the end of 2000, the telecommunications industry faced a liquidity crisis. The debt burden on the big three was increasing for four reasons: a mounting interest bill, a sharp decline in their share prices, a sharp increase in borrowing as they were forced to honor agreements to buy shares in subsidiaries or partners, and weak equity markets that prevented them from selling their non-core assets (Van Duyn, 2002, p.

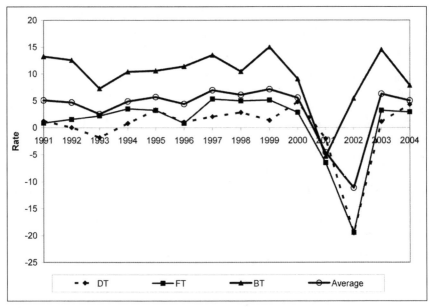

Graph 6.4 Net rate of return on total assets, BT, DT, and FT: 1991–2004[8]

21). A sharp market correction in share prices in 2001 and 2002 suddenly increased their borrowing costs, while halting their acquisitions.

The banking industry was nervous about the dismal situation (Roberts & Van Duyn, 2000, p. 34). The weakest link in the chain was the syndicated loan market ("Lex Column," 2000, p. 24). Given that many upstarts and several old players could not find enough credit, the result was bankruptcy. The number of bankruptcies in the telecommunications industry in the OECD went up from less than three on average in 2000 to 30 by 2002, surpassing all other industries by 20 (OECD, 2003, p. 124). Bankruptcies did not mean that failed firms were inefficient or did not have new technology. The root problem was that the financial sector suddenly stopped its lending activities to the industry after realizing that the promising profit margins could not be realized, even though these bankrupt firms had networks based on the latest available technology on the market.

6.2.2.4. Waning Competition and Depression: 2001–2004

When the telecommunications industry entered into crisis, it faced two major problems: overcapacity and high levels of debt, both of which hurt the profitability of firms. Former national monopolies (such as BT, FT, and DT) were sure that their governments would stand behind them, despite their mountainous debt pile. For instance, thanks to a reckless acquisition spree during the peak of a business cycle, FT ran up debts of more than €70 billion that it was struggling to service. Without access to government funds, FT would have faced default by June 2003, because it would have only €6 billion in cash at the end of 2002, while facing repayments of €4.8 billion in the first quarter of 2003, and €3 billion in the second quarter (Johnson, 2002a, p. 30).

To avoid an impending cash crunch, given that €15 billion of that debt would be maturing early in 2003, FT turned to an obliging state to bail it out of a mess that many other countries would have solved by demanding that the company make drastic divestitures—and possibly forcing it into bankruptcy. Francis Mer, former Finance Minister, said: "The state, as majority shareholder of France Telecom, will behave as a market investor and, if France Telecom has refinancing problems, appropriate measures of support will be taken" (Rudden, 2002, p. 8). The FT bailout was one of the largest government bailouts since that of Credit Lyonnais a decade ago (Johnson, 2002b, p. 25). Similarly, the German government rescued Mobilcom from bankruptcy with a €400 million-bailout scheme to save around 5,000 jobs (Benoit & Johnson, 2002, p. 12). In the UK, Energis, an upstart network operator, went under receivership in 2002, but it did not get any help from the British state (OECD, 2003, p. 16). These three episodes indicate variation in reaction to bankruptcies at the national level.

Dealing with debt became the number-one concern for many companies. Selling non-core assets, reducing employment and refocusing on high-growth mobile and data communications market segments were the three main strategies the firms followed in the aftermath of the crisis (George et al., 2001, p. 20). Against the bleak background in the telecommunications services market, DT had only one option: to refocus away from its fixed-network business towards mobile and Internet activities in 2000 (Harnischfeger, 2000, p. 20). Accordingly, DT disposed of a 10 percent stake in Sprint, the US long-distance telecommunications firm; a 24.5 percent stake in Wind, the Italian mobile phone operator; a 25 percent stake in mobile phone unit Satelindo; an 11 percent stake in Eutelsat, the Paris-based satellite operator; and its regional cable television companies (Wendlandt, 2002, p. 15; Harnishchfeger, 2001, p. 30; Enzweiler, Owen & Roberts, 2000, p. 24). DT also shed 10,000 jobs in May 2002 and announced plans to cut another 22,000 by 2005 (Benoit, 2003, p. 24).

With the purpose of sabotaging its competitors' business by deploying dirty tricks, DT found unconvincing excuses to delay the process of unbundling the local loop. According to Purton (2001): "These include not being able to find the door to an exchange, losing keys, not being able to find wiring and cabling plans, and even losing the high speed link needed to connect the local connections to the backbone network" (p. 5). Such excuses clearly illustrate that DT exercised its power accruing from the ownership of extensive networks. The timing of this exercise was also crucial in that new entrants were cash hungry. Aware of that fragile point, DT aggressively curtailed traffic from its competitors by postponing the process of connection or curtailing the flow of traffic from time to time.

Comparable to DT, BT decided to focus on domestic and Western European markets, concentrating on its mobile, retail and wholesale UK operations. Selling non-core assets, spinning off business units and retreating geographically indicated a clear reversal of the strategy it had been employing since the early 1990s (Barker & Budden, 2002, p. 24). In the new strategy, broadband Internet was at the center ("Stuck on Hold," 2000, p. 28). To reduce its debt pile, BT divested its aeronautical and maritime divisions, as well as its van fleet consisting of 58,000 vehicles, offices and telephone exchange buildings, and the Yell directories business. Selling a string of assets outside Europe was another solution for dire times (Roberts & Waters, 2001, p. 22).

Further, in October 2001, BT dismantled its joint venture company—Concert, established at the beginning of 2000 with AT&T—given the fact that Concert was experiencing huge losses. In other words, the cartel did not work in times of destructive competition, as the incumbents preferred to deal with their problems individually. This break-up marked BT's new strategy of retreating to a more limited and regional position (Waters & Roberts, 2001, p, 25). Additionally, BT cut DSL prices after most of its competitors had run out of capital and had given up trying to gain access to its local network in February 2002 (Arnold, Budden & Grance, 2002, p. 3). Finally, BT announced in 2001 that it would eliminate 13,000 jobs at BT Retail by 2003 (Milmo, 2001). More succinctly, BT successfully reinvented and repositioned itself in high-growth market segments during the depression.

The situation was not different in the case of FT in that divestment and job cuts were part of its business strategy as well. FT sold a number of its holdings (Arnold, 2002b, p. 23). After these divestments, FT, like BT, put broadband and mobile communications at the center of its new business strategy. This was the rationale behind buying minority shares in Orange (mobile communications operator) and Wanadoo (its Internet service provider), as well as integrating the latter into its main body in order to bundle VoIP services with fixed-line offerings. To complete its strategy, in 2003, FT cut 13,000 jobs and decided to shed another 15,000 positions by the end of 2004, reducing its total employment to around 202,500 (Johnson, 2004, p. 29).

The crisis in the telecommunications industry between 2001 and 2002 did not weaken the position of the incumbents due to their ownership of the 'last mile' of the network that runs into homes and offices. This 'local' monopoly gave them a firm grip on their customers and solid revenues or cash flows. As a result, the incumbents emerged from the crisis strong, healthy and nimble. BT, DT and FT, like other incumbents operating in competitive markets, engaged in comparable behavior and analogous market conduct during a crisis. Despite the variation among themselves, the average rate of return for the big three rose to 5.1 percent in 2004, down from -11.18 percent in 2002, showing the structural power of former monopolies. Market competition declined at this stage for two reasons. While the first was voluntary exits from the market in the absence of any attractive profit opportunities, the second was that firms tried to differentiate themselves from their competitors. Given the recent history of liberalization, the services markets were still not stable, but there were signs of stability as of 2005. The next section provides empirical evidence of these conditions.

6.3. POLICY EVALUATION

The common goal of EU competition and telecommunications policies was to create competitive equipment and services markets that, in turn, would offer cheaper and higher quality products and services to consumers, while creating more jobs. The first variable to check is whether the concerned policies achieved their stated objective. In the telecommunications equipment market, the number of major European players declined from 19 to four after two full cycles of market competition between 1980 and 2004, as Table 6.1 below shows. Instead of creating competitive European equipment markets, there was a shift from tight oligopolies at the national level to tight oligopolies at the European level. From a policy point of view, it is surprising, but if one recalls the aim of the model of effective competition, it is very natural in that effective competition is based on the idea of an oligopolistic market structure ensuring profitability of firms in dull and brisk times. This finding indicates the divergence between the stated and real policy goals.

With respect to the nature of competition in telecommunications services, few firms still dominated the market after eight years of full liberalization. For instance, there were only 11 firms controlling more than a 90 percent share in the fixed telephony market in the UK as of December 2005. The respective figures for Germany and France were nine and four (CEC, 2006, p. 12). These figures were not fully stable yet, but they indicate that the services markets are also becoming oligopolistic. As it is clear from Table 6.2, the incumbents still controlled more than half of the local, national long-distance and international markets in 2005. Nonetheless, their average market share in the local calls market declined from 82 percent in 2002 to 69 percent by 2005 in the EU 15. However, there was a significant variation at the individual country level. For instance, DT's market share, as the incumbent, declined from 95 percent to 56 percent. On the contrary, both FT and BT increased their market shares in 2005, after losing some between 2002 and 2004. This upward trend indicates that the incumbents started to control their environment at the local level.

Table 6.1 Industry Consolidation in the European Telecom Equipment Market[9]

1980	1985	1992	1998	2004
CGE-Alcatel	Alcatel	Alcatel	Alcatel	Alcatel
Thomson	ITT			
ITT	Telettra			
Ericsson	Ericsson	Ericsson		Ericsson
Thorn	Thorn			
MET (Matra)	MET (Matra)			
GEC	GEC	GEC	GEC/Marconi	
Plessey	Plessey	GPT		
Siemens	Siemens	Siemens	Siemens	Siemens
		Italtel		
Rolm (IBM)	Rolm (IBM)			
Nixdorf	Nixdorf			
Stromberg-C	GTE			
GTE	Italtel			
Italtel				
Bosch	Bosch	Bosch	Bosch	
Telenorma	Jeumont-Scheider			
ANT				
Jeumont-Scheider				
Nokia	Nokia	Nokia	Nokia	Nokia
Total: 19	Total: 16	Total: 8	Total: 7	Total: 4

In the national long-distance calls market, the incumbents' market share went down from 70 percent in 2002 to 63 percent in 2005. Both DT (from 65 to 57 percent) and BT (from 62 to 52 percent) lost significant market shares. In contrast, FT gained 1 percent market share in 2005, after losing 3 percent between 2002 and 2004. Compared to BT's (52 percent) and DT's (57 percent), FT's (68 percent) market share was higher

Table 6.2 Market Shares of the Incumbents in Fixed Telecommunications (%)[10]

Year	2002	2003	2004	2005
Local Calls				
EU15	82	77	71	69
DT	95	90	57	56
FT	83	81	79	80
BT	68	57	54	60
National Long-Distance Calls				
EU 15	70	67	65	63
Germany	65	62	59	57
France	70	69	67	68
United Kingdom	62	61	54	52
International Calls				
EU 15	62	60	55	52
Germany	59	57	40	39
France	68	69	66	67
United Kingdom	57	58	54	53

in 2005. The incumbents' market share in international calls decreased to 52 percent in 2005, indicating that their competitors attacked the most profitable market segments first, instead of taking the risk of investing in local loops. DT's market share dropped to a mere 39 percent that shows the existence of intense competition in the German market, in contrast to FT's market share of 67 percent. Interestingly, FT improved its market share by 1 percent between 2004 and 2005, paralleling what happened in the French local calls market.

Overall, the incumbents had more than 50 percent of the market share and not all competitors provided services in the national markets. These two facts signal that the services markets were oligopolistic and competition was still asymmetric by the end of 2005. One should be cautious about these conclusions for the reason that the services markets are still dynamic and volatile, as the market shares indicate. What is clear is that the decline in the incumbents' market shares became stable in most cases, and it is possible to see upward trends in a few of them. The next question to ask is: How did the market power translate into prices?

In some cases such as monthly fixed line rental fees, prices increased in real terms after the full liberalization of the telecommunications services

Table 6.3 Monthly Fixed Line Rental Fees (Deflated): 1998–2005[11]

Year	1998	1999	2000	2001	2002	2003	2004	2005
Residential (Including VAT)								
EU15 Weighted Average	12.06	12.48	12.47	13.04	13.45	13.41	14.08	13.82
UK	12.90	15.08	15.91	16.07	14.08	12.72	12.45	15.19
Germany	11.16	11.10	10.94	11.26	11.43	12.92	14.75	14.73
France	10.60	12.21	13.00	12.80	12.55	12.29	12.04	12.74
Business (Excluding VAT)								
EU 15 Weighted Average	12.49	12.95	12.80	12.81	13.51	13.43	13.92	13.44
UK	—	—	17.90	19.08	18.93	18.85	19.28	18.88
Germany	—	—	10.90	10.73	11.11	11.32	12.71	12.74
France	—	—	11.40	10.60	12.67	12.54	12.34	12.10

market in the EU in 1998. Residential fixed line rental fees rose from €12.06 in 1998 to €13.82 in 2006 in the EU15, which is equal to 14.94 percent increase in real terms in seven years, as shown in Table 6.3. Similarly, the figure for business users climbed from €12.49 in 1998 to €13.44 in 2005, which is equal to 7.61 percent increase in real terms. The increase for residential users was 100 percent more than the figure for business users. Parallel to the figures for the EU15, the concerned fees went up in the UK, Germany, and France at varying rates, and residential users were forced to pay higher fees after the full liberalization.

The price of local, national, and international calls is another indicator. As Table 6.4 below illustrates, in contrast to the monthly fixed line subscription fees, there was a dramatic drop in usage fees. For instance, the price of 10-minute local calls in the EU15 declined from €0.41 in 1998 to €0.30 in 2006, after discounting the effect of inflation. In other words, there was a 26.83 percent decrease in real terms. Despite the variances, the UK, Germany and France showed similar tendencies. It is interesting to note that the price became stable and went up in the case of France. These observations are in line with the market share data examined above. The drop in the price of national calls and calls to the US was dramatic. The decline was 71.49 percent in the EU15 between 1998 and 2006. Because of intense competition in the German market, the reduction was 83.61 percent. The UK and France followed suit, but there was an upward trend in 2006, that saw a

Table 6.4 Price of Telecommunications Services (Deflated): 1998–2006[12]

Year	1998	1999	2000	2001	2002	2003	2004	2005	2006
Local Calls (3 km): € of a 10 minute call at 11 am on a weekday, including VAT									
EU 15 Average	0.41	0.41	0.40	0.39	0.37	0.37	0.34	0.32	0.30
France	0.43	0.43	0.42	0.38	0.38	0.37	0.36	0.30	0.32
Germany	0.45	0.44	0.43	0.42	0.41	0.40	0.40	0.36	0.35
UK	0.59	0.58	0.59	0.58	0.58	0.57	0.42	0.41	0.40
National Calls (200km): € of a 10 minute call at 11 am on a weekday, including VAT									
EU 15 Average	2.21	1.70	1.33	1.11	0.99	0.95	0.80	0.62	0.63
France	1.79	1.56	1.19	0.94	0.93	0.91	0.89	0.76	0.80
Germany	2.99	1.89	1.24	1.21	1.19	1.17	1.13	0.45	0.45
UK	1.20	1.18	1.17	1.16	1.14	1.13	0.42	0.41	0.40
Calls to the US: € of a 10 minute call at 11 am on a weekday including VAT									
EU 15 Average	4.65	3.57	3.11	2.59	2.15	2.02	1.73	1.70	1.56
France	3.52	3.10	2.97	2.92	2.26	2.21	2.07	2.07	2.08
Germany	4.41	2.48	2.45	1.21	1.19	1.18	1.16	1.14	0.42
UK	3.58	3.53	3.50	3.46	3.41	3.37	1.98	1.93	2.03

€ 0.04 increase. Finally, price cuts for calls to the US was around 66.45 percent for the EU15, less than the decline in national call prices, but more than local call prices. In contrast to the trend in Germany, prices went up in the UK and France, illustrating that the incumbents established their control over the most competitive market segments. Another fact is that residential users have not benefited as much as business users for the reason that they are the ones who make more local calls and pay more fixed line rental fees.

Concerning the quality of services, it is difficult to find any indicator and for all EU countries. Table 6.5 indicates that faults per 100 main lines were moving upward after a period of decline, reminiscent of trends in the market shares and prices. For instance, the number of complaints or inquires to the German telecommunications agency went up from 9,100 in 1998 to 33,941 in 2006 (Regulatory Authority for Telecommunications and Posts, 1999, p. 6). The Federal Network Agency for Electricity, Gas, Telecommunications, Post and Railway (2006) summarized the nature of complaints as follows:

Table 6.5 Faults Per 100 Main Lines Per Year[13]

Country/Year	1998	1999	2000	2001	2002	2003	2004	2005
United Kingdom	3.9	4.1	4.5	3.7	11			
Austria	6.2	6.3	5.4	5.2	5.7	5.4	5	5.7
Belgium	4.7	4	3.5	4.8	6	5.6	5.9	6.3
Greece	27	17	11.3	12.1	11.2	13.6	13.8	12.8
Portugal	14.7	11.2	10.5	12.1	10.2	10.1	9.7	10.4

> As in the past, complaints still focused on poor customer service of
> telcos in terms of rectifying problems as well as their failure to adhere
> to contractually agreed terms and conditions with regard to charges
> billed, periods of notice and the ability to switch providers. (p. 23)

This indicates that intense competition did not mean better quality services
for Germans. Although it is not conclusive, the empirical evidence suggests
that market competition is not delivering the expected results on the consumer satisfaction front.

In addition to the problems with consumer satisfaction, there seems to be a
problem on the employment front as well. In fact, many European citizens lost

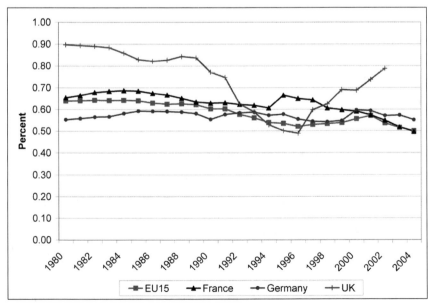

Graph 6.5 Total telephone employees as % of total labor force: 1980–2004.[14]

their jobs in the telecommunications industry over the past quarter century, although the usage of services, revenues from each customer, and the number of firms went up significantly. Graph 6.8 reveals this fact very well. The total number of telecommunications employees as a percentage of the total labor force in the EU15 declined from around 0.64 percent in 1980 to 0.5 percent in 2004. France and Germany demonstrated a similar trend, but there was an upward trend in the UK after 1996, although it had not reached the 1980 level by 2004. As mentioned above, the incumbents such as BT, DT and FT cut their employment by more than half, while the new entrants kept their employment at minimum levels.

Instead of producing new jobs, the industry shed workers over the past 24 years, nullifying the claims of the supranational institutions and national states alike that liberalization, deregulation and privatization would generate new jobs. Even these newly generated jobs are not well-paid and workers do not have job security, as they are often not permitted to unionize. Briefly, workers and residential users have benefitted the least, if one considers the costs and benefits of implementing EU competition policy in the telecommunications industry.

6.4. CONCLUSIONS

The analysis of the telecommunications equipment and services markets has provided an alternative account of the complex and dynamic processes of market competition and concentration, different from what the EU institutions portrayed in their competition decisions. Fluctuations in profitability played a determining role in business strategies, market conduct and the organizational structure of firms. Knowing the four phases of competition and patterns of behavior is essential for understanding the real intentions behind particular market actions.

The first finding is that dominant firms formed alliances to control their markets in the period of growing competition. Such cooperative arrangements exploded during the period of destructive competition as the firms preferred acquisitions. The real motivation behind the merger and acquisition frenzy both in the second half of the 1980s and in the late 1990s was to restore profitability by buying a successful competitor. Similarly, the logic behind alliances between the incumbents in the mid-1990s was mainly to deter new entrants from accessing the newly liberalized areas, an observation contrary to the European Commission's conclusions in its competition law decisions. Partly because of failing to correctly grasp the rationale behind the business strategies of individual firms in different stages of market competition, the European Commission missed a significant opportunity to create genuinely competitive equipment and services markets.

Another interesting finding of this chapter is that there was a divergence in the opinions of politicians and bureaucrats at the national and the EU levels regarding the issue of market concentration. The European Commission particularly overlooked the phenomenon of market concentration and even justified it under the name of increasing 'international competitiveness', even though its British and German counterparts warned the European Commission about the danger of market concentration in a number of occasions.

Strong historical connections between the political institutions at different levels in the EU and the leading firms played a crucial role in determining the future of the firms as well as the evolution of market competition. Concerns about the profitability of the equipment producers as well as the incumbents were the prime motivations behind keeping them intact, and enacting gradual deregulation, liberalization and privatization strategies. The former monopolies were given enough time to adjust themselves to new market conditions. Despite the differences in the regulatory structures, the former monopolies followed business strategies akin to those followed by the European telecommunications equipment makers in different stages of competition. The three incumbents deployed such strategies as forming alliances, offering new products and services, pricing power, and 'dirty tricks' as defensive as well as offensive tools, depending on the stage of competition.

As a result, the European telecommunications industry still remains oligopolistic. In fact, the telecommunications equipment market became a tight oligopoly, further amplifying the market and economic power of the already dominant firms. That the number of prominent firms decreased from around 19 to only four between 1980 and 2004 helped profitability to some extent, but the cyclical nature of the equipment market was not helpful. Ericsson acquired Marconi in 2005; Alcatel and Lucent merged and become one company in 2006; Nokia and Siemens combined their telecommunications equipment business (Belson & Austen, 2006). Similarly, the transition from monopolistic to competitive markets in services is still not successful. The services market remains concentrated. There is even a lingering danger that the market will become more concentrated, as the former monopolies exercise their power in the market as well as outside the market progressively.

Compared to the cost of policy implementation to the public, benefits are not significant, especially to residential users in the first place. Corporate users, especially multinational and transnational corporations, benefited most from the implementation of EU competition policy in the telecommunications industry at the expense of residential users and small firms. There are also significant issues with quality of services and consumer satisfaction as well. Finally, contrary to the expected job creation by the telecommunications industry, there has been a significant trend of job loss over the past quarter century, despite the skyrocketing increase in the number of users and revenues. Briefly, the real picture is not as rosy as EU officials claim regarding the policy outcomes.

7 Concluding Remarks

This study has investigated the political economy of EU competition law and policy by studying its implementation in the telecommunications industry between 1980 and 2004. The model of workable or effective competition was the departure, serving as a yardstick for the EU institutions in making competition law decisions. Building effectively competitive markets was also one of the stated goals of EU competition policy. Rather than treating EU competition policy as a 'technical' issue to be dealt with only by lawyers and economists, this study, considered it 'a matter of high politics', in line with Trebilcock et al.'s (2002) observation (p. 3).

This study has confirmed that uncovering the influential and often divergent economic, political, social interests, contested ideas, values, institutional structures of policy-making and enforcement is essential for a healthy evaluation of public policy outcomes. Because of variations in the balance of power between different social forces and institutional structures involved in policy-making, public policies are an outcome of bargaining and compromise. EU competition policy is no exception to this rule and the policy rationale behind workable or effective competition demonstrates this clearly. This finding is exactly what Ward (2003), an expert on EU law, meant with his following observation: "The law of 'workable' competition is a jurisprudence of such compromises and inconsistencies, [that it is] no more 'perfect' than the free market is 'free'" (p. 159). The preceding chapters have provided ample theoretical as well as empirical evidence for the compromises and inconsistencies in the model of effective competition during the application of EU competition law.

The rest of this chapter will summarize the findings of this study, briefly identifying a number of areas for future studies, and evaluating the implications of the theoretical framework developed here. While the first section of the chapter recapitulates the findings with respect to EU competition policy and the telecommunications industry, the second section highlights the key issues in EU competition policy and telecommunications to be considered in future studies. The implications of this study for theorizing about market competition and competition policy (dynamic market competition or DMC) are discussed in a few words in the third section before stating some concluding comments in the final section.

7.1. EU COMPETITION POLICY AND THE TELECOMMUNICATIONS INDUSTRY

It is clear by now that there was continuity between the pre- and post-EEC/EU competition policy practices in Europe. The institutional structure of the EEC/EU involved in the enforcement of competition law was centralized, and political power was concentrated in the hands of the European Commission and the Council of Ministers in the early years. The situation has not changed very much since then, despite various attempts to empower the Parliament over the past 20 years. This finding is in line with Gill's (2003) claim of centralization of political power in the executive branches of the EU such as the Directorate-General for Competition within the European Commission (pp. 66–7).

Gill is not alone in his observation. After studying the effects of the modernization of EU competition policy, Wilks (2005) concluded that "[t]he reforms in policy implementation are of historic importance. While they appear to promise decentralization to national competition authorities, more sophisticated analysis points to an increase in the centralized power of the Commission" (p. 431). This finding supports the assertion made in the second chapter regarding the institutional requirements of the model of effective competition, while further strengthening the conclusions of Chapter 3.

Another finding is that EU competition law was not against market concentration, cartels or state aids *per se*, as long as they did not 'harm' effective' competition. After an in-depth analysis of the theory of effective competition, it was clear that effective competition favoured loosely oligopolistic markets. This finding is in line with Haack's (1983) early realization of the true nature of competition policy: "Competition policy and the emerging industrial policy of the EC therefore seem to take a stand somewhere in between competition and concentration" (p. 371). EU competition law and policy perceived loosely oligopolistic markets as the ideal market structure where effective competition could flourish. This is the source of the chasm between the stated and real objectives of EU competition policy.

That profitability played a determining role in the historical evolution of EU competition policy is a significant finding because most of those who studied EU competition law from the legal, political, and administrative perspectives categorically underestimated this point. Of course, some critical scholars did not miss it. For instance, Lewis (1971) stated that "[t]he Commission's approach is not doctrinaire: it is concerned to prevent distortions to competition which results not only in excessive concentration of economic power but excessively small profits as well" (p. 33). Nevertheless, such critical studies in the field of EU competition law and policy have been rare. Finally, this study illustrated that the process of enforcing EU competition law was far from being smooth. Conflict, competition, and cooperation were the three predominant modes of behavior between various market, social, and political actors at the industry, national, and supranational levels.

As for EU telecommunications policy, deregulation, liberalization, and privatization strategies were a collective response to conjectural changes in the 1970s and early 1980s, especially to the fluctuations in the rate of profit in the first place. Given that EU telecommunications policy was part of the broader process of European integration in which EU competition policy has played a central role, this study, unlike others on the subject, recognized that the first concrete policy actions appeared when the overall profit rate of European firms plunged in the mid-1970s. If one considers further market integration as a solution to the problem of profitability, the period after 1980 definitely provides rich empirical evidence to achieve this goal in the telecommunications industry by means of competition policy.

In EU telecommunications policy, technical standards were the common denominator that brought the supranational institutions, the member states and major telecommunications firms together, after they had failed to realize their goals individually. These actors preferred gradual or progressive liberalization and deregulation of telecommunications markets, starting with the segments that were least important economically to the former monopolies in terms of revenue contribution, yet most essential to the European multinationals. Consequently, privatization of the former national telecommunications operators has been gradual as this was a crucial requirement that allowed the member states to continue their control over the former monopolies, while extracting revenues to reduce government deficit to comply with EU monetary policy.

Regarding the links between liberalization, privatization, profitability and state revenues, Bauer (2005) made the following observation after examining interconnection prices in fixed telecommunications networks for 2000, 2002, and 2004: "It was revealed that public and mixed ownership generally coincided with higher interconnection prices" (p. 170). High interconnection prices naturally increased competitors' costs and helped the incumbents maintain higher market shares, while generating higher revenues for the incumbents and the member states as their shareholders. These observations uphold the point that EU telecommunications policy ensured the profitability of European firms, while serving the interests of the member states at the expense of ordinary citizens and working people.

Analysis of the implementation of Articles 81, 82, 87, and the merger regulation in the telecommunications industry in Chapter 5 offered further empirical evidence for the assertion that EU competition policy was aimed at assuring profitability and supporting market concentration up to a certain degree. Chapter 5 also demonstrated the impact of the two visions of market competition for delineating the relevant market, and analyzing market power, besides illustrating the dominance of the static view of competition in EU competition law cases. The policy outcome of this was that the EU institutions used a shorter time scale in their competition law cases, and this observation is in line with Korah's (2004) general conclusion about EU competition law (p. 8). Short-term analysis and narrow delimitation of product and geographical markets meant the loss of the whole picture of the historical evolution of the markets and the disappearance of market power. Finally, Chapter 5 showed that the existence of the two visions of competition caused inconsistency and unpredictability in EU competition law decisions.

Chapter 6 provided an in-depth analysis of EU telecommunications equipment and services markets between 1980 and 2004. By focusing on the behavior of the individual firms and the member states in four stages of market competition, the crucial role of the structural characteristics of the relevant markets such as technology, firm size and firm-customer relations in the process of competition was demonstrated. State regulation was also significant in terms of its effects on the business strategies of firms and, hence, the intensity of market competition. Chapter 6 clarified that the intensity of market competition depended on profit margins as well as available profit sources, not on the number of competitors directly. Depending on the rate of profit, firms developed business strategies that, in turn, influenced their organizational structure and market behavior.

Concentration in the telecommunications equipment market increased significantly, with the number of major players declining from 19 in 1980 to only four in 2004. The four remaining equipment producers are the oldest ones as well, indicating the intractability of economic power. In the case of the services market, the situation was not very rosy, either. Despite the entrance of a large number of new firms, four to nine firms controlled more than 90 percent of the markets as of 2005. The former monopolies accounted for more than 69 percent of the local calls market, 63 percent of the national calls markets, and 52 percent of the international calls markets on average in the EU15 at the end of 2005. The former monopolies reduced the rate of the decline in their market shares in most cases. Not surprisingly, the incumbents increased their market share at the expense of their new competitors in a few cases.

After adjusting for the effects of inflation, residential users paid fourteen percent more in monthly fixed line rental fees in the EU15 in 2005 than they had paid in 1998. The rate increase was only seven percent for business users during the same period. Price decline in phone calls was quite significant between 1998 and 2005, but again, local call prices did not drop as much as long distance and international call prices in the EU15. Based on the findings in Chapter 6, it is safe to conclude that corporations benefited most in comparison to small firms and residential users, in line with the real intentions of EU competition and telecommunications policies. These findings also support the conclusions made in Chapter 4. With respect to the quality of service, the results were mixed, if not all negative. Finally, the share of employment in the telecommunications industry, in contrast to the stated policy objective of creating more employment, went down in the EU15 from around 0.62 percent of the total labor force in 1980 to 0.50 by 2004. In addition, most newly created jobs in the industry are precarious. This study is not alone with respect to these conclusions. Thatcher (2004), a prominent student of EU telecommunications policy, concluded that the Europeanization of telecommunications policy had favored the member states and incumbent telecommunications operators at the expense of residential users, small-business users, workers and trade unions.

These conclusions strengthen three general statements about the EU. First, the EU, as Moss (2005) argued, is "a neo-liberal construction that functioned on behalf of employers and the owners of capital to ensure market competition, sound money and profitability . . ." (p. xi). Second, according to Allen (2005), supply-side-oriented German ordoliberalism played a crucial role in EU economic policy during the formative and subsequent stages of European integration (p. 200). Finally, in line with the conclusions of Maurer et al. (2003), the project of European integration has resulted in the centralization of political power both at the national and European levels (p. xvi). Nugent and Paterson (2003) supported this assessment with the following words: "The fact is that an effect of European integration has been to strengthen national executives and weaken legislatures" (p. 107). There has been a process of de-parliamentarization and bureaucratization in the evolution of the state in Europe with the process of European integration (Mittag & Wessels, 2005, pp. 445–7). According to Galés (2003), this is functional for the state:

> Most central governments have been able to make use of 'the constraints of Europe', which they have been active in developing, in order to impose reforms on national actors. Conversely, many decentralization reforms have allowed central governments to 'decentralize penury', giving regions the responsibility of managing scarcity and painful restructuring. (p. 394)

On the whole, EU competition and telecommunications policies corroborate the fact that the EU is a new kind of polity that is not a substitute for the member states, but is a new stage in the evolution of the European states in response to the changing nature of capitalism.

7.2. KEY ISSUES IN EU COMPETITION AND TELECOMMUNICATIONS POLICIES

Both EU competition and telecommunications policies entered a new phase in 2004, after the addition of ten new member states to the EU, the completion of the process of modernizing EU competition law, and finally, the adoption of a new regulatory framework for telecommunications. For an adequate understanding of the key issues for EU competition policy, it is necessary to recall the serious setback that the European Commission suffered in 2002, when the CFI annulled its three merger decisions.

In *Airtours v Commission* in 2002, the (CFI) Court of First Instance found that the Commission failed to provide enough empirical evidence to support its contention for the link between collective dominance and restriction of competition in capacity setting. The CFI also stated that the Commission did not consider the volatile nature of the main tour operators' market shares before the case, which was pointing to the existence of a competitive market. In other words, the Commission failed to assess market competition correctly in the relevant market before the notification (Airtours v Commission, 2002, para. 120). The CFI concluded that the Commission misinterpreted the data available to it when outlining the growth in demand over the past ten years, in that there was a clear tendency to considerable growth, despite the volatility in demand from one year to another. Indeed, the pace of growth increased in the relevant market during the years before the case, whereas the Commission characterized the market as low-growth (Airtours v Commission, 2002, para. 33).

According to the CFI, the Commission's analysis fell short of an adequate examination of market competition between the main tour operators. There were grave mistakes in the Commission's assessment of the evolution of the concerned market (Airtours v Commission, 2002, para. 181). The CFI commented that:

> The Court observes, *in limine*, that . . . the prospective analysis of the market necessary in any assessment of an alleged collective dominant position must not only view that position statically at a fixed point in time—the point when the transaction takes place and the structure of competition is altered—but must also assess it dynamically, with regard in particular to its internal equilibrium, stability, and the question as to whether any parallel anti-competitive conduct to which it might give rise is sustainable over time. (Airtours v Commission, 2002, para. 192)

This observation by the CFI was striking in that it pointed out the core of the problem in the Commission's vision of market competition that the ECJ had observed in the 1960s. As the CFI correctly stated, the static and ahistorical view of competition made it possible to analyze competition at one point in time for the reason that it associated market competition with market structure. It is very hard, if not impossible, therefore, to comprehend the market conduct of firms and assess their future implications correctly. Such analysis, in fact, requires the recognition of competition as a dynamic process playing out over a longer time-period.

The CFI also found similar errors in the Commission's examination of market competition in the *Schneider Electric v Commission* judgment in 2002. It particularly discovered that the European Commission did not properly investigate the structure of competition in the relevant geographical markets, while overestimating the economic power of the merged entity. The CFI annulled the decision, after concluding that the economic analysis behind the decision was inadequate (Schneider Electric v Commission, 2002, p. 419). These setbacks prepared the ground for the Commission to initiate a major revision in its implementation of EU competition policy.

The year 2004 was a turning point for EU competition policy. After realizing the main defects in its analysis of market competition, completing the modernization process and the historic enlargement of the EU, the Commission adopted a new approach, 'pro-active competition policy', which was described as follows:

> Pro-active enforcement will be founded on economic analysis of market structures and behavior which will help in prioritizing the enforcement efforts according to the nature and the gravity of the competition problem and according to the extent a sector or an industry falls behind in performance. (CEC, 2004c, p. 16)

The main thrust of the new pro-active competition policy approach is to bring more economic analysis to individual competition cases, as stated in the policy paper. There seems to be a fundamental shift in the Commission's vision of market competition, at least in theory, but experience will show whether the change is cosmetic or substantial.

In tandem with the substantial change in its vision of market competition, the Commission created the post of chief competition economist as of September 1, 2003 and appointed an economist to the position for three years. Moreover, it also dedicated a staff of around ten specialized economists to work with the chief competition economist. Three major tasks of the chief economist are: providing direction on economics and econometrics in the application of EU competition rules, including contributions to the development of general policy instruments; supervision in individual competition cases and detailed help in the key competition cases that involve complex economic issues; and finally making connections with the academic world by organizing meetings, seminars, conferences and discussions (CEC, 2004d, pp. 11–2).

The last innovation in the sphere of EU competition policy is that the Commission finally remembered consumers and established a Consumer Liaison Officer within the Commission's Competition Directorate-General in 2003, ensuring 'healthy' communication between itself and consumers (CEC, 2004d, p. 6). Nonetheless, the recent move by the Commission held up one of the major claims of this study: profitability and thus, the interests of firms, not those of consumers, had been the major concern for EU competition policy up until 2004. Willemien Bax, deputy director of the European Consumers' Association, or Bureau Européen des Consommateurs (BEUC), complained recently about the lack influence the association has had on decisions taken by the European Commission. He was quoted by Beattie (2005): "The industry and the retailers have much bigger voices in Brussels." The new policy initiative aimed to change this fact, and the future experience of this new body will demonstrate whether the EU institutions' concern about consumers is genuine.

As for the administrative side of the implementation of the competition rules, one of the objectives of the modernization was decentralization of the implementation process. Paradoxically, the process became more centralized. According to Article 3 of Regulation 1/2003, the national courts and competition authorities cannot ignore EU competition law and base their decisions solely on national laws. They are obliged to follow EU case law (Lowe, 2003, pp. 2–3). As a result, studying EU competition law decisions after 2004 would be important to understand the impact of all these changes.

In the field of telecommunications, member states began to implement the new regulatory framework for electronic communications networks and services on July 25, 2003. The purpose was to consolidate the internal market in telecommunications, while ensuring that competition continues to exist by establishing a unified framework for creating and maintaining the conditions for competition to exist (European Parliament and Council, 2002a; Bavasso, 2004). Despite the new regulatory framework, even Mario Monti (2003a), former European commissioner for competition policy, acknowledged at the end of 2003 that the evolution of the services market was not very promising in all areas, especially in local loop unbundling and broadband. The European Commission adopted proposals to review the existing regulatory framework in November 2007 to realize the following goals: more competition, better regulation, a stronger internal market, and better consumer protection (CEC, 2007). These new policy goals for the revised framework, in fact, corroborate the findings in Chapter 6.

The root cause of the problem is that instead of building new networks, new competitors have mostly been buying their services from the incumbents at wholesale prices and reselling them at competitive market prices. As a result, competition at the network level has yet to develop. Moreover, such an arrangement has given leverage to the incumbents over their competitors. Authorities have recently started to question the effectiveness of liberalization and deregulation in telecommunications on both sides of the Atlantic. Even the incumbents have stated that attempts to encourage more competitors to take advantage of unbundling would not work in the long term, unless new operators build alternative networks to compete with them (Larsen & Budden, 2003, p. 1).

There is not much space for consolidation in the European telecommunications equipment market ("Britain: Business Past," 2005, p. 36). The situation is slightly different in the services market because there are many new and weak competitors. After several years of stability, consolidation in the services market has accelerated since 2004. The largest companies, especially the former monopolies, have been acquiring new entrants in distress recently ("European Telecoms," 2005). These deals will continue until the number of competitors diminishes significantly in the coming years and the European telecommunications services landscape will be very different over the next decade.

With respect to the future implications of these developments, analyzing the effects of the new communications framework law on business strategies of firms is important to understand the evolution of the market in the first place. Secondly, investigating the nature of the relationship between EU competition and the new communications law can reveal whether there is a conflict between them. Thirdly, studying technological evolution in the telecommunications industry is also significant for understanding the impact of new technologies on business strategies of the firms in the industry. Finally, examining the evolution of market competition in the telecommunications equipment and services markets would be helpful to comprehend the factors behind an ongoing process of market consolidation and its future implications.

A major limitation of this study is that two significant issues were left out. One of them is the impact of EU telecommunications policy on trade unions and workers (and their reaction), as the scope of the study is limited to market competition, its regulation and policy outcomes regarding market concentration. Trade unions and workers were investigated to the extent that they are closely related to market competition and its regulation. However, the subject needs an in-depth analysis. The second is the broader repercussions of liberalization, deregulation and privatization in the telecommunications industry for democratic communications. This topic is too important to be treated within a few pages.

7.3. THEORIZING MARKET COMPETITION AND COMPETITION POLICY

This study has exposed the conceptual and methodological difficulties of the conservative and liberal perspectives in dealing with the notion of power in their approach to state-market relations. This is in line with a general criticism directed against mainstream theories of European integration. Talani (2004) has suggested that: "Critical political economists contend that mainstream theory ignores relations of power and interest that are contained within the market-integration process itself" (p. xi). By putting power at the center of the analysis, distinction between different forms of power, and the complex and dynamic relations between them, were emphasized without prioritizing one over others or conflating economic power with market power.

Based on the case of the EU, it is possible to state several general conclusions. First, the state is not a homogeneous entity. Different departments within the state may have conflicting goals and can offset each other. Second, once in power, political parties with different ideological stances are often forced to follow more or less similar policies in certain times due to the structural exigencies. This shows that there are structural barriers or constraints to state policies under given social, economic, and political conditions. Third, the state has a responsibility to assure the profitability in the market in capitalist societies. Fourth, the state protects its own interests, besides those of social forces cooperating with it, as long as they do not conflict with its own. The auctioning of 3G licenses provided ample evidence of how the state assured its own interests, even at the expense of those of capitalists and ordinary citizens. Finally, EU member states played a determining role in EU policy-making, even at the expense of the European Commission. However, instead of dictating their own preferences, compromise was the common feature of EU policy-making and implementation. Informal politics has also played as significant a role as formal politics, as demonstrated by the complex relations between the former incumbents, member state officials, and the European Commission in the DT case.

These broader conclusions have three major implications for a dynamic theory of market competition. In the first place, it is important to consider informal aspects of public policy-making and implementation when drawing conclusions about policy outcomes. This is especially true in the EU case where actors express their positions on specific policy matters and sharpen their arguments through informal politics before sitting around the table and announcing formal conclusions. This is also the case for implementing EU competition policy, as the European Commission communicates its opinion about individual cases and hears the voices of parties through the media before making its final decision. Besides formal procedures, paying more attention to the informal dimension of implementation would be helpful in theorizing as well as understanding EU competition policy.

The second implication is that a theory of market competition should pay adequate attention to relations within and between political institutions. The EU is a complex ensemble of institutions and operates at different levels simultaneously. Agenda setting, policy-making and implementation include a range of actors at various times in formal as well as informal contexts. A realistic assessment of public policies and their enforcement in the EU engenders a serious consideration of the political institutions that are involved in the process as well as the historical ties between them and the social forces that shape them. Finally, as it has become clear by now, this study investigated market competition in transitional or rapidly changing markets. Studying competition in consolidated markets would be very useful for applying competition rules.

7.4. FINAL REMARKS

As this study has revealed, hopes for a democratic communications industry at this point in history does not seem very promising. Market concentration will definitely encourage firms to seek more profits in depressed markets, fostering collusion and abusive behavior. Unlike telecommunications, agriculture or transportation, competition policy does not have a powerful political constituency for supporting market competition. Nor does the European Commission have adequate financial resources and staff to resist pressures from big corporations and lobby groups in Brussels. Regulatory bodies such as the European Commission and NRAs (National Regulatory Authorities) follow firms, not the other way around, especially in telecommunications because of the highly technical nature of the industry. As a result, market imperatives may prevail over the needs of ordinary citizens in the long term.

It is true that the balance of forces shifted to large corporations after the 1980s with the internationalization of capital and Europeanization of public policy-making. Instead of feeling alienated, EU residential users, workers, and small businesses should exploit opportunities that information communication technologies (ICTs) provide them. EU citizens should make use of the discourse of the digital divide and form strong grassroot coalitions to force their governments to close the gap. Then, they can exploit the possibilities of participation provided by electronic government (e-government) to follow EU policies regardless of their physical location and put pressure on politicians in Brussels. In this way, they can encourage and shape electronic democracy (e-democracy) as a second step. Finally, they can determine the political agenda, play active role in policy-making and implementation.

Notes

NOTES TO CHAPTER 1

1. Thatcher (2004) mentioned winners and losers, but did not show any empirical evidence.
2. Whereas Americans prefer the concept *antitrust* policy, the rest of the world uses the term *competition* policy. Different from American antitrust policy, EU competition policy regulates the market behavior of firms as well as the financial relations of member states with firms.
3. As indicated by Rothschild (2002, p. 433), this vision of economic power is either absent or restricted to price formation in the mainstream theories of competition and competition analysis of the EU institutions.
4. This does not mean that it may not have other purposes. Profit is the rationale for the formation of a business enterprise in the first place in a capitalist market economy.
5. These concepts and distinctions are heuristic devices often deployed in the literature and crucial for understanding the implementation of EU competition policy, as their definition determines the way market power is defined. As such, they are historical and highly contested categories.
6. In this study, the net rate of return on net capital stock for the European economy and the net rate of return on total assets for European telecommunications firms are used for the sake of simplicity.
7. The areas for which the CFI has responsibility are agriculture, state aid, competition, commercial policy, regional policy, social policy, institutional law, trademark law, transport and staff regulations. All judgments by the CFI relative to points of law may be appealed to the Court of Justice.

NOTES TO CHAPTER 2

1. Ordoliberalism or German neoliberalism is a set of ideas advanced by a group of German economists, political scientists, lawyers and sociologists at Freiburg University to find solutions to Germany's grave problems during in the 1930s and 1940s. Prominent members of the Freiburg School include Walter Eucken, Franz Böhm, and Hans Grossman-Doerth and Wilhelm Ropke. (Gerber, 1998; Hermann-Pillath, 1994; Oswalt-Eucken, 1994; Yeager, 1994; Barry, 1989; Moschel, 1989; Peacock & Willgerodt, 1989; Rothschild, 1964; Oliver, Jr., 1960; Ropke, 1960; Friedrich, 1955).
2. The underlying difference between Classicals and Austrians on the one hand and ordoliberals on the other originates from their perception of market

competition. Whereas the former contend that monopolies would simply disappear in a 'gale of creative destruction' like 'soap bubbles' burst under competitive pressure, the latter were convinced that creative destruction within the private sector would not be a sufficiently potent force to burst the bubble. Thus, they saw the need for states to pursue competition policies to prevent the spontaneous growth of trusts and combines (Peacock & Willgerodt, 1989, p. 7; Clark, 1955, p. 457).

3. Both Clark and the ordoliberals were against the welfare state, because they saw it as the main source of inflation (Barry, 1989, pp. 114–5; Moschel, 1989, pp. 118 and 149; Clark, 1969, p. 168; Oliver, Jr., 1960, p. 130).

4. This contradiction is the source of ambiguity, arbitrariness, uncertainty and unpredictability in implementing the EU competition rules, as we shall see in the fifth chapter while examining European Commission, ECJ and CFI decisions in the telecommunications industry. For understanding the contradiction theoretically, see Janberg, 2001, p. 47.

5. Smith also mentioned that firms may make secret agreements to restrict competition occasionally, drawing attention to the dangers of cartels (Richardson, 1975, p. 350).

6. The economic or structural power of the business is variable, while business interests are not monolithic in that there are different business groups with different objectives (Hacker & Pierson, 2002, p. 282; Lindblom, 1977; Poulantzas, 1973).

7. According to Marx, centralization of capital is not a unilinear process because firms may be partitioned by their owners. Competition and credit lever the centralization of capital as well (Marx, 1967, pp. 474–5).

8. Obstructing traffic means that dominant firms do not supply essential raw materials or intermediate commodities to their competitors (Veblen, 1964c, p. 100).

NOTES TO CHAPTER 3

1. According to the cooperation and assent procedures, the European Parliament gained the right to give its opinion on new draft laws and assent in the case of international agreements negotiated by the Commission, enlargement and a number of other issues including any changes in election rules respectively (Campbell, 1986).

2. Regulations are general in their scope, binding in their entirety and directly applicable in all member states. In contrast to regulations, the member states have the freedom to choose different methods to implement directives. The latter are also general in their scope and directly applicable in all member states, as long as the stated objectives are realized. Decisions are binding in their entirety upon those to whom they are addressed (member states, individuals, or firms). There are also non-obligatory acts such as recommendations and opinions that do not have any binding force (Lasok and Lasok, 2001).

3. This does not mean that there was no action in this sphere in Italy. For further information about the Italian case, see: (Torre, 1965; Venturini, 1964).

4. The inclusion of a rule dealing with mergers and acquisitions in the Treaty of Paris reflects the significant role that US authorities played in its drafting (Gerber, 1998, p. 341).

5. In referring to article numbers in the EEC Treaty, the new numbering adopted with the Treaty of Amsterdam in 1997, which came into effect in 1999, is used in this study. However, old numbers may be referred to along with new ones in dealing with the most important EU competition rules.

6. The EEC also contained Article 91 that was applied to prevent dumping between the member states during the transitional period, lasting until January 1, 1970. It gave the European Commission the right to authorize a member state to take appropriate measures to prevent dumping, if it could not find a solution to the problem after addressing "recommendations to the person or persons with whom such practices originate for the purpose of putting an end to them," as stated in Article 91. Having ceased to have an effect on 1 January 1970, the provisions of Article 91(1) were incorporated into Article 187 (ex-Article 136 of the Act of Accession). Article 91 was finally repealed with the Treaty of Amsterdam in 1997.

7. Article 226 (ex-Article 169) and Article 227 (ex-Article 170) confer on the European Commission and the member states the right to take a dispute to the ECJ, if a member state does not fulfill its obligation under the Treaty, and the European Commission has not found a solution to the infringement.

8. The total number of staff at the DG for Competition in 2006 was 750. Whereas 357 people were dealing with Articles 81, 82, 86, and Merger Control Regulation cases, 188 people were handling Article 87 cases. The rest of the personnel were responsible for international cooperation (10), policy, strategy, and coordination (108), and administrative support (87). The DG for Competition budget for 2006 was Euros 12,569,960 (CEC, 2006a, pp. 9–10).

9. The main source of information in this section is the Commission's annual *Reports on Competition Policy*. They summarize the year's main developments, while serving as a platform for expressing the Commission's opinion and its future intentions on all aspects of EU competition policy (Holmes, 2004, p. 444).

10. Net operating surplus =Total gross value added at basic prices—(compensation of employees + taxes less subsidies on products +consumption of fixed capital), calculated from OECD, *Annual National Accounts—volume I—Main aggregates Vol 2007 release 02*. The total net capital stock for each country was obtained from Kiel Institute for World Economics. Retrieved May 25, 2006, from, http://www.uni-kiel.de/ifw/forschung/netcap/netcap.htm (Accessed August 15, 2007). Denmark, Ireland, and the UK were added to the series in 1973; Greece in 1981; Spain and Portugal in 1987; and Austria, Sweden and Finland in 1996.

11. The author does not agree with the periodization made by Gerber and Wesseling because it does not take into account the factor of profitability (Wesseling, 2000, p. 9–10; Gerber, 1998, chapter IX; Gerber, 1994, p. 111).

12. Based on the data from Graph 3.2, the correlation computed between profitability and accepted state aid decisions was negative, strong (r = -0.804) and statistically significant at the 0.01 (two-tailed). In other words, as profitability declined, the number of state aids accepted increased between 1970 and 1983). This fact supports the main thesis of this study that the primary objective of state aids was to assure profitability, although political actors and institutions had to consider other objectives such as unemployment and regional equality.

13. Agricultural aids were not included (CEC, 1983, p. 113).

14. Denmark was the only country to reject the TEU.

15. Data were reported in the Commission's annual reports on competition policy published between 1995 and 2003.

16. Full-function joint ventures refer to firms created by two or more firms to carry out economic activities, but they act on the market independently from their mother companies.

17. Source: European Merger Control—Council Regulation 139/2004—Statistics 21 September 1990 to 31 August 2007. Retrieved September 26, 2006, from http://ec.europa.eu/comm/competition/mergers/statistics.pdf.
18. European Commission, State Aid Control: Part 2- Comparative Tables (Table: Total State Aid by Member State as a Percentage of GDP). Retrieved, September 14, 2005, from http://ec.europa.eu/comm/competition/state_aid/studies_reports/k1_2.xls.

NOTES TO CHAPTER 4

1. There are four different arguments with respect to liberalization, deregulation, re-regulation and privatization of the telecommunications industry. Whereas the first position takes *technology* as a basis for its explanation, the second perspective explains the transformation by taking *the modern state* as a key variable. The third thesis combines the first two to understand complex processes at the national as well as the international level. The fourth position considers *profit* as its starting point. Findings of this study support the fourth position, albeit with minor differences. For detailed discussion see: Schneider, 2001; Curwen, 1995; Schneider, Dang-Nguyen & Werle, 1994; Grande, 1994; Luthje, 1993; De Bernis, 1990; Dyson & Humphreys, 1990; Symeonidis, 1990; Thimm, 1989; Neu, Neumann & Schnöring, 1987; Locksley, 1986; Dyson, 1986; Shearman, 1986; CEC, 1985; Montella, 1984.
2. The ranking was as follows: Western Electric (United States), ITT (United States), Siemens (Germany), L. M. Ericsson (Sweden), Northern Telecom (Canada), NEC (Japan), Philips (Netherlands), CGE (France), Thomson Brandt (France), GEC (United Kingdom), Plessey (United Kingdom) and Italtel (Italy) (OECD, 1983, p. 130).
3. There was a change of trade nomenclature in 1988 that makes a comparison of pre-1987 and post-1988 figures risky (CEC, 1991, pp. 12–9).
4. The twelve companies involved were General Electric Company (GEC), ICL and Plessey from the UK; Thomson–Brandt, CIT-Alcatel (GCE) and Bull from France; Siemens, AEG and Nixdorf from Germany; Olivetti and STET from Italy; and Philips from the Netherlands (Stevers, 1990, p. 65, footnote 118).
5. CEC, 2004a, p. 62.
6. The scheme was adopted from the EU website and modified: Information Society, Policies: eCommunications. Retrieved August 28, 2006, from http://ec.europa.eu/information_society/policy/ecomm/history/index_en.htm#brief_history.
7. European Information Technology Observatory, *EITO Update 2003: ICT Market*, October 2003. Retrieved June 15, 2005, from http://www.eito.com.
8. (CEC, 1999b, p. 17).
9. In some cases, member states used golden shares to maintain control over privatized firms. The data were obtained from company web sites on August 6, 2004.

NOTES TO CHAPTER 5

1. Roaming in wireless telecommunications refers to the extending of connectivity service in a network that is different than the network with which a cellular phone or digital personal assistant is registered.
2. For similar cases, see Phoenix/GlobalOne, 1996; Atlas, 1996; Uniworld, 1997; Unisource, 1997.

3. The Court of Justice dropped the case because the party that violated Article 86 was not in a dominant position on the relevant market (Alsatel/Novasam, 1990, para. 23).
4. The local loop means the physical circuit between the customer's premises and the telecommunications operator's local switch (CEC, 2003b, p. 1).

NOTES TO CHAPTER 6

1. Articles from *Financial Times* (London), *The Economist*, and *Business Week* were retrieved from Lexis-Nexis database between 2003 and 2004.
2. That telecommunications contracts are in billions in amount and spreading over several years makes it almost impossible to identify price wars.
3. Source OECD Telecommunications Database, Vol. 2005, Release (ISSN 1608–1315). The member states were added to the calculation a year after becoming EU members.
4. American Telephone and Telegraph (AT&T) was the only company in the world that produced and put into operation the first digital switch in 1976 (OECD, 1988, p. 73).
5. Telettra and Italtel attempted to merge in November 1985, but the initiative failed after two years of effort (Buxton, 1985, p. 19; Friedman, 1987, p. 46).
6. Moody's International Manual (various years); company reports from Investext Plus; and Mergent Online.
7. ITU, Key Global Telecom Indicators for the World Telecommunication Service Sector. Retrieved November 9, 2007, from http://www.itu.int/ITU-D/ict/statistics/at_glance/KeTelecom99.html.
8. Data were obtained from Mergent Online, Investext Plus, and BT's website. Retrieved March 25, 2005, from http://www.btplc.com/.
9. Adopted with substantial modifications from Roobek & Broeders, 1993, p. 304.
10. Eurostat, Structural Indicators. Retrieved on November 27, 2006, from http://epp.eurostat.ec.europa.eu/portal/page?_pageid=1996,45323734&_dad=portal&_schema=PORTAL&screen=welcomeref&open=/strind/ecoref&language=en&product=EU_strind&root=EU_strind&scrollto=0.
11. Data were collected from ITU (2007) and various reports drafted by the European Commission (2005, 2003, 2001, and 2000) on the implementation of the telecommunications regulatory package. Retrieved November 15, 2006,http://ec.europa.eu/information_society/policy/ecomm/library/communications_reports/annualreports/11threport/index_en.htm.
12. Eurotat, Structural Indicators. Retrieved on December 14, 2006, from http://epp.eurostat.ec.europa.eu/portal/page?_pageid=1996,45323734&_dad=portal&_schema=PORTAL&screen=welcomeref&open=/strind/ecoref&language=en&product=EU_strind&root=EU_strind&scrollto=0.
13. ITU, 2007.
14. Austria, Finland, Italy, Netherlands and the UK were not included in the calculation between 2001 and 2004. World Bank, *World Development Indicators' database (Old WDI Online)*. Retrieved December 20, 2006, from http://0-devdata.worldbank.org.innopac.lib.ryerson.ca/dataonline/.

Bibliography

PRIMARY SOURCES

Aerospatiale/Alcatel Espace (Case IV/34/422) (1994). *Common Market Law Reports*, 4, 705–11.

Airtours v Commission (T-342/99) (2002). Retrieved March 15, 2005, from http://eurlex.europa.eu/smartapi/cgi/sga_doc?smartapi!celexplus!prod!CELEXnumdoc&numdoc=61999A0342&lg=en.

Alcatel/AEG Kabel (Case No IV/M.165) (1991). *Official Journal*, L-2985, 18.12.1991. Retrieved April 2003, 2004, from http://ec.europa.eu/comm/competition/mergers/cases/decisions/m165_en.pdf .

Alsatel/Novasam SA (Case 247/86) (1990). *Common Market Law Reports*, 4, 434–48.

Aniline Dyes (69/243/EEC) (1969). *Common Market Law Reports*, (R.P. Supplement), 3, D23-D40.

ATES/ANT (Case IV/32.006) 1990, *Common Market Law Reports*, 4, 16–22.

Atlas (Case No IV/35.337), *Official Journal*, L 239, 19.09.1996, 23–56.

AT&T/Philips (Case No IV/M.651). Brussels, 05.02.1996. Retrieved April 12, 2004, from http://ec.europa.eu/comm/competition/mergers/cases/decisions/m651_en.pdf.

Belgacom/Tele Danmark/Tulip (Case No IV/M.1177). Brussels, 19.05.1998. Retrieved April 15, 2004, from http://ec.europa.eu/comm/competition/mergers/cases/decisions/m1177_en.pdf.

BT/Airtel (Case No Comp/JV.3). Brussels, 08.07.1998. Retrieved June 1, 2004, from http://ec.europa.eu/comm/competition/mergers/cases/decisions/jv3_en.pdf.

BT/Astra (Case IV/32/745) (1994). *Common Market Law Reports*, 5, 226–52.

BT/AT&T (Case No IV/JV.15), 30.03.1999.

BT-MCI (Case IV/34.857). *Official Journal*, L 223/36, 27.08.1994, 36–55.

Cable & Wireless/VEBA Veba (Case No IV/M.618). Brussels, 16.08.1995. Retrieved April 12, 2004, from http://ec.europa.eu/comm/competition/mergers/cases/decisions/m618_en.pdf.

CEC. (1958). *First general report on the activities of the Community*. Brussels: The Publications Department of European Communities.

———. (1959). *Second General Report on the Activities of the Communities*. Brussels: The Publications Department of European Communities.

———. (1960). *Third General Report on the Activities of the Communities*. Brussels: The Publications Department of European Communities.

———. (1962). *Fifth General Report on the Activities of the Communities*. Brussels: The Publications Department of European Communities.

———. (1963). *Sixth General Report on the Activities of the Community*. Brussels: The Publications Department of European Communities.

————. (1964). *Seventh General Report on the Activities of the Community*. Brussels: The Publications Department of European Communities.

————. (1965). *Eighth General Report on the Activities of the Community*. Brussels: The Publications Department of European Communities.

————. (1966). *Ninth General Report on the Activities of the Community*. Brussels: Publishing Services of the European Community.

————. (1972). *First Report on Competition Policy*. Brussels-Luxembourg: Office for Official Publications of the European Communities.

————. (1973). *Second Report on Competition Policy*. Brussels-Luxembourg: Office for Official Publications of the European Communities.

————. (1974). *Third Report on Competition Policy* (Brussels-Luxembourg: Office for Official Publications of the European Communities.

————. (1975). *Fourth Report on Competition Policy*. Brussels-Luxembourg: Office for Official Publications of the European Communities.

————. (1976). *Fifth Report on Competition Policy*. Brussels-Luxembourg: Office for Official Publications of the European Communities.

————. (1977). *Sixth Report on Competition Policy*. Brussels-Luxembourg: Office for Official Publications of the European Communities.

————. (1978a). *Seventh Report on Competition Policy*. Brussels, Luxembourg: Office for Official Publications of the European Communities.

————. (1978b). *Eleventh General Report on the Activities of the Communities, 1977*. Brussels: The Publications Department of European Communities.

————. (1979a). *Eighth Report on Competition Policy*. Brussels, Luxembourg: Office for Official Publications of the European Communities.

————. (1979b). *Twelfth General Report on the Activities of the Communities 1978*. Brussels: The Publications Department of European Communities.

————. (1980a). *Ninth Report on Competition Policy*. Brussels, Luxembourg: Office for Official Publications of the European Communities.

————. (1980b). *Thirteenth General Report on the Activities of the Communities 1979*. Brussels: The Publications Department of European Communities.

————. (1981a). *Tenth Report on Competition Policy*. Brussels, Luxembourg: Office for Official Publications of the European Communities.

————. (1981b). *Fourteenth General Report on the Activities of the Communities*. Brussels: Office for Official Publications of the European Communities.

————. (1982a). *Eleventh Report on Competition Policy*. Brussels, Luxembourg: Office for Official Publications of the European Communities.

————. (1982b). *The Competitiveness of the Community Industry*. Brussels, Luxembourg: Office for Official Publications of the European Communities.

————. (1983a). *Twelfth Report on Competition Policy*. Brussels: Office for Official Publications of the European Communities.

————. (1983b). *Sixteenth General Report on the Activities of the Communities 1982*. Brussels: The Publications Department of European Communities.

————. (1984). *Thirteenth Report on Competition Policy*. Brussels: Office for Official Publications of the European Communities.

————. (1985). *Fourteenth Report on Competition Policy*. Brussels, Luxembourg: Office for Official Publications of the European Communities.

————. (1987a). *Sixteenth Report on Competition Policy*. Brussels, Luxembourg: Office for Official Publications of the European Communities.

————. (1987b). *Esprit—The First Phase: Progress and Results, Communication from the Commission to the Council*. Luxembourg: Office for Official Publications of the European Communities.

————. (1987c). Towards A Dynamic European Economy: Green Paper on the Development of the Common Market for Telecommunications Services and Equipment COM(87) 290 final, Brussels, June 30, 1987.

————. (1988a). Towards a competitive Community-wide telecommunications market in 1992 COM (88) 48 final, Brussels, 9 February 1988.

————. (1988b). *Working towards Telecom 2000: Launching, the Programme RACE*. Luxembourg: Office for Official Publications of the European Communities.

————. (1988c). Commission Directive (88/301/EEC) of 16 May 1988 on competition in the markets in telecommunications terminal equipment. *Official Journal*, L 131, 27.05.1988, 73–77.

————. (1989). *Eighteenth Report on Competition Policy*. Luxembourg: Office for Official Publications of the European Communities.

————. (1990a). *Nineteenth Report on Competition Policy*. Luxembourg: Office for Official Publications of the European Communities.

————. (1990b). Industrial policy in an open and competitive environment: Guidelines for a Community approach COM(90) 556 final. Retrieved May 12, 2002, from http://aei.pitt.edu/5690/01/003082_1.pdf.

————. (1990c)., Commission Directive (90/388/EEC) of 28 June 1990 on competition in the markets for telecommunications services, *Official Journal*, L 192, 24.07.1990, 10–16.

————. (1991a). XXth *Report on Competition Policy*. Brussels, Luxembourg: Office for Official Publications of the European Communities.

————. (1991b) Guidelines (92/C 233/02) on the Application of EEC Competition Rules in the Telecommunications Sector *Official Journal*, C 233/2, 09.06.1991

————. (1992). XXIth *Report on Competition Policy*. Luxembourg: Office for Official Publications of the European Communities.

————. (1993a). *XXIInd Report on Competition Policy*. Luxembourg: Office for Official Publications of the European Communities.

————. (1993b). *Growth, Competitiveness, Employment: The Challenges and Ways Forward into the 21st Century: White Paper*. Luxembourg: Office for Official Publications of the European Communities.

————. (1994a). *XXIIIrd Report on Competition Policy 1993*. Luxembourg: Office for Official Publications of the European Communities.

————. (1994b). Commission Directive (94/46/EC) of 13 October 1994 Amending Directives 88/301/EEC and 90 388/EEC in Particular With Regard to Satellite Communications, *Official Journal*, L 268, 19.10.1994, 15–21.

————. (1994c). Green Paper on a Common Approach in the Field of Mobile and Personal Communications in the European Union (COM(94) 145—final, 27.04.1994.

————. (1994d), Green Paper on the Liberalization of Telecommunications Infrastructure and Cable Television Networks COM (94) 440 Final, Brussels, 25.10.1994.

————. (1995). *XXIVth Report on Competition Policy 1994*. Luxembourg: Office for Official Publications of the European Communities.

————. (1996a). *XXVth Report on Competition Policy 1995*. Luxembourg: Office for Official Publications of the European Communities.

————. (1996b). Commission Directive (96/2/EC) of 16 January 1996 Amending Directive 90/388/EEC With Regard to Mobile and Personal Communications, *Official Journal*, L 020, 26.01.1996, 59–66.

————. (1997a). *XXVIth Report on Competition Policy 1996*. Brussels: Office for Official Publications of the European Communities.

————. (1997b). Green Paper on the Convergence of the Telecommunications, Media and Information Technology Sectors, and the Implications for Regulation: Towards an Information Society Approach COM (97) 623, Brussels, 03.12.1997.

————. (1998a). *XXVIIth Report on Competition Policy 1997*. Luxembourg: Office for Official Publications of the European Communities.

———. (1998b). Notice on the Application of the Competition Rules to Access Agreements in the Telecommunication Sector: Framework, relevant markets and principles. Official Journal, C 265/2, 22.08.1998, 2–28.

———. (1999a). *XXVIIIth Report on Competition Policy 1998*. Luxembourg: Office for Official Publications of the European Communities.

———. (1999b). Towards a New Framework for Electronic Communications Infrastructure and Associated Services: The 1999 Communications Review COM (1999)539.

———. (2000). Commission Recommendation (2000/417/EC) of 25 May 2000 on Unbundled Access to the Local Loop: Enabling the Competitive Provision of a Full Range of Electronic Communications Services Including Broadband Multimedia and High-Speed Internet. *Official Journal*, L 156, 29.06.2000, 44–50.

———. (2001a). *XXXth Report on Competition Policy 2000*. Luxembourg: Office for Official Publications of the European Communities.

———. (2001b). Commission Working Document on Proposed New Regulatory Framework for Electronic Communications Networks and Services COM (2001) 175, Brussels. 28.03.2001. Retrieved November 4, 2004, from http://ec.europa.eu/archives/ISPO/infosoc/telecompolicy/en/com2001-175-5en.pdf.

———. (2002a). Commission Directive 2002/77/EC of 16 September 2002 on Competition in the Markets for Electronic Communications Networks and Services. *Official Journal*, L 249/21, 17.09.2002, 21–6.

———. (2002b). Commission intends to clear 3G network sharing agreements between T-Mobile and MM02 in the UK and Germany (IP/02/1277). Brussels, 10.09.2002. Retrieved June 27, 2003, from http://europa.eu/rapid/press ReleasesAction.do?reference=IP/02/1277&format=HTML&aged=0&langu age=EN&guiLanguage=en.

———.(2002c).CommissionsuspectsDeutscheTelekomofcharginganti-competitive tariffs for access to its local network (IP/02/686). Brussels, 08.04. 2002. Retrieved June 30, 2004, from http://europa.eu/rapid/pressReleasesAction.do?reference=IP/ 02/686&format=HTML&aged=1&language=EN&guiLanguage=en.

———. (2003a). Commission approves 3rd generation mobile network sharing in the United Kingdom (IP/03/589). Brussels, 30.04.2003. Retrieved June 28, 2004, from http://europa.eu/rapid/pressReleasesAction.do?reference=IP/03/1026&for mat=HTML&aged=1&language=EN&guiLanguage=en.

———. (2003b). Commission fines Deutsche Telekom for charging anti-competitive tariffs for access to its local networks (IP/03/717). Brussels, 21.04.2003. Retrieved June 23, 2004, from http://europa.eu/rapid/pressReleasesAction.do?reference=IP/ 02/686&format=HTML&aged=1&language=EN&guiLanguage=en.

———. (2004a). Commission staff working document: Annex to the report from the Commission on 'research and technological development activities of the European Union 2003 annual report COM(2004)533 Final SEC (2004) 1023. Brussels, 02.08.2004. Retrieved, July 14, 2005, from http://www.insme.info/ documenti/report-working-doc-2004_en.pdf.

———. (2004b). Five-year assessment of the European Union research framework programmes: 1999–2003. Brussels, 15.12.2004. Retrieved May 23, 2005, from http://www.euractiv.com/29/images/five_year_assessment_tcm29-135412.pdf.

———. (2004c). Communication from the Commission: A pro-active competition policy for a competitive Europe COM (2004a) 293 final. Brussels, 20.4.2004. Retrieved April 2, 2005, from http://eurlex.europa.eu/smartapi/cgi/sga_doc ?smartapi!celexplus!prod!DocNumber&lg=en&type_doc=COMfinal&an_ doc=2004&nu_doc=293.

———. (2004d). *XXXIIIrd report on competition policy 2003*, SEC (2004) 658 final. Brussels, 04.06.2004. Retrieved April 25, 2005, from http://ec.europa. eu/comm/competition/annual_reports/2003/en.pdf.

————. (2006a). DG Competition annual management plan 2006 (final). Retrieved December 12, 2006, from http://ec.europa.eu/comm/competition/publications/annual_management_plan/amp_2006_en.pdf.

————. (2006b). Commission staff working document, annex to the Communication from the Commission to the Council, the European Parliament, the European Economic and Social Committee, and the Committee of Regions: European electronic communications regulation and markets 2005 (11th Report), COM(2006)68 final. Retrieved December 10, 2006, from http://ec.europa.eu/information_society/policy/ecomm/doc/library/annualreports/11threport/sec_2006_193_vol2bis.pdf.

————. (2007). Commission proposes a single European telecoms market for 500 million consumers (IP/07/1677). Brussels, 13.12.2007. Retrieved November 17, 2007, from http://www.europa.eu/rapid/pressReleasesAction.do?reference=IP/07/1677&format=HTML&aged=0&language=EN&guiLanguage=en.

Commission Notice on the definition of relevant market for the purposes of Community competition law (1997). *Official Journal*, 09.12. 1997, 5–13. Retrieved May 12, 2004, from http://eur-lex.europa.eu/LexUriServ/LexUriServ.do?uri=C ELEX:31997Y1209(01):EN:HTML

Continental Can Company Incorporated (72/21/EEC) (1972). *Common Market Law Reports*, (R.P. Supplement), 2, D 11–35.

Council of Ministers. (1962). Council regulation No17/62 of 6 February 1962. *Official Journal*, 13, 21.02.1962, 204–11.

————. (1965–6). Council regulation 19/65 of the Council of 2 March 1965 on the application of Article 85(3) of the Treaty to certain categories of agreements and concerted practices (1965–66). *Official Journal*, 36/533, 02.03.1965, 533–5.

————. (1974). Council resolution of 15 July 1974 on a Community policy on data processing. *Official Journal*, C 086, 20.07.1974, 1.

————. (1979). Council resolution of 11 September 1979 on a Community action promoting microelectronic technology. *Official Journal*, C 231, 13.09.1979, 1–2.

————. (1984). Council recommendation (84/549/EEC) of 12 November 1984 concerning the implementation of harmonization in the field of telecommunications. *Official Journal*, L 298, 16.11. 1984, 49–50.

————. (1985). Council decision of 25 July 1985 on a definition phase for a Community action in the field of telecommunications technologies: R&D programme in advanced communication technologies for Europe (RACE) (85/372/EEC). *Official Journal*, L 210/24, 07.08.1985, 24–27.

————. (1986a). Council directive of 24 July 1986 on the initial stage of the mutual recognition of type approval for telecommunications terminal equipment. *Official Journal*, L 217, 05.08.1986, 21.

————. (1986b), Council recommendation (86/659/EEC) of 22 December 1986 (86/659/EEC) on the coordinated introduction of the integrated services digital network (ISDN) in the European Community. *Official Journal*, L 382, 31.12.1986, 36–41.

————. (1987). Council decision (87/95/EEC) of 22 December 1986 on standardization in the field of information technology and telecommunication, *Official Journal*, L 036, 07.02.1987, 31–7.

————. (1988a). Council decision of 14 December 1987 on a Community programme in the field of telecommunications technologies: Research and development (R&D) in advanced communications technologies in Europe (RACE Programme), (88/28/EEC). *Official Journal*, L 16/35, 21.01.1988, 35–43.

————. (1988b). Council resolution (88/C 257/01) of 30 June 1988 on the development of the Common Market for telecommunications services and equipment up to 1992. *Official Journal*, C 257, 04.10.1988, 1–3.

———. (1989). Council Regulation (EEC) No 4064/89 of 21 December 1989 on the control of concentrations between undertakings. *Official Journal*, L 395, 30.12.1989, 1–12.

———. (1990a). Council directive (90/387/EEC) of 28 June 1990 on the establishment of the internal market for telecommunications services through the implementation of open network provision. *Official Journal*, L 192, 24.07.1990, 1–9.

———. (1990b). Council recommendation (90/543/EEC) of 9 October 1990 on the coordinated introduction of pan-European land-based public radio paging in the Community. *Official Journal*, L 310, 09.11.1990, 23–7.

———. (1990c). Council directive (90/544/EEC) of 9 October 1990 on the frequency bands designated for the coordinated introduction of pan-European land-based public radio paging in the Community. *Official Journal*, L 310, 09.11.1990, 28–9.

———. (1991). Council recommendation (91/288/EEC) of 3 June 1991 on the coordinated introduction of digital European cordless telecommunications (DECT) into the Community. *Official Journal*, L 144, 08.06.1991, 47–50.

———. (1992a). Council directive (92/44/EEC) of 5 June 1992 on the application of open network provision to leased lines. *Official Journal*, L 165/27, 19.06.1992, 27.

———. (1992b). Council recommendation (92/383/EEC) of 5 June 1992 on the provision of harmonized integrated services digital network (ISDN) access arrangements and a minimum set of ISDN offerings in accordance with open network provision (ONP) principles. *Official Journal*, L 200, 18.07.1992, 10–19.

———. (1992c). Council resolution (92/C 158/01) of 5 June 1992 on the development of the integrated services digital network (ISDN) in the Community as a European-wide telecommunications infrastructure for 1993 and beyond. *Official Journal*, C 158, 25.06.1992, 1–2.

———. (1992d). Council recommendation (92/382/EEC) of 5 June 1992 on the harmonized provision of a minimum set of packet-switched data services (PSDS) in accordance with open network provision (ONP) principles. *Official Journal*, L 200 , 18.07.1992, 1–9.

———. (1992e). Council directive (92/13/EEC) of 25 February 1992 coordinating the laws, regulations and administrative provisions relating to the application of Community rules on the procurement procedures of entities operating in the water, energy, transport and telecommunications sectors. *Official Journal*, L 76, 23.03.1992, 14–20.

———. (1992f). Council resolution (92/C 8/01) of 19 December 1991 on the development of the Common Market for satellite communications services and equipment. *Official Journal*, C 8, 14.01.1992, 1.

———. (1993a). Council directive (91/263/EEC) of 29 April 1991 on the approximation of the member states concerning telecommunications terminal Equipment, including the mutual recognition of their conformity. *Official Journal*, L 128/1, 23.05.1991, 1–18.

———. (1993b). Council directive (93/97/EEC) of 29 October 1993 supplementing directive 91/263/EEC in respect of satellite earth station equipment. *Official Journal*, L 290/1, 24.11.1993, 1–8.

———. (1993c). Council directive (93/38/EEC) of 14 June 1993 coordinating the procurement procedures of entities operating in the water, energy, transport and telecommunications sector. *Official Journal*, L 199, 09.08.1993, 84–138.

———. (1993d). Council resolution (93/ C 399/01) of 7 December 1993 on the introduction of satellite personal communication services in the Community. *Official Journal*, C 339, 16.12.1993, 1–2.

————. (1994). Council resolution (94/C 379/03) of 22 December 1994 on the principles and timetable for the liberalization of telecommunications infrastructures. *Official Journal*, C 379, 31.12.1994, 4–5.

————. (1995). Council resolution (95/C 258/01) of 18 September 1995 on the implementation of the future regulatory framework for telecommunications. *Official Journal*, C 258, 03.10.1995, 1–3.

————. (2003). Council regulation EC No 1/2003 of 16 December 2002 on the implementation of the rules on competition laid down in Articles 81 and 82 of the Treaty. *Official Journal*, L 1, 04.01.2003, 1–25.

————. (2004). Council regulation (EC) No 139/2004 of 20 January 2004 on the control of concentrations between undertakings (the EC Merger Regulation). *Official Journal*, L 24, 29.01.2004, 1–22.

ECR 900 (Case IV/32.688) (1992). *Common Market Law Reports* 4, 54–60.

Enel/FT/DT (Case No IV/JV.2). Brussels, 22.06.1998. Retrieved on April 19, 2004, from http://ec.europa.eu/comm/competition/mergers/cases/decisions/jv2_en.pdf.

Ericsson/Nokia/Psion (Case No Comp/JV.6), 11.08.1998. Retrieved August 9, 2004, from http://ec.europa.eu/comm/competition/mergers/cases_old/index/by_nr_jv_0.html#jv_6.

European Parliament and Council of Ministers (1997a). Decision No 710/97/EC of the European Parliament and of the Council of 24 March 1997 on a coordinated authorization Approach in the field of satellite personal-communication services in the Community. *Official Journal*, L 105, 23.04.1997, 4–12.

————. (1997b). Decision No 1336/97/EC of the European Parliament and of the Council of 17 June 1997 on a series of guidelines for trans-European telecommunications networks. *Official Journal*, L 183, 11.07.1997, 12–20.

————. (1997c). Directive (97/33/EC) of the European Parliament and of the Council of 30 June 1997 on interconnection in telecommunications with regard to ensuring universal service and interoperability through application of the principles of open Network provision (ONP). *Official Journal*, L 199, 26.07.1997, 32–52.

————. (1998). Directive (98/61/EC) of the European Parliament and of the Council of 24 September 1998 amending directive 97/33/EC with regard to operator number portability and carrier pre-selection. *Official Journal*, L 268, 03.10.1998, 3–38.

————. (2000). Regulation (EC) No 2887/2000 of the European Parliament and of the Council of 18 December 2000 on unbundled access to the local loop. *Official Journal*, L 336, 30.12.2000, 4–8.

————. (2002a). Directive 2002/21/ EC of the European Parliament and of the Council of 7 March 2002 on a common regulatory framework for electronic communications networks and services (Framework Directive). *Official Journal*, L 108/33, 24.4.2002, 33–50.

————. (2002b). Directive 2002/20/EC of the European Parliament and of the Council of 7 March 2002 on the authorization of electronic communications networks and services (Authorization Directive). *Official Journal*, L 108/21, 24.4.2002, 21–32.

————. (2002c). Directive 2002/19/EC of the European Parliament and of the Council of 7 March 2002 on access to, and interconnection of, electronic communications networks and associated facilities (Access Directive). *Official Journal*, L 108/7, 24.4.2002, pp. 7–20.

————. (2002d). Directive 2002/22/EC of the European Parliament and of the Council of 7 March 2002 on universal service and users' rights relating to electronic communications networks and services (Universal Service Directive). *Official Journal*, L 108/51, 24.4.2002, 51–77.

————. (2002e). Directive 2002/58/EC of the European Parliament and of the Council of 12 July 2002 concerning the processing of personal data and the protection of privacy in the electronic communications sector (Directive on Privacy and Electronic Communications). *Official Journal*, L 201/37, 31.07.2002, pp. 37–47.

Europemballage Corporation and Continental Can Company Inc. v. EC Commission (Case 6/72) (1973). *Common Market Law Reports*, 68, 199–239.

Flaminio Costa *v* ENEL (Case 6/64) (1964). Retrieved December 13, 2002, from http://europa.eu.int/.

Ford Tractor (Belgium) Limited (64/651/EEC) (1965). *Common Market Law Reports*, 13, 32–5.

France, Italy and the United Kingdom (France Intervening) *v.* EC Commission (Netherlands and Germany Intervening) (Cases 188–190/80) (1982). *Common Market Law Reports*, 35(3), 144–76.

France Telecom/Orange (Case No Comp/ M. 2016). Brussels, 11.08.2000. Retrieved June 13, 2004, from http://ec.europa.eu/comm/competition/mergers/cases/decisions/m2016_en.pdf.

France Telecom (2005/709/EC) 2005. *Official Journal*, L 269/30, 14.10.2005, 30–41. Retrieved September 26, 2006 from http://eur-lex.europa.eu/LexUriServ/site/en/oj/2005/l_269/l_26920051014en00300041.pdf.

France Telecom (2006/621/EC) 2006. *Official Journal*, L 257/11, 20.09.2006, 11–67. Retrieved September 28, 2006 from http://eur-lex.europa.eu/LexUriServ/site/en/oj/2006/l_257/l_25720060920en00110067.pdf.

GEC/ANT/Telettra/SAT (Case IV/32.011) (1988). *Common Market Law Reports*, 4, 815–20.

Gema (71/224/EEC) (1971) *Common Market Law Reports*, (R.P. Supplement), 3, D 35–61.

Grundig Verkaufs-MmbH (64/566/EEC) (1964). *Common Market Law Reports*, 12, 489–504.

Guidelines on the application of EEC competition rules in the telecommunication sector. *Official Journal*, C 233/2, 06.09.1991, 2.

Hoffman-La Roche & Co. AG v. Commission of the European Communities (Case 85/76), (1979), *Common Market Law Reports*, 26(3), 211–344.

Istituto Chemioterapico Italiano SpA and Commercial Solvents Corporation v. EC Commission (Case 6–7/73) (1974). *Common Market Law Reports*, 1, 309–46.

Italy v. EC Commission (Case 41/83) (1985). *Common Market Law Reports*, 2, 368–96.

Mannesmann/Orange (Case No Comp/M. 1760). Brussels, 20.12.1999. Retrieved on June 17, 2004, from http://ec.europa.eu/comm/competition/mergers/cases/decisions/m1760_en.pdf.

MCI WorldCom/Sprint (Case No COMP/M.1741). Brussels, 28.06.2000. Retrieved from May 17, 2004, from http://ec.europa.eu/comm/competition/mergers/cases/decisions/m1741_en.pdf.

Metro-SB-Groß-Märkte GmbH & Co. KG v. EC Commission (Case 26/76) (1978). *Common Market Law Reports*, 22(2), pp. 1–45.

Mobilcom AG (2005/346/EG) 2005. *Official Journal*, L 116/55, 04.05.2005, 55–75. Retrieved September 12, 2005, from http://eur-lex.europa.eu/LexUriServ/site/en/oj/2005/l_116/l_11620050504en00550075.pdf.

Nortel/Bay (Case No IV/M.1263). Brussels, 21.08.1998. Retrieved December 24, 2004, from http://ec.europa.eu/comm/competition/mergers/cases/decisions/m1263_en.pdf.

Notice on the application of the competition rules to access agreements in the telecommunication sector: Framework, relevant markets and principles. *Official Journal*, C 265/02, 22.08.1998, 2–28.

Omega Watches (70/488/EEC) (1970). *Common Market Law Reports*, (R.P. Supplement), 4, D49-D65.

Phoenix/GlobalOne (Case No IV/35.617). *Official Journal*, L 239, 19.09.1996, 57–78.

Plessey/General Electric/Siemens (Case IV.33.018) (1992). *Common Market Law, Reports*, 4, 471–85.

Quinine (69/240/EEC) (1969). *Common Market Law Reports*, (R.P. Supplement), 4, D41-D76.

Regulatory Authority for Telecommunications and Posts (1999). *Annual Report 1999*. Retrieved December 14, 2006, from http://www.bundesnetzagentur.de/media/archive/2038.pdf.

Schneider Electric v Commission (T-310/01). Brussels, 10.12.2002. Retrieved March 17, 2005, from http://eurlex.europa.eu/LexUriServ/LexUriServ.do?uri=CELEX:62001A0310:EN:HTML

Siemens/Italtel (Case No IV/M.468), 17.02.1995. Retrieved on April 23, 2004, from http://ec.europa.eu/comm/competition/mergers/cases/decisions/m1717_en.pdf.

Solectron/Ericsson Switches (Case No Comp/M.1849). Brussels, 29.02.2000. Retrieved on June 12, 2004, from http://ec.europa.eu/comm/competition/mergers/cases/decisions/m1849_en.pdf.

STET/Italtel-SIT/AT&T (Case IV/33/232) (1993). *Common Market Law Reports*, 4, 276–85.

Telespeed Services Limited/United Kingdom Post Office (Case 82/861/EEC) (1983). *Common Market Law Reports*, 1, 457–69.

Telia/Sonera (Case No COMP/M.2803). Brussels, 10.7.2002. Retrieved July 6, 2004, from http://ec.europa.eu/comm/competition/mergers/cases/decisions/m2803_en.pdf.

Unisource (Case No IV/35.830. *Official Journal*, L 318, 20.11.1997, 1–23.

Uniworld (Case No IV/35.738). *Official Journal*, L 318, 20.11.1997, 24–41.

Van Katwijk's Industrieen N.V. (70/487/EEC) (1970). *Common Market Law Reports*, (R.P. Supplement), 4, D43-D48.

Viag/Orange UK (Case No IV/JV.4), Brussels, 11.08.1998. Retrieved July 12, 2004, from http://ec.europa.eu/comm/competition/mergers/cases/decisions/jv4_en.pdf.

Wanadoo Interactive (COMP/38.233). Brussels, 16.07.2003. Retrieved on June 19, 2004, from http://ec.europa.eu/comm/competition/antitrust/cases/decisions/38233/en.pdf.

SECONDARY SOURCES

A market where the US lacks. (1980, February 11). *Business Week*(Industrial Edition), 73.

A mobile phone maker finds a hookup in the US. (1984, July 2). *Business Week*, 40.

Addleson, M. (1994). Competition. In P. J. Boettke (Eds.), *The Elgar companion to Austrian economics*. Aldershot: Edward Elgar.

Adonis, A. (1993a, September 15). BT's Pounds 400m Spanish venture. *Financial Times* (London), 28.

———. (1993b, December 9). A brief encounter, now line is engaged. *Financial Times* (London), 23.

———. (1994a, June 15). Survey of telecommunication in business. *Financial Times* (London), 4.

———. (1994b, January 18). Nokia and Hewlett in alliance. *Financial Times* (London), 9.

———. (1994c, September 27). BT alliance with three Nordic partners. *Financial Times* (London), 21.

———. (1994d, October 17). Survey of international telecommunications. *Financial Times* (London), 13.

Adonis, A. & Tait, N. (1993, June 3). BT takes global step with Dollars 4.3bn US deal: MCI agrees to joint venture. *Financial Times* (London), 1.

Adonis, A. & Dickson, M. (1994, June 8). Sprint warms up for race to link world telecoms. *Financial Times* (London), 31.

AEG/Robert Bosch: If you can't make it, buy it, (1981, December 12). *The Economist*, 82.

Albaek, S., et al. (1998). The Danish competition act and barriers to entry. In S. Martin (Eds.), *Competition policies in Europe*. Amsterdam: Elsevier.

Albo, G. (1997). A world of market of opportunities? Capitalist obstacles and Left economic policy. In L. Panitch (Ed.), *Socialist Register 1997*. London: Merlin Press.

Albo, G. & Zuege, A. (1999). European capitalism today: Between the *Euro* and the third-way. *Monthly Review*, 51(3), 100–20.

Albors-Llorens, A. (2002). Competiton policy and the shaping of the single market. In C. Barnard & J. Scott (Eds.), *The law of the single european market: Unpacking the premises*. Oxford: Hart Publishing.

Alcatel—One name, one company. (1987, October). *Telecommunications: Telecom 87 Supplement*(International Edition), 146–7.

Alcatel goes broadband. (1991, July). *Telecommunications* (International Edition, 13.

Alcatel Lex Column. (2001, February 1). *Financial Times* (London Edition 1), 22.

Alcatel Alsthom: Power play. (1991, August 3). *The Economist*, 65.

Allen, C. S. (2005). 'Ordoliberalism' trumps Keynesianism: Economic policy in the federal republic of Germany and the EU. In B. H. Moss (Eds.), *Monetary union in crisis: The European Union as a neo-liberal construction*. New York: Palgrave Macmillian.

Americanization of L.M. Ericsson. (1983, October) *Business Week*, 63.

Arnold, M. (2002a, December 13). Alcatel falls on bond launch. *Financial Times* (London Edition 2), 28.

———. (2002b, July 30). France Telecom sells stake. *Financial Times* (London Edition 1), 23.

———. (2003, February 5). France Tel sells Eutelsat stake. *Financial Times* (London Edition 2), 18.

Arnold, M., Budden, R. & Grande, C. (2002, February 27). BT in battle for fast-Internet customers. *Financial Times* (London Edition 3), 3.

Arrow, K. J. (1975). Thorstein Veblen as an economic theorist. *American Economist*, 19(1), 5–9.

Asch, P. (1970). *Economic theory and the antitrust dilemma*. New York: John Wiley & Sons, Inc.

Atkins, R. (1997, March 12). Telekom set for launch of 'VIP' service. *Financial Times* (London Edition 1), 25.

———. "Germany's Telephone Price War Escalates," *Financial Times* (London Edition 2), August 24, 1998, 16.

———. (1999a, March 16). Telekom set to slash call prices. *Financial Times* (London Edition 1), 30.

———. (1999b, October 5). Deutsche Telekom cuts Internet prices. *Financial Times* (London Edition 1), 44.

Baimbridge, M., Harrop, J. & Philippidis, G. (2004). *Current economic issues in EU integration*. New York: Palgrave Macmillan.

Baker, S. (1999, March 22). Phone giants on the prowl. *Business Week*(International Edition), 20.

Barker, T. & Budden, R. (2002, February 8). BT starts to ring the changes. *Financial Times* (London Edition 2), 24.

Baker, S. & Echikson, W. (1998, November 30). A shaken CEO at Philips. *Business Week*, 26.

Baker, S., Resch, I. & Crockett, R. O. (2000, August 14). Nokia's costly stumble. *Business Week*, 42.

Baran, P. A. & Sweezy, P. M. (1968). *Monopoly capital: An essay on the American economic and social order* (12th ed.). New York and London: Monthly Review Press.

Barber, T., Benoit, B. & Calusen, S. (2002, May 21). Siemens sells Internet hardware to Juniper. *Financial Times* (London), 31.

Barket, T. (2000, December 7). Freeserve taken over for Pounds 1.6bn: Search for partner ends in France Telecom deal. *Financial Times* (London Edition 1), 27.

Barnard, K. E. (1990). Doing business in Europe. *Telecommunications Policy*, 14(4), 279–82.

Barnes, H. (1982, June 16). Big companies increase share: Financial Times Survey; Finland V; Electronics, *Financial Times* (London), 5.

———. (1983, August 19). Telenokia finds fresh two-way connection: Finland pushes forward in telecommunications. *Financial Times* (London), 17.

Barry, N. P. (1989). Political and economic thought of German neo-liberals. In A. Peacock & H. Willgerodt (Eds.), *German neo-liberals and the social market economy*. New York: St. Martin's Press.

Barry, F. & O'Toole, F. (1998). Irish competition policy and the macroeconomy. In S. Martin (Ed.), *Competition policies in Europe*. Amsterdam: Elsevier.

Bartle, I. (2006). Globalization and EU policy-making: Neo-liberal transformation of telecommunications and electricity. Manchester: Manchester University Press.

Bauer, J. M. (2005). Regulation and state ownership: Conflicts and complementarities in EU telecommunications. *Annals of Public and Cooperative Economics*, 76(2), 151–77.

Baumol, W. (1982). Contestable markets: An uprising in the theory of industry structure. *American Economic Review*, 72(1), 1–15.

Bavasso, A. (2004). Electronic communications: A new paradigm for European Regulation. *Common Market Law Review*, 41, 87–118.

Beattie, A., et al. (2005, August 26). EU consumers ambiguous on low-cost clothing. *Financial Times*. Retrieved August 25, 2005, from http://search.ft.com/ftArticle?queryText=EU+Consumers+Ambiguous+on+Low-Cost+Clothing&aje=true&id=050826000368&ct=0.

Bebr, G. (1953). The European coal and steel community: A political and legal innovation. *Yale Law Journal*, 63(1), 1–43.

Bellamy, C. & Child, G. D. (1987). *Common Market law of competition* (3rd ed.). London: Sweet & Maxwell.

Belson, K. & Austen, I. (2006, June 20). A mania in telecom to merge. *New York Times*. Retrieved December 18, 2006, from http://www.nytimes.com/2006/06/20/technology/20telecom.html.

Benoit, B. (2000a, August 30). Deutsche Telekom signals end to run of large acquisitions. *Financial Times* (London Edition 1), 21.

———. (2000b, May 22). DT weathers liberalization storm; Survey: Germany. *Financial Times* (Monday Surveys GER1), 15.

———. (2001a, February 23). Electronics chief spoils the party with tales of a slowdown. *Financial Times* (London), 29.

———. (2001b, August 13). The failures that meant the head of ICN had to go. *Financial Times* (London), 20.

———. (2003, January 18). German business held back by nation's social conscience. *Financial Times* (London Edition), 24.

Benoit, B. & Waters, R. (2000, March 28). Deutsche Telekom invests in IT sector. *Financial Times* (London Edition 1), 34.

Benoit, B. & Johnson, J. (2002, September 14). Germany in pledge to help Mobilcom telecommunications. *Financial Times* (London Edition), 12.

Bernholz, P. (1989). Ordoliberals and the control of the money supply. In A Peacock & H. Willgerodt (Eds.), *German neo-liberals and the social market economy.* New York: St. Martin's Press.

Besen, S. M. (1990). The European telecommunications standards institute: A preliminary analysis. *Telecommunications Policy,* 14(6), 521–30.

Betts, P. (1984, August 24). CIT-Alcatel raises stake in US group. *Financial Times* (London), 14.

———. (2000, July 1). Telecom Italia sells Italtel stake to Cisco. *Financial Times* (London), 18.

Betts, P. & Ellis, W. (1983, January 6). AT&T to join Philips in digital switching venture. *Financial Times* (London), 1.

Betts, P. & Housego, D. (1987, April 24). Row erupts as Ericsson wins control of CGCT. *Financial Times* (London), 1.

Black, J. (2002). Oxford dictionary of economics. Oxford: Oxford University Press.

Block, F. (1987). *Revising state theory: Essays in politics and postindustrialism.* Philadelphia: Temple University Press.

Bogler, D. (1999, April 27). GEC agrees $4.2bn Fore deal. *Financial Times* (London Edition 1), 23.

Bohlin, E., & Granstrand, O. (1991). Strategic options for national monopolies in transition: The case of Swedish telecom. *Telecommunications Policy,* 15(5), 453–76.

Bolbol, A. A. & Lovewell, M. A. (2001). Three views on stock markets and corporate behavior: Tobin, Veblen, and Marx. *Journal of Post Keynesian Economics,* 23(3), 527–43.

Bork, R. H. (1967). The goals of antitrust policy. *American Economic Review,* 57(2), pp. 242–53.

Brenton, M. E. The role of standardization in telecommunications. In OECD (ed.), *Trends of change in telecommunications policy.* Paris: OECD.

Britain: Business past, business future: Takeover of Marconi. 2005, October 29). *The Economist,* 36.

Brittan, S. L. (1991). Competition policy and merger control in the single European *market.* Cambridge: Brotius Publications Limited.

Brown-Humes, C. (2000, April 28). Nokia ahead sharply in term. *Financial Times* (London Edition 2), 27.

———. (2001a, April 24). Sony and Ericsson set to unveil joint venture. *Financial Times* (London Edition 2), 26.

Brown-Humes, C., Budden, R. & Gowers, A. (2002, November 18). There are challenges ahead but the Finnish group's chief believes the tide has turned for the handset industry. *Financial Times* (London Edition 1), 21.

Brown-Humes, C. & Heavens, A. (2001, March 14). Nokia plans to outsource two network plants. *Financial Times* (London Edition 2), 36.

Brown-Humes, C. & Waters, R. (2000, December 7). Ericsson sells Juniper shares to raise Dollars 1.5bn. *Financial Times* (London Edition 1), 34.

Bruce, R. R., Cunard, J. P., & Director, M. D. (1988). *The telecom mosaic: Assembling the new international structure.* London: Butterworths.

Brusse, W. A. & Griffiths, R. (1998). Paradise lost or paradise regained? Cartel policy and cartel legislation in the Netherlands. In S. Martin (Ed.), *Competition policies in Europe.* Amsterdam: Elsevier.

Brussels clears Telekom offer. (1996, November 1). *Financial Times* (London Edition 1), 2.

Bryan, R. (1985). Monopoly in Marxist method. *Capital & Class*, 26, pp. 72–92.

Buck, T., Johnson, J. & Minder, R. (2004, July 21). Brussels rules against France Telecom state aid. *Financial Times* (London 1st Ed.), p. 27.

Buck, T., Blitz, J. & Bickerton, I. (2007, June 24). EU treaty breaks years of deadlock. *Financial Times*. Retrieved August 24, 2005, from http://www.ft.com/cms/s/0/c8880f8c-228b-11dc-ac53-000b5df10621.html.

Buchan, D. (1996, January 13). France Telecom to join the Internet. *Financial Times* (London), 2.

Buchan, D. & Ridding, J. (1995, March 14). Elite searches for safety in numbers: The bonds between French business and the state are weakening. *Financial Times* (London), 21.

Budden, R. (2002, September 7). F Telecom shares hit by rumors. *Financial Times* (USA Edition 1), 8.

Bulmer, S. J. (1996). The European Council and the Council of the European Union: Shapers of a European confederation. *Publius: The Journal of Federalism*, 26(4), 17–42.

Burt, T. (1999, March 1). Nokia aims to increase staff by 25%. *Financial Times* (London Edition 1), 24.

Burton, J. (1991, August 23). Ericsson profits down 26% as orders shrink. *Financial Times* (London), 18.

Buxton, J. (1982, June 25). Planning a new strategy for telecommunications: Financial Times survey, Italian engineering V; Electronics. *Financial Times* (London), 6.

———. (1985, November 28). Stet and Fiat agree to merge subsidiaries. *Financial Times* (London), 19.

Camesasca, P. & Van Der Bergh, R. J. (2002). Achilles uncovered: Revisiting the European commission's 1997 market definition notice. *The Antitrust Bulletin*, 47(1), 143–86.

Campbell, A. (1986). The single European act and the implications. *International and Comparative Law Quarterly*, 35(4), 932–9.

Campbell-Smith, D. (1982, March 18). Plessey in £19m sale of four businesses. *Financial Times* (London), 28.

Cane, A. (1982, June 17). Plessey leaps in the office with Ibis. *Financial Times* (London), 17.

———. (1994, November 18). Siemens in multimedia alliance. *Financial Times* (London), 24.

———. (1995a, March 1). Asia-Pacific will head spenders; Financial Times IT Review of Information Technology (18), *Financial Times* (London), p. 8.

———. (1995b, October 3). Survey of international telecommunications. *Financial Times* (London), 3.

———. (1995c, January 19). Competition down the line. *Financial Times* (London), 15.

———. (1996a, August 22). BT cuts cost of business link to superhighway. *Financial Times* (London Edition 1), 8.

———. (1996b, January 20). Telecoms competition hots up: European operators need to ring big changes *Financial Times* (London), 2.

———. (1998a, April 9), Nokia signs global alliance with CSC. *Financial Times* (London Edition 2), 36.

———. (1998b, July 25). Industrial logic adds up to confirm tell-tale signs of a transatlantic connection. *Financial Times* (London Edition 1), 19.

———. (1999a, March 30. Deal on third generation mobile phone standards boosts European prospects. *Financial Times* (London Edition 1), 8.

———. (1999b, January 20). GEC decides to turn its back on the past. *Financial Times* (London Edition 1), 24.

———. (1999c, February 10). Europe's operators add up to a wrong number. *Financial Times* (London Edition 3), 32.

———. (1999d, March 12). BT pays £90m for 20% stake in ImpSat. *Financial Times* (London Edition), 22.

———. (1999e, July 2). BT expands in US via $340m Syntegra deal. *Financial Times* (London Edition 1), 22.

———. (2000a, April 4). Cisco and Nokia in mobiles pact. *Financial Times* (London Edition 1), 15.

———. (2000b, April 22). Marconi expands in wireless with Pounds 391m MSI deal. *Financial Times* (London Edition 1), 21.

———. (2000c, October 6). Marconi to sell commodity manufacturing business. *Financial Times* (London Edition 1), 23.

———. (2000d, March 1). BT cuts subscriptions to increase market share. *Financial Times* (London Edition 1), 4.

Cane, A. & Owen, D. (1996, September 27). BT hopes £1bn deal will boost European aims. *Financial Times* (London Edition 1), 1.

Carchedi, G. (2001). *For another Europe: A class analysis of economic integration.* London: Verso.

Carnegy, H. (1993a, November 17). Ericsson retains its Swedish style—But the Group's background has drawbacks. *Financial Times* (London), 32.

———. (1993b, July 9). Nokia shrugs off the turmoil of the 1980s. *Financial Times* (London), 26.

———. (1995, September 1). Ericsson to cut jobs, sell units. *Financial Times* (London), 17.

———. (1996a, June 13). Companies and finance: Europe; Nokia to offload struggling TV unit to Semi-Tech. *Financial Times* (London), 31.

———. (1996b, June 17). People: North Star seeks another way to shine. *Financial Times* (London), 11.

Carpentier, M. (1995). Foreword. In J-E. De Cocbrone, C. Berben & P. Scott (Eds.), *Telecommunications for Europe 1995: The CEC sources, Volume 3.* Amsterdam: IOS Press.

Carson, R. B., Thomas, W. L., & Hecht, J. (2002). *Economic issues today: Alternative approaches* (7th ed.). Armonk, New York: M. E. Sharpe.

CGE/Thomson: Connecting. (1985, April 20). *The Economist,* 72.

Chamberlin, E. H. (1937). Monopolistic or imperfect competition? *Quarterly Journal of Economics,* 51(4), 557–80.

———. (1950). *The theory of monopolistic competition: A re-orientation of the theory of value* (6th ed.). Cambridge: Harvard University Press.

———. (1961). The origins and early development of monopolistic competition theory. *Quarterly Journal of Economics,* 75(4), 515–43.

Chang, H. (1997). The economics and politics of regulation: A critical survey. *Cambridge Journal of Economics,* 21(6), 703–28.

Chryssochoou, N. D. (2001). *Theorizing European integration.* London: Sage Publications.

Chryssouchoou, N. D., Tsinisizelis, M. J., Stavridis, S. & Ifantis, K. (1999). *Theory of reform in the European Union* (2nd ed.). Manchester: Manchester University Press.

Cini, M. & McGowan, L. (1998). *Competition policy in the European Union.* (New York: St. Martin's Press.

Clark, J. M. (1940). Toward a concept of workable competition. *American Economic Review,* 30(2), 241–56.

———. (1943). Imperfect competition theory and basing-point problems. *American Economic Review,* 33(2), pp. 283–300.

———. (1955). Competition: static models and dynamic aspects. *American Economic Review,* 45(2), 450–62.

————. (1960). *Alternative to serfdom: Five lectures delivered on the William W. Cook foundation at the University of Michigan, March 1947* (2nd ed.). Vintage Books.

————. (1961). *Competition as a dynamic process*. Washington DC: Brookings Institution.

————. (1967). *Preface to social economics: Essays on economic theory and social problems*. New York: Augustus M. Kelley Publishers.

————. (1969). *Social control of business* (2nd ed.). New York: Augustus M. Kelley Publishers.

Clarke, S. (2001). The globalization of capital, crisis and class struggle. *Capital & Class*, 75, 93–101.

Clements, B. (1998). The impact of convergence on regulatory policy in Europe. *Telecommunications Policy*, 22(3), 197–205.

Cocks, P. (1980). Towards a Marxist theory of European integration. *International Organization*, 34(1), 1–40.

Corbett, J. & Vines, D. (1999). Asian currency and financial crises: Lessons from vulnerability, crisis, and collapse. *World Economy*, 22(2), 155–77.

Corbey, D. (1995). Functionalism—Stagnation as a booster of European integration. *International Organization*, 49(2), 253–84.

Coy, P., Levine, J. B., Gross, N. & Schares, G. E. (1991, October 7). Super phones. *Business Week*, 138.

Crawford, L. & Owen, D. (2000, February 24). Alcatel down after Newbridge buy. *Financial Times* (London Edition 2), 30.

Curwen, P. (1995). Telecommunications policy in the European Union: Developing the information superhighway. *Journal of Common Market Studies*, 33(3), 331–60.

Dalum, B., et al. (2000). Europe and the information and communications technologies revolution. In Fagerberg, J., Guerrieri, P., & Cerspagen, P. (Eds.), *The economic challenge for Europe: Adapting to innovation based on growth*. Cheltenham: Edward Elgar.

Daniel, C. (2000, August 8). Inside Track: Offspring seeks to shed its parent's culture. *Financial Times* (London), 10.

Dawkins, W. (1989, July 19). Moves to break monopolies' stranglehold. Survey: International telecommunications. *Financial Times* (London), 12.

————. (1990, December 13). Alcatel buys 10% Telettra stake. *Financial Times* (London), 28.

————. (1992, January 28). Alcatel sells postal units in record buy-out. *Financial Times* (London), 22.

De Bernis, D. (1990). On a Marxist theory of regulation. *Monthly Review* 41(8), 28–37.

De Búrca, G. & Weiler, J. H. H. (Eds.) (2001). *The European Court of Justice*. Oxford: Oxford University Press.

De Jonquieres, G. (1985, July 5). Crossed lines in an $80bn industry: European telecommunications. *Financial Times* (London), 14.

————. (1986, December 1). World Telecommunications 4: Old Patchwork Begins to Come Apart, Survey. *Financial Times* (London), IV.

De Jonquieres, G. & Barber, L. (1985, December 4). GEC floats merger worth £1.16bn in overture to Plessey. *Financial Times* (London), 1.

Delcourt, B. (1991). EC decisions and directives on information technology and telecommunications. *Telecommunications Policy*, 15(1), 15–21.

Del Marmol, C. (1963, September). *Rules applicable to dominant positions in the common market (Article 86 of the Rome Treaty)*. In Proceedings: Conference on antitrust and the European communities, Brussels and Luxembourg.

Dennis, K. (1977). *Competition in the history of economic thought*. New York: Arno Press.

Deutsche Telekom: Wrung out. (1998, February 7). *The Economist*(US Edition), 68.

Dinan, D. (2004). *Europe recast: A short history of European Union.* Boulder, Colorado: Lynne Rienner Publishers.

Dixon, H. (1988, July 25). Telefonica in bid to reassert role of telephone networks. *Financial Times* (London), 4.

———. (1992, January 8). Sprint makes the running in challenging telecoms policy. *Financial Times* (London), 9.

Dixon, R. C. (1958). European policies on restrictive business practices. *American Economic Review,* 48(2), 442–51.

Dodsworth, T. (1982, April 13). French strives to catch up. *Financial Times* (London), 16.

Dodsworth, T. & Dixon, H. (1989, September 9). Plessey concedes defeat to GEC-Siemens. *Financial Times* (London), 22.

Done, K. (1987, October 21). Ericsson to sell office equipment operations. *Financial Times* (London), 31.

Drake, W. J. (1994). The transformation of International telecommunications standardization: European and global dimension. In C. Steinfield, J. M. Bauer & L. Caby (Eds.), *Telecommunications in transition: policies, services and technologies in the European community.* Thousands Oaks: Sage Publications.

Dyrberg, T. B. (1997). *The circular structure of power: Politics, identity, community,* London: Verso.

Dyson, K. (1986). West European states and communications revolution. *Western European Politics,* 9(4), 10–55.

———. (1990). West European states and the communications revolution. In K. Dyson & P. Humphreys (Eds.), *The politics of the communications revolution in Western Europe.* London: Frank Cass.

Dyson, K. & Humphreys, P. (1990). Introduction: Politics, markets and communications policies. In K. Dyson & P. Humphreys (Eds.), *The political economy of communications: International and European dimensions.* London: Routledge.

Edmondson, G. (1988, April 6). Alcatel doesn't look like an also-ran anymore. *Business Week*(International Edition), 20.

Edmondson, G. et al. (1995, April 24). Telecom giants still have the lines tied up. *Business Week*(International Edition), 20.

———. (1999, October 25). Time is running out. *Business Week*(International Edition), 26.

Eatwell, J. (1987). Competition: Classical conceptions. In J. Eatwell, M. Milagate, & P. Newman (Eds.), *The new palgrave: A dictionary of economics, Vol. 1 A to D.* The Macmillan Press Limited.

Egeberg, M. (2003). The European Commission. In M. Cini (Ed.), *European Union Politics.* Oxford: Oxford University Press.

Eichengreen, B. (1993). European monetary integration. *Journal of Economic Literature,* 31(3), 1321–57.

EITO, (2007, March). ICT markets. http://www.eito.org/download/EITO%202 007%20-%20ICT%20markets,%20March%2020071.pdf (retrieved July 23, 2007).

El-Agraa, A. (2004). A history of European integration and the evolution of the EU. In A. El-Agraa (Ed.). *The European Union economics and policies* (7th ed.). Essex: Pearson Education Limited.

Eliassen, K. A., Mason, T, & Sjovaag, M. (1999). European telecommunications policies—Deregulation, re-regulation or real Liberalization?. In K. A. Eliassen & M. Sjovaag (Eds.), *European telecommunications liberalization.* London: Routledge.

Elixmann, D. (1989). Introduction: Current issues in European communications policy. In D. Elixmann & H.- H. Neuomann (Eds.), *Communications policy in Europe.* Berlin: Springer-Verlag.

Endres, A. M. (1997). *Neoclassical microeconomic Theory: The founding Austrian version.* London and New York: Routledge.

Enzweiler, T., Owen, D. & Roberts, D. (2000, July 19). Deutsche Telekom leaves Wind venture. *Financial Times* (London Edition 2), 34.

Equipment Lex Column. (2000, December 30). *Financial Times* (London Edition 1), 24.

Ericsson Deal Survey: Telecommunications Review. (1997, March 19). *Financial Times* (London), 11.

Ericsson in Java deal with Sun. (1997, March 25). *Financial Times* (USA Edition 1), 22.

Ericsson Milestones, Survey: FT Telecoms: (1997, November 19). *Financial Times* (London), 2.

Euro telecom alliances. (1993, December 8). *Financial Times* (London), 23.

European telecoms: Spanish step. (2005, July 28). *The Economist.* Retrieved August 24, 2005, from http://www.economist.com/research/articlesbysubject/displaystory.cfm?subjectid=349005&story_id=4234155.

European electronics: Dinosaurs' picnic. (1988, November 19). *The Economist,* 78.

Federal Network Agency for Electricity, Gas, Telecommunications, Post and Railway (2006). *Annual Report 2006.* Retrieved December 17, 2006, from http://www.bundesnetzagentur.de/media/archive/10417.pdf

Ferguson, P. R., & Ferguson, G. J. (1994). *Industrial economics: Issues and perspectives* (2nd Ed.). New York: New York University Press.

Field, A. R. (1986, October 6). DEC and Ericsson: A new team in electronics tellers. *Business Week*(Industrial/Technology Edition), 86.

Fisher, A. (1990, January 11). Siemens takeover of Nixdorf shakes up computer industry. *Financial Times* (London), 1.

Fishwick, F. (1993). *Making sense of competition policy.* London: Kogan Page Limited.

Fleming, S. (1982, April 28). Telecommunications struggle to catch up. Financial Times Survey; West German industry. *Financial Times* (London), 5

Flynn, J. (1994, November 18). An ever-quicker trip from R&D to customer. *Business Week,* 88.

Foss, N. J. (2000). Hunt's *A General Theory of Competition*: The dangers and attractions of theoretical eclecticism. *Journal of Marketing,* 20(1), 65–7.

Foster, J. B. (2002). Monopoly capital and the new globalization. *Monthly Review,* 53(8), 1–16.

France Telecom Lex Column. (2003, January 16), *Financial Times* (London Edition 1), 20.

Fransman, M. (2002). *Telecoms in the Internet age: From boom to burst to . . . ?.* Oxford: Oxford University Press.

Frazer, T. (1988). *Monopoly, competition and the law: The regulation of business activity in Britain, Europe and America.* New York: St. Martin's Press.

Friedrich, C. J. (1955). The political thought of neo-liberals. *American Political Science Review,* 49(2), 509–25.

Friend, M. & Ridyard, D. (1991, November 28). The limits of price competition. *Financial Times,* 13.

Friedman, A. (1987, November 6). Fiat calls off telecoms merger. *Financial Times* (London), 46.

Fuchs, G. (1992). ISDN–Telecommunications highway for Europe after 1992? *Telecommunications Policy,* 16(8), 635–45.

Gadrey, J. (2003). *New economy, new myth.* London: Routledge.

Gagliardi, D. (1989). Experience with the European Telecommunications Standards. In T. M. Schuringa (Ed.), *EuroComm 88: Proceedings of the international congress on business, public and home communications, Amsterdam, 6–9 December 1988.* Amsterdam: North-Holland.

Galés, P. L. (2003). The changing European state: Pressures from within. In J. Hayward & A. Menon (Eds.), *Governing Europe*. Oxford: Oxford University Press.

Garzaniti, L. (2003). *Telecommunications, broadcasting and the Internet: EU competition law & regulation*. London: Sweet & Maxwell.

GEC: Pick of LEX. (1999, January 23). *Financial Times* (London M Edition 1), 4.

GEC-Plessey: The Red Light (1986, August 10), *The Economist*, 51.

Geisst, C. R. (2000). *Monopolies in America: Empire builders and their enemies from Jay Gould to Bill Gates*. Oxford: Oxford University Press.

George, N. (2000a, October 21). Ericsson warns of huge mobile phone losses. *Financial Times* (London Edition 3), 21.

———. (2000b, October 23). Ericsson receives an alarm call from mobile phone unit. *Financial Times* (London Edition 2), 34.

George, N. (2000c, July 28). Fears for the future hit Nokia. *Financial Times* (London Edition 2), 32.

———. et al. (2001, August 24). European telecoms jobs slashed. *Financial Times* (London Edition 2), 20.

Gerber, D. (1994). The transformation of European community competition law?. *Harvard International Law Journal*, 35(1), 97–142.

———. (1998). *Law and competition in the twentieth century Europe: Protecting Prometheus*. Oxford: Clarendon Press.

Gertler, M. & Gilchrist, S. (1994). Monetary policy, business cycles, and the behavior of small manufacturing firms. *Quarterly Journal of Economics*, 109(2), 309–40.

Gill, S. (2003). A Neo–Gramscian approach to European integration. In A. W. Cafruny & M. Ryner (Eds.), *A ruined fortress?: Neoliberal hegemony and transformation in Europe*. Oxford: Rowman & Littlefield Publishers.

Gillingham, J. (2003). *European integration, 1950–2003: Superstate or new market economy?*. Cambridge: Cambridge University Press.

Gilpin, A. (1977). *Dictionary of economic terms*. London: Butterworths.

Gluntz, P. (1989). Opportunities in the worldwide telecommunications market. In T. M. Schuringa (Ed.), *EuroComm 88: Proceedings of the international congress on business, public and home communications, Amsterdam, 6–9 December 1988.* Amsterdam: North-Holland.

Golob, J. (1992). Will telecommunications remain a golden sector? *Telecommunications Policy*, 6(9), 738–43.

Goodman, J. W. (2006). *Telecommunications policy-making in the European Union*. Cheltenham, UK: Edward Elgar.

Goyder, D. G. (1998). *EC competition* law (3rd ed.). Oxford: Oxford University Press.

Gram, H. & Walsh, V. (1983). Joan Robinson's economics in retrospect. *Journal of Economic Literature*, 21(2), pp. 518–50.

Grande, E. (1994). The new role of the state in telecommunications. *Western European Politics*, 17(3), 138–57.

Grin, G. (2003). *The battle of the single European market: Achievements and economic thought 1985–2000*. London: Kegan Paul.

Gray, D. E. (2004). *Doing research in the real world*. London: Sage Publications.

Haack, W. G. C. N. (1983). The selectivity of economic integration theories. *Journal of Common Market Studies*, 21(4), 365–87.

Hacker, J. S., & Pierson, P. (2002). Business power and social policy: Employers and the formation of the American welfare state. *Politics & Society*, 30(2), 277–325.

Hahn, H. J. (1962). Continuity in the law of international organization. Part two: Continuity from OEEC to OECD. *Duke Law Journal*, 4, 522–57.

Hallstein, W. (1963). The european economic community. *Political Science Quarterly*, 78(2), 161–78.

Hanson, J. L. (1977). *A Dictionary of economics and commerce* (7th ed.). Estover, Plymouth: Macdonald and Evans.

Harnischfeger, U. (2000, April 20). Deutsche Telekom fails to dispel fears. *Financial Times* (USA Edition 1), 20.

———. (2001, February 19). Telekom set to outline disposals. *Financial Times* (London Edition 1), 30.

Hartley, T. C. (1993). Constitutional and institutional aspects of the Maastricht agreement. *International and Comparative Law Quarterly*, 42(2), 213–37.

Hawkins, R. W. (1992). The doctrine of regionalism: A new dimension for international standardization in telecommunications. *Telecommunications Policy*, 16(4), 339–53.

Hay, C. (2002). *Political analysis: A critical introduction.* New York: Palgrave.

Hayek, F. A. (1948). *Individualism and economic order.* Chicago: University of Chicago Press.

———. (1978). *New studies in philosophy, politics, economics and the history of ideas.* Chicago: Chicago University Press.

Hermann-Pillath, C. (1994). Methodological aspects of Eucken's work. *Journal of Economic Studies*, 21(4), 40–60.

He's putting Siemens on the American map. (2002, February 4). *Business Week*, 16B.

Hess, G. D. & Shin, K. (1997). International and intranational business cycles. *Oxford Review of Economic Policy*, 13(3), 93–109.

High, J. (1984–85). Bork's paradox: Static vs. dynamic efficiency in antitrust analysis. *Contemporary Policy Issues*, 3, 21–32.

Hilderbrand, D. (1998). *The role of economic analysis in the EC competition policy.* The Hague: Kluwer International Law.

Hilferding, R. (1981). *Finance capital: A study of the latest phase of capitalist development.* London: Routledge.

Holmes, J. (2004). Commission's annual report on competition policy. *Antitrust Bulletin*, 49(1–2), 444.

Holscher, J. & Stephan, J. (2004). Competition policy in Central Eastern Europe in the light of EU accession. *Journal of Common Market Studies*, 42(2), 321–45.

Hooghe, L. (1999). Images of Europe: Orientations to European integration among senior officials of the commission. *British Journal of Political Science*, 29(2), 345–67.

How Europe's phone monopolies are warding off the US giants (1984, August 20). *Business Week* (Industrial/Technology Edition), 110A.

Huber, P. (1998, December 14). The electronic economy. *Forbes*, 136.

Huebner, K. (n.d). Reputation failure: The economic and monetary union and its institutional flaws. Retrieved September 12, 2003, from http://www.yorku.ca/nerg/doc/unpublished-papers/.

Hudson, H. E. (1997). *Global connections: International telecommunications infrastructure and policy.* New York: Van Nostrand Reinhold.

Hudson, R. (2004). Editorial: Thinking through the geographies of the new Europe in the new millennium, dialectics of circuits, flows and spaces. *European Urban and Regional Studies*, 11(2), 99–102.

Humpreys, P. (1990). The political economy of telecommunications in France: A case study of 'telematics'. In K. Dyson & P. Humphreys (Eds.), *The political economy of communications: International and European dimensions.* London: Routledge.

————. (2004). Globalization, regulatory competition, and EU policy transfer in the telecoms and broadcasting sector. In D. Levi-Faur & E. Vigoda-Gadot (Eds.), *International public policy and management: Policy learning beyond regional, cultural, and political boundaries.* New York: Marcel Dekker.

Humpreys, P. & Simpson, S. (2005), *Globalization, convergence and European telecommunications regulation.* Cheltentam, UK & Northampton, MA, USA: Edward Elgar.

Hunt, E. K. (1979). *History of economic thought: A critical perspective.* Belmont, California: Wadsworth Publishing.

Hunt, S. D. (2000). *A general theory of competition: Resources, competences, productivity, economic growth.* Thousands Oaks, California: Sage Publications.

Hunt, B. (2002a, July 24). Marconi sales drop 22% as net debt rises. *Financial Times* (London Edition 3), 19.

————. (2002b, August 30). Marconi rebuilds from wreckage of a dream. *Financial Times* (London Edition 3), 21.

Hunt, B. & Kapner, F. (2002, August 2). Marconi agrees Italian disposal. *Financial Times* (London Edition 2), 21.

In the shark pond. (1998, January 13). *The Economist*(US Edition), 59.

Interview with Etienne Davignon: 'We cannot be myopic (1984, August 20). *Business Week* (Industrial/Technology Edition), p. 110B.

ITU, *Yearbook of Statistics: Telecommunications Services 1996–2005,* (Geneva: ITU, 2007.

Jack, A. (1995, March 21). Alcatel Cable sells US interests. *Financial Times* (London), 27.

————. (1996, March 12). Alcatel joins sharp in mobile phone initiative. *Financial Times* (London), 30.

Jackson, T. & Cane, A. (1995, June 23). Sprint signs telecoms deal with European partners. *Financial Times* (London), 22.

Jacobs, D. M. & Stewart-Clark, J. (1991). *Competition law in the european community* (2ⁿᵈ Ed.). London: Kogan Page Limited.

Jacquemin, A. P. & De Jong, H. W. (1977). *European industrial organization.* New York: John Wiley & Sons.

Janberg, V. J. (2001). *The constitution of markets: Essays in political economy.* London: Routledge.

Johnson, J. (2002a, December 6). Breton faces up to his greatest challenge. *Financial Times* (London Edition 2), 30.

————. (2002b, December 6). Regulators to look at France Telecom's Euros 9bn state loan. *Financial Times* (London Edition 3), 25.

————. (2004, January 20). 15,000 jobs to go at France Telecom restructuring. *Financial Times* (London Edition 2), 29.

Just, N. & Latzer, M. (2000). EU competition policy and market power control in the mediamatics era. *Telecommunications Policy,* 24(5), 395–411.

Kalecki, M. (1971). *Selected essays on the dynamics of the capitalist economy,1933–1970.* London and New York: Cambridge University Press.

Kaminsky, G. L. & Reinhart, C. M. (2000). On crises, contagion and confusion. *Journal of International Economics,* 51(1), 145–68.

Kapteyn, P. J. G. & Van Themaat, P. V. (1998). *Introduction to the law of the European Communities: From Maastricht to Amsterdam (3ʳᵈ ed.).* (London, the Hague and Boston: Kluwer Law International.

Kaufer, T. E. (1997). The problem of market definition under EC competition law. *Fordham International Law Journal,* 20(4), 1682–1767.

Kay, G. (1986). Macroeconomics and monopoly capitalism: Review article. *Capital & Class,* 30, 215–22.

Kehoe, L. (1992, May 8). IBM sell remaining interest in Rolm. *Financial Times* (London), 24.

Keller, J. J. & Miller, F. A. (1986, August 4). Siemens and GTE a little bit married. *Business Week*, 62.

Keller, J. J., et al. (1989, March 13). Special report: Dealmakers are burning up the phone lines. *Business Week*, 138.

Kemp, J. (1994). The competition policy of the European Union. In F. McDonald & S. Dearden, (Eds.), *European economic integration* (2nd ed.). London: Longman.

Keppler, J. (1994). *Monopolistic competition theory: Origins, results, and implications.* Baltimore: The John Hopkins University Press.

Kirzner, I. M. (1985). *Discovery and the capitalist process.* Chicago and London: University of Chicago Press.

Klein, A. (1988). Power and economic performance: The institutionalist view. In M. R. Tool (Ed.), *Evolutionary economics: Vol.I, foundations of institutionalist thought.* Armonk, New York: M. E. Sharpe Inc.

Knight, F. H. (1951). *The ethics of competition and other essays* (2nd ed.). London: George Allen & Unwin Ltd.

Knopf, K. A. (1991). *A lexicon of economics.* San Diego, California: Academic Press.

Kojima, K. (2000). The 'flying geese' model of Asian economic development: Origin, theoretical extensions, and regional policy implications. *Journal of Asian Economics*, 11(4), 375–401.

Kok, B. (1992). Privatization in telecommunications: Empty slogan or strategic tool? *Telecommunications Policy*, 16(9), 699–704.

Kolasky, W. J. (2001). Conglomerate mergers and range effects: It's a long way from Chicago to Brussels," An Address Before the George Mason University Symposium, Washington, DC., November 9. Retrieved April 13, 2004, from http://www.justice.gov/atr/public/speeches/9536.pdf.

———. (2002). Comparative merger control analysis: Six guiding principles for antitrust agencies," Presented at the International Bar Association Conference on Competition Law and Policy in a Global Context Cape Town, South Africa, March 18. Retrieved March 12, 2003, from http://www.usdoj.gov/atr/public/speeches/10845.htm.

Kolko, G. (1965). *Railroads and regulation: 1877–1916.* Princeton, New Jersey: Princeton University Press.

Korah, V. (2000). *An introductory guide to EC competition law and practice* (7th ed.). Oxford: Hart Publishing.

———. (2004). *An Introductory Guide to EC Competition Law and Practice* (8th ed.). Oxford: Hart Publishing.

Lalor, E. (1987). Action for telecommunications development: STAR—a European community programme. *Telecommunications Policy*, 11(2), 115–20.

Landes, M. & Posner, R. A. (1981). Market power in antitrust cases. *Harvard Law Review*, 94(5), 937–96.

Lang, J. T. (1997). Media, multimedia and European Community antitrust law. Retrieved July 10, 2003, from http://ec.europa.eu/comm/competition/speeches/text/sp1997_070_en.pdf.

Larouche, P. (1998). EC competition law and the convergence of the telecommunications and broadcasting sectors. *Telecommunication Policy*, 22(3), 219–42.

———. (2000). *Competition law and regulation in European telecommunications.* Oxford: Hart Publishing.

Larsen, P. T. (2000, June 29). RealNetworks in Nokia deal. *Financial Times* (USA Edition 1), 23.

Larsen, P. T. & Budden, R. (2003, February 27). Telecoms dinosaurs refuse to go extinct. *Financial Times* (London), 1.

Lasok, K. P. & Lasok, D. (2001). *Law and Institutions of the European Union* (7th ed.). London: Butterworths.

Latzer, M. (1998). Comment: European medimatics policies: Coping with convergence and globalization. *Telecommunications Policy*, 22(6), 457–66.

Lavin, D. (1995, September 27). Alcatel to slate restructuring: profit fall seen. *The Wall Street Journal*, A10.

Lenel, H. (1989). Evolution of the social market economy. In A. Peacock & H. Willgerodt, (Eds.), *German neo-liberals and the social market economy*. New York: St. Martin's Press.

Lenin, V. I. (1963). *Imperialism: The highest stage of capitalism: A popular outline*. New York: International Publishers.

Lera, E. (2000). Changing relations between manufacturing and service provision in a more competitive telecom environment. *Telecommunications Policy*, 24/5, (2000), 413–37.

Leadbeater, C. (1990, May 11). BT squares up to its international competition. *Financial Times* (London), 8.

Levine, J. B. (1993, October 4). Plugged into the wireless world. *Business Week*, 106.

Lewis, W. R. (1971). *Rome or Brussels . . . ?: An economist's comparative analysis of the development of the European community and the aims of the Treaty of Rome*. Sussex: The Institute of Economic Affairs.

Lex column: Limited mobility. (2000, December 8). *Financial Times* (London Edition 1), 24.

Lindahl, H. & Van Roermund, B. (2000). Law without a state? On representing the Common Market. In Z. Bankowski & A. Scott (Eds.), *The European Union and its order: The legal theory of European Integration*. Oxford: Blackwell Publishers.

Lindblom, C. E. (1977). *Politics and markets: The world's political-economic systems*. New York: Basic Books.

Lindemann, M. (1996a, February 1). Telecoms operators launch global alliance. *Financial Times* (London), 27.

———. (1996b, June 4). Deutsche Telekom turns its talent to global networking. *Financial Times* (London), 29.

———. (1996c, January 5). Deutsche Telekom under attack. *Financial Times* (London), 2.

Lipsey, R. G., Ragan, C. T. S., & Couragant, P. N. (1997). *Economics* (9th Canadian ed.). Toronto: Addison-Wesley Publishers Limited.

Listen, Mario (2002, October 26). *The Economist* (US Edition).

Littlechild, S C. (1978). *The fallacy of the mixed economy: An 'Austrian' critique of conventional 'mainstream' economics and of British economic policy*. London: Institute of Economic Affairs.

———. (1981) Misleading calculations of the social costs of monopoly power. *Economic Journal*, 91(362), 348–63.

Loasby, B. J. (1971). Hypothesis and paradigm in the theory of the firm. *Economic Journal*, 81(324), 863–85.

Locksley, G. (1986). Information technology and capitalist development *Capital & Class*, 27, 85–102.

Lorenz, C. (1983, May 9). Living with state control in France. *Financial Times* (London), 12.

Lowe, P. (2003, October 2).Current issues of EU competition law: The new competition enforcement regime. Key lecture at the study days of the International League of Competition Law, Barcelona. Retrieved August 2005, fromhttp://ec.europa.eu/comm/competition/speeches/text/sp2003_035_en.pdf.

Lucas, L. (1997, July 2). BT service for Hong Kong: Companies 7, finance. *Financial Times* (London Edition), 26.

Lukes, S. (1974). *Power: A radical view*. London: Macmillan Press.

Luthje, B. (1993). On the political economy of 'post-fordist' telecommunications: The US experience. *Capital & Class*, 51, 83–93.

Mahant, E. (2004). *Birthmarks of Europe: The origins of the European community considered*. Aldershot and Burlington: Ashgate Publishing.

Mallet, V. (2001, October 4). Alcatel to cut 3,000 jobs in two sectors. *Financial Times* (London Edition 1), 26.

Marsh, D. (1983, November 3). French get 10% stake in Olivetti to seal new links. *Financial Times* (London), 1.

Marconi to cut 1,000 more jobs. (2002, August 9). *Financial Times* (London Edition 1), 1.

Marx, K. (1952). *Wage labor and capital*. Moscow: Progressive Publishers.

———. (1963). *The poverty of philosophy*. Moscow: Foreign Languages Publishing House.

———. (1967). *Capital: A critique of political economy, Vol. 1 the process of capitalist production*. New York: International Publishers.

———. (1968). *Theories of surplus-value: Volume IV of capital, part II*. Moscow: Progress Publishers.

———. (1973). *Grundrisse: Foundations of the critique of political economy*. (1973). Middlesex: Penguin Books.

———. (1976). *Capital: A critique of political economy, Vol. 3*. London: Penguin Books.

———. (1994). *Selected Writings*. Simon, L. H. (Ed.). Indianapolis, Indiana: Hackett Publishing Company, Inc.

Matlack, C. & Reinhardt, A. (2003, February 17). Vive La Telecom?. *Business Week* (International Edition), 26.

Maurer, A. et al. (2003). Preface and major findings. In W. Wessels et. al. (Eds.), *Fifteen into one? The European Union and its member states*. Manchester: Manchester University Press.

McGowan, L. & Cini, M. (1999). Discretion and politicization in EU competition policy. *Governance*, 12(2), 175–200.

McLachlan, D. L. & Swan, D. (1963), Competition policy in the Common Market. *Economic Journal*, 73(289), 54–79.

———. (1967). *Competition policy in the European Community: The rules in theory and practice*. London: Oxford University Press.

McCartney, N. (1999, March 18). Sector enjoys its most successful year: European View; Survey: Financial Times telecoms. *Financial Times* (London Survey Edition), 13.

McNulty, P. (1967). A note on the history of perfect competition. *Journal of Political Economy*, 75(4), 395–9.

———. (1968). Economic theory and the meaning of competition. *Quarterly Journal of Economics*, 82(4), 639–56.

Meckstroth, T. W. (2000), Marx and the logic of social theory: The capitalist state. *Science & Society*, 64(1), 55–86.

Merkin, R. & Williams, K. (1984). *Competition law: Antitrust policy in UK and the EEC*. London: Sweet & Maxwell.

Microsoft Corporation, (2002). *Microsoft computer dictionary* (5th ed.) [electronic version]. Redmond, Washington: Microsoft Press.

Miller, J. P. (1955). Measures of monopoly power and concentration: Their economic significance. In National Bureau of Economic Research (Ed.), *Business concentration and price policy: A conference of the universities-national bureau committee for economic research*. Princeton: Princeton University.

Miller, K. L. (1995, May 1). Siemens shapes up. *Business Week*, 52.

Milward, A. (1992). *The European rescue of the nation-state*. Berkeley: University of California Press.

Milmo, D. (2001, December 4). BT confirms job losses. *Guardian Unlimited*. Retrieved, April 15, 2004, from http://www.guardian.co.uk/recession/story/0,,611944,00.html.

Minder, R. (2002, January 16). Alcatel gets back in the 3G race. *Financial Times* (London), 26.

Mittag, J. & Wessels, W. (2003). The 'one' and the 'fifteen'? The member states between procedural adaptation and structural revolution. In W. Wessels et al. (Eds.),*Fifteen into one? The European Union and its member states*. Manchester: Manchester University Press.

Montella, L. (1984). Global competition and EEC policy in telecommunications: An Italian perspective. *Telecommunications Policy*, 8(3), 205–12.

Montgomery, C. A. (1985). Product market diversification and market power. *Academy of Management Journal*, 28(4), 789–98.

Monti, M. (2003a, October 24). EU competition policy after May 2004. Fordham Annual Conference on International Antitrust Law and Policy, New York. Retrieved May 24, 2004, from http://www.eurunion.org/.

———. (2003b, December 10). *Competition and regulation in the telecom industry: The way forward*. Presented at the ECTA Conference, Conrad Hotel, Brussels. Retrieved November 17, 2005, from http://europa.eu/rapid/pressReleasesAction.do?reference=SPEECH/03/604&format=HTML&aged=0&language=EN&guiLanguage=en.

———. (2004). Introduction. In P. A. Buigues and R. Rey, (Eds.), *The economics of antitrust and regulation in telecommunications: Perspectives for the new European regulatory framework*. Cheltenham, UK: Edward Elgar.

Moschel, W. (1989). Competition policy from an Ordo point of view. In A. Peacock & H. Willgerodt (Eds.), *German neo-liberals and the social market economy*. New York: St. Martin's Press.

———. (2000). Guest editorial: Change of policy in European competition law. *Common Market Law Review*, 37(3), 495–500.

Moss, B. H. (2005). Preface and acknowledgments. In B. H. Moss (Ed.), *Monetary union in crisis: The European Union as a neo-liberal construction*. New York: Palgrave Macmillan.

Muellerbauer, J. (1997). The assessment: Business cycles. *Oxford Review of Economic Policy*, 13(3), 1–18.

Munchau, W. (1995, December 20). Old rival finds the winning formula. *Financial Times* (London), 25.

Narjes, K-H. (1988). The RACE programme: The European route towards integrated broadband communications. *Telecommunications Policy*, 12(2), 106–8.

Nakamoto, M. & Owen, V. (2000, May 3). Fujitsu, Alcatel in mobiles link. *Financial Times* (London Edition 2), 33.

Natalicchi, G. (2001). *Wiring Europe: Reshaping the European telecommunications regime*. Lanham: Rowman & Littlefield Publishers.

Neu, W., Neumann, K-H., & Schnöring, T. (1987). Trade patterns, industry structure and industrial policy in telecommunications. *Telecommunications Policy*, 11(1), 31–44.

Neumann, F. L. (1950). Approaches to the study of political power. *Political Science Quarterly*, 65(2), 161–80.

Neumann, M. (1998). The evolution of cartel policy in Germany. In S. Martin (Ed.), *Competition policies in Europe*. Amsterdam: Elsevier.

New Telekom, Netscape link. (1997, February 6). *Financial Times* (London Edition 1), 22.

Newing, R. (1996, February 7). Lotus is first to use BT's new public servers—global network service: Review of information technology. *Financial Times* (London), 18.

Newman, M. (1994, March 16). A tricky balancing act for leading vendors—Telecom equipment suppliers: Survey of Information and Communications Technology (13). *Financial Times* (London), 8.

Nicholson, W. E. (1997). *Intermediate microeconomics and its application* (7th ed.). Fort Worth, TX: The Dryden Press.

Nitzan, J. (2001). Regimes of differential accumulation: Mergers, stagflation and the logic of globalization. *Review of International Political Economy*, 8(2), pp. 226–74.

No one said building a brand was easy. (2005, December 5). *Business Week*. Retrieved November 8, 2006, http://www.businessweek.com/magazine/content/05_49/b3962064.htm.

Nugent, N. (2001). *The European commission*. New York: Palgrave.

Nugent, N. & Paterson, W. (2003). The political system of the European integration. In J. Hayward & A. Menon (Eds.), *Governing Europe*. Oxford: Oxford University Press.

OECD. (1983). *Telecommunications: Pressures and policies for change*. Paris: OECD.

———. (1988). *The telecommunications industry: The challenges and structural change*. Paris: OECD.

———. (1991). *Information technology standards: The economic dimension*, Paris: OECD.

———. (2003). *OECD telecommunications outlook 2003*. Paris: OECD.

Offe, C. (1972). Political authority and class structures: An analysis of late capitalist societies. *International Journal of Sociology*, 2(1), 73–108.

———. (1975). The theory of the capitalist state and the problem of policy formation. In L. N. Lindberg et. al. (Eds.), *Stress and contradiction in modern capitalism: Public policy and the theory of the state*. Lexington, Massachusetts: D.C Heath and Company.

———. (1996). *Modernity and the state: East, west*. Cambridge, Massachusetts: The MIT Press.

Offe, C. & Ronge, V. (1975). Theses on theory of the state. *New German Critique*, 6, 37–47.

Oliver, Jr., H. M. (1960). German neoliberalism. *Quarterly Journal of Economics*, 74(1), pp. 117–49.

Oswalt-Eucken, I. (1994). Freedom and economic power: Neglected aspects of Walter Eucken's work. *Journal of Economic Studies*, 21(4), 38–45.

Owen, D. (1991, February 12). Europe's largest cellular phone makers join forces. *Financial Times* (London), 26.

———. (1996a, June 19). Companies and finance: Europe: Lines to profit still open as Bouygues enters French mobile market. *Financial Times* (London), 31.

———. (1997, September 18). New round of rate cuts at France Telecom. *Financial Times* (London Edition 1), 38.

———. (1999, February 10). Telecoms shares fall on price fears. *Financial Times* (London Edition 1), 32.

———. (2000a, March 24). France Telecom in Germany link. *Financial Times* (London Edition 1), 38.

———. (2000b, September 7). France Telecom gearing set to rise by year-end. *Financial Times* (London Edition 1), 34.

Pal, L. A. (2006). *Beyond policy analysis: Public issue management in turbulent times* (3rd ed.). Toronto: Nelson.

Palim, M. R. A. (1998). Worldwide growth of competition law: An empirical analysis. *Antitrust Bulletin,* 43(1), 105–45.

Parkes, S. (2000, November 15). Capacity mushrooms as fibre networks grow; Survey: FT telecomms. *Financial Times* (Wednesday Surveys TCH1), 6.

Parkes, C. & Fisher, A. (1992, November 23). Charmed by the simple life -Heinrich von Pierer, chief executive of Siemens. *Financial Times* (London), 32.

Palley, T. I. (1996). "Out of the closet: The political economy of neo-classical distribution theory. *Review of Radical Political Economics,* 28(3), 57–68.

Panitch, L. & Gindin, S. (2005). Superintending global capital. *New Left Review,* 35, 101–23.

Peacock, A. & Willgerodt, H. (1989). Overall view of the German liberal movement. In A. Peacock & H. Willgerodt (Eds.), *German neo-liberals and the social market economy.* New York: St. Martin's Press.

Pearce, D. W. (186). *The MIT dictionary of modern economics* (3rd ed.). Cambridge, Massachusetts: The MIT Press.

Peltzman, S. (1988). Toward a more theory of general theory of regulation. In G. Stigler (Ed.), *Chicago studies in political economy.* Chicago: The University of Chicago Press.

Peterson, J. & Bomberg, E. (1999). *Decision-making in the European Union.* New York: St. Martin's Press.

Peterson, T., et al. (1987, May 18). Now that CGE is a heavyweight, it will have to fight like one. *Business Week,* 98.

Petrella, R. (1998). The limits of European Union competition policy. *New Political Economy,* 3(2), 292–5.

Pinder, J. (2001). *The European Union: A very short introduction.* Oxford: Oxford University Press.

Poulantzas, N. (1973). *Political power and social classes.* London: Verso.

Price, C. (1997, November 19). Liberalization: New year Deadline is largely symbolic. Survey: FT telecoms surveys. *Financial Times* (Wednesday Surveys T), 12.

Purton, P. (2001, January 17). Consolidation may temper incumbents' advantages; Survey: FT telecoms. *Financial Times* (Wednesday Surveys ITB1), 5.

Pye, R. & Lauder, G. (1987). Regional aid for telecommunications in Europe: A force for economic development. *Telecommunications Policy,* 11(2), 99–113.

Ragin, C. C. (1987). *The comparative method: Moving beyond qualitative and quantitative strategies.* Berkeley: University of California Press.

Raines, J. P. & Leathers, C. G. (1996). Veblenian stock markets and the efficient markets hypothesis. *Journal of Post Keynesian Economics,* 19(1), 137–148.

Ratner, J. & Roberts, D. (2000, September 1). BT sagging under mountain of debt. *Financial Times* (London Edition 2), 20.

Rawsthorn, A. (1992, March 3). Alcatel Cable rises 16% to FFr1.27bn. *Financial Times* (London), 28.

———. (1993, March 5). Alcatel poised for telecom stake. *Financial Times* (London), 16.

Ready, Steady . . . Whoops. (1997, September 13). *The Economist* (US Edition), 5.

Reder, M. W. (1982). Chicago economics: Permanence and change. *Journal of Economic Literature,* 20(1), 1–38.

Reed, S. (2000, July 10). Ericsson: Wireless workhorse. *Business Week,* 48

Ricardo, D. (1981). *On the principles of political economy and taxation.* Cambridge, New York: Cambridge University Press.

Rich, C. J. (1988). European telecommunications policy: A US view. *Telecommunications Policy,* 12(1), (1988), 2–7.

Richardson, G. B. (1975). Adam Smith on competition and increasing returns. In A. Skinner & T. Wilson (Eds.), *Essays on Adam Smith*. Oxford: Clarendon Press.

Ridding, J. (1995, September 27). Alcatel set to announce reorganization. *Financial Times* (London), 26.

Riesman, D. (1953). *Thorstein Veblen: A critical interpretation*. New York: Charles Scribner's Sons.

Roberts, D. (2001, March 7). Telecoms struggles show US gloom is spreading. *Financial Times* (London Edition 1), 30.

———. (2000a, June 22). BT retreats in mobile 'lock' row. *Financial Times* (London Edition 3), 1.

———. (2000b, May 31). Pounds 31bn deal for Orange leaves Snook on top. *Financial Times* (London Edition 1), 25.

Roberts, D. & Van Duyn, A. (2000, September 29). Confidence in telecoms is far from buzzing: Operators' shares are on the slide. *Financial Times* (London Edition 1), 34.

Roberts, D. & Waters, R. (2001, July 4). BT sells stake in Rogers Wireless of Canada. *Financial Times* (London Edition 2), 22.

Robinson, J. (1932). Imperfect competition and falling supply price. *Economic Journal*, 42(168), 544–54.

———. (1934). What is perfect competition? *Quarterly Journal of Economics*, 49(1), pp. 104–20.

———. *The economics of imperfect competition*. London: Macmillan.

Roobek, A. & Broeders, J. (1993). Telecommunications: Global restructuring at full speed. In H. W. de Jong, (Ed.), *The Structure of European Industry (3rd Revised Ed.)*. Dordrecht: Kluwer Academic Publishers.

Rothschild, K. W. (1964). The old and the new-some recent trends in the literature of German economics. *American Economic Review*, 54(2), p. 1–33.

———. (2002). The absence of power in contemporary economic theory. *Journal of Socio-Economics*, 31(5), 433–42.

Ropke, W. (1960). *A humane economy: The social framework of the free market*. Chicago: Henry Regnery Company.

Sally, R. (1996). Ordoliberalism and the social market: Classical political economy from Germany. *New Political Economy*, 1(2), 233–57.

Sandholtz, W. (1993). Institutions and collective action: The new telecommunications in Western Europe. *World Politics*, 45(2), 242–70.

Sauter, W. (1997). *Competition law and industrial policy in the EU*. Oxford: Clarendon Press.

———. (1998). The economic constitution of the European Union. *Columbia Journal of European Law*, 4(1), 27–68.

Sawyer, M. C. (1981). *The economics of industries and firms*. New York: St. Martin's Press.

———. (1989). *The challenge of radical political economy: An introduction to the alternatives to neo-classical economics*. Savage, Maryland: Barnes & Noble Books.

———. (1994). Post-Keynesian and Marxian notions of competition: Towards a synthesis. In M. A. Glick (Ed.), *Competition, technology and money: Classical and post-Keynesian perspectives*. Aldershot: Edward Elgar.

Shearman, C. (1986). European collaboration in computing and telecommunications: A policy approach. In K. Dyson & P. Humphreys (Eds.), *The politics of the communications revolution in Western Europe*. London: Frank Cass.

Schmidt, J. (2004). The new ECMR: 'Significant impediment' or significant improvement'? *Common Market Law Review*, 41(6), 1555–82.

Schneider, V. (2001). Institutional reform in telecommunications: The European Union in transitional policy diffusion. In M. G. Cowles., J. Caporaso, & T.

Risse (Eds.), *Transforming Europe: Europeanization and domestic change.* Ithaca and London: Cornell University Press.

Schneider, V., & Werle, R. (1990). International regime or corporate actor?: The European community in telecommunications policy. In K. Dyson & P. Humphreys (Eds.), *The political economy of communications: International and European dimensions.* London: Routledge.

Schneider, V., Dang-Nguyen, G., & Werle, R. (1994). Corporate actor networks in European policy-making: Harmonizing telecommunications policy. *Journal of Common Market Studies,* 32(4), 473–94.

Schneider, V. & Werle, R. (2007). Telecommunications policy. In P. Graziano & M. P. Vink (Eds.), Europeanization: New research agendas. New York: Palgrave MacMillan.

Schnoring, T. (1994). European telecommunications R&D systems in transition. In C. Steinfield, J. M. Bauer & L. Caby (Eds.), *Telecommunications in transition: Policies, services and technologies in the European community.* Thousand Oaks: Sage Publications.

Schumpeter, J. A. (1950). *Capitalism, socialism and democracy* (3rd ed.). New York: Harper and Row.

Scully, R. (2003). The European parliament. In M. Cini (Ed.), *European Union politics.* Oxford: Oxford University Press.

Semmler, W. (1982). Theories of competition and monopoly. *Capital & Class,* 18, 91–117.

Shaw, J. (2000). *Law of the European Union* (3rd ed.). Hampshire: Palgrave.

Shearman, C. (1986). European collaboration in computing and telecommunications: A policy approach. In K. Dyson & P. Humphreys (Eds.), *The politics of the communications revolution in Western Europe.* London: Frank Cass.

Shepherd, W. G. (1984).'Contestability' vs. competition. *American Economic Review,* 74(4), 572–87.

Shepherd, W. G. (1990). *The economics of industrial organization* (3rd ed.). Englewood Cliffs, New Jersey: Prentice Hall.

Shim, J. K. & Siegel, J. G. (1995). *Dictionary of economics.* New York: John Wiley & Sons.

Siemens to cut handset operation. (2001, April 11). *Financial Times,* 25.

Simonian, H. (1989, July 7). Siemens reshape aims at flexibility. *Financial Times* (London), 30.

Simonian, H. (1999, December 28). Siemens set to buy Bosch mobile phone arm. *Financial Times* (London), 11.

Smith, A. (1994). *An inquiry into the nature and causes of wealth of nations,* Vol. 2. New York: Modern Library.

Smith, P. M. (1982). Multinational corporations and merger law control in community antitrust law. In K. J. Kopt (Ed.), *European merger control: Legal and economic analyses on multinational enterprises,* Vol. I. Berlin: Walter de Gruyter.

Solomon, J. H. (1987). The EEC green paper: A faltering step in the right direction. *Telecommunications Policy,* 11(4), 322–4.

Sommer, R. (1995, October 3). Survey of international telecommunications. *Financial Times* (London), 39.

Sounam, S. (1987). French competition policy. In S. Martin (Ed.), *Competition policies in Europe.* Amsterdam: Elsevier.

Spaak, F. & Jaeger, J. N. (1961). The rules of competition within the European common market. *Law and Contemporary Problems,* 26(3), 485–507.

Sraffa, P. (1926). The laws of return under competitive conditions. *Economic Journal,* 36(144), 535–50.

Sosnick, S. H. (1958). A critique of workable competition. *Quarterly Journal of Economics,* 72(3), 380–423.

Sowell, T. (1967). The 'evolutionary' economics of Thorstein Veblen. *Oxford Economic Papers*, 19(2), pp. 177–99.

Steindl, J. (1947). *Small and big business: Economic problems of the size of firms.* Oxford: Basil Blackwell.

———. (1952). *Maturity and stagnation in American capitalism.* Oxford: Basil Blackwell.

Steiner, J. & Woods, L. (2001). *Textbook on EC law* (7th ed.). London: Blackstone Press.

Stevers, E. (1990). *Telecommunications regulation in the European community: The commission of the European communities as regulatory actor* (EUI Working Paper No89/421). Florence: European University Institute.

Stewart, A. (1997, July 2). Retail revolution ahead. Survey: FT information technology. *Financial Times* (London), 6.

Stigler, G. (1988). The theory of economic regulation. In G. Stigler (Ed.), *Chicago studies in political economy.* Chicago: The University of Chicago Press.

Stockman, A. C. (1998). New evidence connecting exchange rates to business cycles. *Economic Quarterly*, 84/2, (1998), 73–89.

Streit, M. E. (1992). Economic order, private law and public policy: The Freiburg school of law and economics in perspective. *Journal of Institutional and Theoretical Economics*, 148, 675–704.

Stuck on hold Lex column. (2000, May 19). *Financial Times* (London Edition 1), 28.

Studemann, F. (1997, February 4), Siemens to sell its TV cable network. *Financial Times* (London), 26.

Styliadou, M. (1997). Applying EC competition law to alliances in the telecommunications sector. *Telecommunications Policy*, 21(1), 47–58.

Surviving the telecoms jungle. (1998, April 4). *The Economist*(US Edition), 13.

Swann, D. (1983). *Competition & industrial policy in the European community.* London and New York: Methuen.

Sweezy, P. A. (1984). Competition and monopol. In H. B. Foster & H. Szlajfer (Eds.), *The faltering economy: The problem of accumulation under monopoly capitalism.* New York: Monthly Review Press.

Symeonidis, G. K. (1990). European telecommunications environment in the 1990s. *Telecommunications Policy*, 14(6), 451–6.

Symeonidis, G. K. (1998). The evolution of UK cartel policy and its impact on market c conduct and structure. In S. Martin (Ed.), *Competition policies in Europe.* Amsterdam: Elsevier.

Sztompka, P. (1994). Evolving focus on human agency in contemporary social theory. In P. Sztompka (Ed.), *Agency and structure: Reorienting social theory.* Reading: Gordon and Breach.

Talani, L. S. (2004). *European political economy: Political science perspectives.* Aldershot: Ashgate.

Taylor, R. S. (1988). The future of the European telecoms industry. In T. M. Schuringa, (Ed.), *EuroComm 88: Proceedings of the international congress on business, public and home communications, Amsterdam, 6–9 December 1988.* Amsterdam: North-Holland.

Taylor, R. (1990, May 9). Ericsson strategist takes the lead. *Financial Times* (London), 34.

Taylor, P. (1996a, August 13). Europe telecoms deals rise after deregulation. *Financial Times* (London Edition 1), 15.

———. (1996b, July 31). Oftel to probe BT on 'wrong advice'. *Financial Times* (London Edition 1), 7.

———. (1999, December 9). Microsoft and Ericsson forge link-up in wireless computing. *Financial Times* (USA Edition 2), 1.

Telecoms groups confirm talks: Telecom Italia and Deutsche Telekom discuss merger (1999, April 19). *Financial Times* (London Edition 1), 23.

Telecommunications Lex Column. (2001, October 26). *Financial Times* (London Edition 1), 20.

Tessieri, E. (1991a, May 30). Nokia concentrate on electronics. *Financial Times* (London), 30.

———. (1991b, October 4). Hopes built on telecommunications; Profile of Nokia: Survey, Finland 3. *Financial Times* (London), 35.

Thatcher, M. (1999). *The politics of telecommunications: National institutions, convergence, and change in Britain and France.* Oxford: Oxford University Press.

———. (2004a). Winners and losers in Europeanization: Reforming the national regulation of telecommunications. *West European Politics*, 27(2), pp. 284–309.

———. (2004b). Varieties of capitalism in an internationalized world: Domestic institutional change and in European telecommunications. *Comparative Political Studies*, 37(7), 102–27.

The short arm of the law. (1997, September 13). *The Economist* (US Edition), 14.

The Great Telephone Debate, (1996, March, 23). *The Economist* (US Edition), 70.

Thimm, A. L. (1989). The European community's telecommunication strategy: A European perspective. In W. F. Averyt & A. C. Averyt (Eds.), *Managing global telecommunications: North American perspective.* Burlington, Vt.: University of Vermont, School of Business Administration.

———. (1992). *America's stake in European telecommunications policies.* Westport, Connecticut: Quorum Books.

To keep on top: It is no longer enough to be big. (1995, September 30). *The Economist* (US Edition), 25.

Tomkins, A. (1999). Responsibility and resignation in the European commission. *Modern Law Review*, 62(5), 744–65.

Torelli, H. B. (1955). *The federal antitrust policy: Origination of an American tradition.* Baltimore: Johns Hopkins University Press.

Torre, R. J. (1965). Italian antitrust law. *American Journal of Comparative Law*, 14(3), 489–503.

Toy, S. (1996, May 6). A talk with Alcatel's Serge Tchuruk. *Business Week* (International Edition), 17.

Trebilcock, M., et al. (2002). *The law and economics of Canadian competition policy.* Toronto: University of Toronto Press.

Trebing, H. M. (1969). Government regulation and modern capitalism. *Journal of Economic Issues*, 3(1), 87–109.

Triffin, R. (1947). *Monopolistic competition and general equilibrium theory.* Cambridge: Harvard University Press.

Truell, P. & Hudson, R. L. (1994, July 6). For Alcatel chief, charges cap bad year. *The Wall Street Journal*, A14.

Trusbusting: Will Economics Bless this Union (1997, August 2). *The Economist* (US Edition), 61.

Tyson, K. W. M. (1997). *Competition in the 21st century.* Delray Beach, Florida: St. Lucie Press.

Ungerer, H. (1990). *Telecommunications in Europe: Free choice for the user in Europe's 1992 market, the challenge for the European community.* Brussels: Office for Official Publications of the European Communities.

Van Duyn, A. (2002, June 14). Debt troubles dog European telecom giants. *Financial Times* (London Edition 1), 21.

Vanberg, V. J. (1998). Freiburg school of law and economics. In P. Newman (Ed.), *The new palgrave dictionary of economics and the law, Vol. 2.* London: Macmillan.

Van Gerven, W. (1974). Twelve years EC competition law (1962–1973) revisited. *Common Market Law Review*, 11(1), 38–61.

Van Themaat, P. V. (1963). The anti-trust policy of the European Economic Community. In The British institute of international and comparative law (Ed.), *Comparative aspects of anti-trust law in the United States, the United Kingdom and the European Economic Community*. London: The Eastern Press.

Veblen, T. (1932). *The theory of business enterprise*. New York: Charles Scribner's Sons.

———. (1964a). *Absentee ownership and business enterprise in recent times: The case of America*. New York: Sentry Press.

———. (1964b). *Essays in our changing order*. New York: Sentry Press.

———. (1964c). *The vested interests and the common man: The modern point of view and the new order*. New York: Sentry Press.

———. (1965). *The engineers and the price system*. New York: The Viking Press.

Veljanovski, C. (2004). EC merger policy after GE/Honeywell and Airtours. *Antitrust Bulletin*, 49(1/2), 153–94.

Venit, J. S. (2003). Brave new world: The modernization and decentralization of enforcement under Articles 81 and 82 of the EC Treaty. *Common Market Law Review*, 40(3), 545–80.

Venturini, V. G. (1964). Monopolies and restrictive practices in Italy. *International and Comparative Law Quarterly*, 13(2), 617–64.

Virtanen, O. (1987, April 24). Nokia-Mobira buys US paging operator. *Financial Times* (London), 29.

———. (1989, April 7). Nokia reshapes its operations. *Financial Times* (London), 22.

Von Weizsäcker, C. C. (1984). Free entry into telecommunications?. *Information Economics and Policy*, 1, 197–216.

Von Wieser, F. (1927). *Social economics*. New York: Adelphi Company.

Wagstyl, S. (1998, February 14). GEC sells chipmaker to Mitel for $225m disposal ends 30 years' effort to develop significant UK-owned semiconductor industry. *Financial Times* (London Edition 3), 21.

Walker, D. A. (1977). Thorstein Veblen's economic systems. *Economic Inquiry*, 15(2), 213–37.

Wallenstein, G. (1990). *Setting global telecommunication standards*. Norwood, MA: Artech House, Inc.

Wallace, H. & Edwards, G. (1976). European Community: The evolving role of the presidency of the Council. *International Affairs*, 52(4), 535–50.

Walton, C. C. (1953). Background for the European defense community. *Political Science Quarterly*, 68(1), 42–69.

Ward, I. (2003). *A critical introduction to European law* (2nd ed.). London: LexisNexis.

Waters, R. (1997, June 24). Alcatel Alsthom and Cisco unveil networks tie-up. *Financial Times* (USA Edition 1), 22.

Waters, R. & Roberts, D. (2001, October 16). Concert sounded off key almost from opening bars. *Financial Times* (London Edition 1), 25.

Waters, R. & Taylor, P. (1999, September 170. BT and AT&T link up in global wireless alliance. *Financial Times* (London Edition 1), 1.

Webb, S. (1987a, April 14). Ericsson to buy remaining shares in Spanish concern. *Financial Times* (London), 34.

———. (1987b, September 10). Nokia buys rubber goods maker. *Financial Times* (London), 37.

Weeks, J. (2001). The expansion of capital and uneven development on a world scale. *Capital & Class*, 74, 9–31.

Weil, G. L. (1967). The merger of the institutions of the European Communities. *American Journal of International Law*, 61(1), 57–65.

Weintraub, S. (1955). Revised doctrines of competition. *American Economic Review* 45(2), 463–479.

Wendlandt, A. (2002, December 14). DT sells stake in Eutelsat. *Financial Times* (London Edition 1), 15.

Wesseling, R. (2000). *The modernization of EC antitrust law.* Oxford: Hart Publishing.

Wheelock, J. (1983). Competition in the Marxist tradition. *Capital & Class*, 21, 18–49.

White, Jr., H. G. (1936). A review of monopolistic and imperfect competition theories. *American Economic Review*, 26(4), 637–49.

Wilks, S. (2005). Agency escape: Decentralization or dominance of the European commission in the modernization of competition policy? *Governance: An International Journal of Policy, Administration, and Institutions*, 18(3), 431–452.

Willams, E. (1982a, April 5). Horizons widen for new markets: Section III, Financial Times survey; electronic components. *Financial Times (London)*, 1

———. (1982b, December 20). Growing market for telecommunications industry: Financial Times survey, Swedish industry and technology. *Financial Times* (London), 14.

Williamson, J. (1991a, October 7). Intervention is the slogan: Profile, European Commission. *Financial Times* (London), 6.

———. (1991b, October 7). World Telecommunications 26: Characteristics of enlightened paternalism—France. *Financial Times* (London), 26.

Wilks, S. (1996). The prolonged reform of United Kingdom competition policy. In G. B. Doern & S. Wilks (Eds.), *Comparative competition policy: National institutions in a global market.* Oxford: Clarendon Press.

Wilks, S. & McGowan, L. (1996). Competition policy in the European Union: Creating a federal agency? In G. B. Doern & S. Wilks (Eds.), *Comparative competition policy: national institutions in a global market.* Oxford: Clarendon Press.

Willis, F. R. (1978). Origins and evolution of the European communities. *Annals of the American Academy of Political and Social Science*, 440, 1–12.

Yeager, L. B. (1994). Eucken on capital and interest. *Journal of Economic Studies*, 21(4), 61–75.

Yoo, J. H. & Moon, C. W. (1999). Korean financial crisis during 1997–1998: Causes and challenges. *Journal of Asian Economics*, 10(2), 263–77.

Yalem, R. J. (1959). Prospects for European Political unification. *Western Political Quarterly*, 12(1), 50–63.

Yataganas, X. A. (2001). The treaty of nice: The sharing of power and the institutional balance in the European Union: A continental perspective. *European Law Journal*, 7(3), 242–91.

Young, D. (1992). Austrian views on monopoly: Insights and problems. *Review of Political Economy*, 4(2), 203–26.

Young, D. & Metcalfe, S. (1997). Competition policy. In M. Artis & N. Lee (Eds.), *The economics of the European Union: Policy and analysis.* Oxford: Oxford University Press.

Zahariadis, N. (2003). *Ambiguity & choice in public policy: Political decision making in modern democracies.* Washington, D.C.: Georgetown University Press.

Zysman, J. & Borrus, M. (1994). From failure to fortune? European electronics in a changing world economy. *Annals of the American Academy of Political and Social Science*, 531, 141–67.

Index